DOING THE BEST WE CAN

PHILOSOPHICAL STUDIES SERIES
IN PHILOSOPHY

VOLUME 35

FRED FELDMAN

Department of Philosophy,
University of Massachusetts at Amherst

DOING
THE BEST
WE CAN

An Essay in Informal Deontic Logic

D. REIDEL PUBLISHING COMPANY

A MEMBER OF THE KLUWER ACADEMIC PUBLISHERS GROUP

DORDRECHT / BOSTON / LANCASTER / TOKYO

Library of Congress Cataloging-in-Publication Data

Feldman, Fred, 1941–
    Doing the best we can.

    (Philosophical studies series in philosophy ; v. 35)
    Includes index.
    1. Ethics. 2. Duty. 3. Social ethics. 4. Deontic
logic. I. Title. II. Series.
BJ1012.F43   1986   170   86–3888
ISBN 90–277–2164–5

Published by D. Reidel Publishing Company,
P.O. Box 17, 3300 AA Dordrecht, Holland.

Sold and distributed in the U.S.A. and Canada
by Kluwer Boston Inc.,
190 Old Derby Street, Hingham, MA 02043, U.S.A.

In all other countries, sold and distributed
by Kluwer Academic Publishers Group,
P.O. Box 322, 3300 AH Dordrecht, Holland.

Printed in The Netherlands.

TABLE OF CONTENTS

v

PREFACE

Several years ago I came across a marvelous little paper in which Hector-Neri Castañeda shows that standard versions of act utilitarianism are formally incoherent.[1] I was intrigued by his argument. It had long seemed to me that I had a firm grasp on act utilitarianism. Indeed, it had often seemed to me that it was the clearest and most attractive of normative theories. Yet here was a simple and relatively uncontroversial argument that showed, with only some trivial assumptions, that the doctrine is virtually unintelligible.

The gist of Castañeda's argument is this: suppose we understand act utilitarianism to be the view that an act is obligatory if and only if its utility exceeds that of each alternative. Suppose it is obligatory for a certain person to perform an act with two parts — we can call it '*A & B*'. Then, obviously enough, it is also obligatory for this person to perform the parts, *A* and *B*. If act utilitarianism were true, we apparently could infer that the utility of *A & B* is higher than that of *A*, and higher than that of *B* (because *A & B* is obligatory, and the other acts are alternatives to *A & B*). Furthermore, since *A* is obligatory, and *B* is obligatory, it seems that we can also infer that the utility of *A* is higher than that of *A & B*, and that the utility of *B* is higher than that of *A & B*. Clearly enough, this is impossible.

I subsequently found that a number of philosophers, equally perplexed by Castañeda's puzzle, had attempted to reformulate the main thesis of act utilitarianism. While some of their work (for example, that of Åqvist, Bergström, and Sobel) seemed to me to be ingenious and very carefully worked out, most of it was quite complicated.[2] Castañeda's own proposals were, by his own admission, "rather complex".[3]

I am convinced that the truth in philosophy must be simple. Perhaps this conviction arises from the combination of my hope to come to know the truth, and my inability to understand complicated philosophical theories. At any rate, it seemed to me that the utilitarian insight had to be capable of some simple and tidy formulation. It was with the hope of providing a simple, clear, and recognizably utilitarian normative theory that I tried out the main idea of 'World Utilitarianism'.[4] As I then saw it, the acts still possible for a person at a time organize themselves into possible "life histories" — sequences of acts he still can perform. For each such life history, there is a life history world. A life history world is the possible world that would exist if some life history were lived out. These life history worlds have values. A "best" is a world than which there is none better. Moral obligation, I proposed, can be understood as truth in all the bests. I made a number of claims in behalf of this view. Among these was the claim that it would solve the puzzle Castañeda had set.

At about the same time, I began to think seriously about Roderick Chisholm's enormously perplexing 'Contrary to Duty Imperatives and Deontic Logic'.[5] At first, this seemed to me to raise a problem having only technical interest for specialists in deontic logic. Chisholm had pointed out that there are cases in which, as a matter of ordinary English, a quartet of sentences relevantly like the following would be true:

(1)   Jones ought to go to the aid of his neighbors.
(2)   If Jones goes to the aid of his neighbors, then he ought to tell them he is coming.
(3)   It ought to be that if he does not go to the aid of his neighbors, then he does not tell them he is coming.
(4)   Jones does not go to the aid of his neighbors.

These may seem unproblematic. However, in the systems of deontic logic current at the time, they could not be represented adequately. Those systems provided for what I call "materially conditioned absolute obligation", but they did not provide for "conditional obligation". Thus, in some of these systems, we could derive a contradiction from the formal analogues of (1)—(4). From (1) and (2) we could derive a statement to the effect that Jones ought to tell his neighbors that he is coming. From (3) and (4) we could derive a statement to the effect that Jones ought not to tell them he is coming. This is a conflict of obligations. In most systems, it would be easy then to derive an outright contradiction. Jones would have an obligation, and also not have an obligation, to tell them he is coming.

Further relection on Chisholm's puzzle, in the context of the theory of 'World Utilitarianism', made me realize that there is a truly profound problem here. The Chisholm puzzle and the Castañeda puzzle are just two manifestations of this deeper concern. This deeper concern may be conceived of as the problem of laying out the logical structure of the concept of moral obligation. Special emphasis would have to be placed on the logic of the "iffy oughts" — sentences with both an 'if' and an 'ought' such as (2) and (3) above.

The difficulty of discerning the formal structure of moral obligation, I soon realized, is compounded by the fact that moral obligation is easily confused with a remarkable variety of other concepts of obligation — prudential, civic, social, and others. Furthermore, the problem is again compounded by the fact that different moral philosophers have profoundly different views about what we ought to do, morally. Some of these views are so different that they cannot be accommodated within a single logical system. Thus, in order to do justice to the topic at hand, I found that I would have to do a great deal of sorting and sifting. I would have to distinguish among these concepts of obligation, and attempt to spell out at least some of the crucial formal features of each. Inevitably, this would require committing myself on some extremely controversial normative and axiological questions.

The present book is the product of my reflections on these questions, and on some of the further questions to which these have given rise. The book is divided into three parts. Part One is about absolute moral obligation. In Chapter 1, I present a traditional formulation of act utilitarianism, and I explain some of its main formal difficulties. Then, in Chapter 2, I present my own neo-utilitarian view about absolute moral obligation. By appeal to the concept of intrinsic value and the concept of "accessibility", I try to do justice to the idea that all of our moral obligations boil down to one — we morally ought to do the best we can. This I take to mean that we morally ought to do what we do in the intrinsically best possible worlds still accessible to us. This normative theory yields a number of relatively formal results, including a solution to Castañeda's original puzzle.

Chapter 3 contains a presentation and evaluation of some of the most interesting objections to the sort of approach to absolute moral obligation that I advocate. Several of these objections are fundamentally moral in tone. Such objections may be thought of as attempts to show that my approach yields morally objectionable results. My intention in Chapter 3 is to answer the objections and, in the process, make my own view, and its purpose, clearer.

Chisholm's puzzle has to do with "contrary to duty imperatives". These are statements such as 'if you injure your friend, you ought to apologize'. They are iffy oughts purporting to tell us what to do if we fail to do what we should have done in the first place. Consideration of these opened the door to consideration of iffy oughts of many other kinds. Part Two of the book is about all these iffy oughts. The fundamental thesis is that there are very many different logical structures confusingly expressed in ordinary English by sentences with 'if' and 'ought'. In order to understand them, we must first distinguish them from each other.

In Chapter 4, I present my account of the four most basic sorts of iffy ought. These are materially-, subjunctively-, and strictly conditioned absolute moral obligation and conditional moral obligation. I have attempted to provide a unified analysis of as many sorts of obligation as possible, so my account of these concepts is stated in terms of the same notions used in Part One to explain absolute moral obligation — intrinsic value and accessibility. By appeal to these formal structures, I show how Chisholm's puzzle may be solved.

Kant drew attention to a class of statements he called 'hypothetical imperatives'. These are iffy oughts of a different sort, not to be confused with any form of conditioned or conditional moral obligation. They raise some of the most interesting problems on the formal side of moral philosophy. One of these is a puzzle about detachability. We may agree that the hypothetical imperative:

(5)   If you want to kill him, you ought to use a double dose.

is true. Perhaps a smaller dose would be ineffective. We may also agree that, monster that you are, you do want to kill him. Thus,

(6)   You want to kill him.

is also true. Yet we may be unwilling to "detach" the absolute prescription, and conclude that:

(7)   You ought to use a double dose.

is true. Does this mean that we have to regard modus ponens as being invalid in normative contexts?

I present my analysis of hypothetical imperatives in Chapter 5. I explain, by appeal to that analysis, why the inference from (5) and (6) to (7) fails. I also attempt to spell out the other important formal features of such sentences. In addition to this, I introduce and explain the grander Kantian principle nowadays known as "The Hypothetical Imperative". This is the doctrine sometimes formulated as "he who wills the end, wills the means".

One of the most perplexing types of iffy ought is illustrated by such examples as 'if you have made a promise, then you ought to keep it', 'if you have borrowed something, then you ought to return it', etc. Such statements seem to be used to express the idea that the fact mentioned in the antecedent commits one to the action mentioned in the consequent. However, the commitment here is of a deeply defeasible sort. From the fact that you have made a promise, we may conclude only that you have a "prima facie" obligation to keep it. In the final chapter of Part Two, I try to show how problematic these statements of defeasible commitment really are. One of my main theses is that they have little in common with statements of conditioned and conditional moral obligation.

In Part Three, I turn to some extensions of the theory. The first of these, discussed in Chapter 7, has to do with the relations between what individuals ought to do and what groups ought to do. Because of some often misunderstood features of the accessibility relations, it turns out that individuals may fail to be obliged to do their parts in the things their societies are obliged to do. Furthermore, it turns out that, no matter how utilitarian our original assumptions, our moral obligations do not "harmonize". Even if each of us does the best he can, we as a group may fail to achieve the best possible outcome. By appeal to a novel concept ("civic obligation") I try to account for the contrary intuition. I also discuss the remarkably ingenious view ("cooperative utilitarianism") recently developed by Donald Regan. The chapter as a whole may be seen as an attempt to spell out the connections between what individuals ought to do and what groups ought to do. As I try to show, the connection is very tenuous.

In Chapter 8, I turn to another problem whose importance has been brought to light by Castañeda. This has to do with the distinction between the ought-to-do and the ought-to-be. I suspect that many moral philosophers once conceived this to be a merely rhetorical distinction, perhaps having something to do with the scope of the 'ought', or the content of the obligation. Chisholm, for example, once said that 'S ought to do A' means the same as 'it ought to be that S does A'.[6] I try to explain the irreducibility of the ought-to-be and the ought-to-do, and, by appeal to a proposed account of the ought-to-be, I try to explain why some plausible bridge principles fail.

I maintain that there are many sorts of obligation. Among these are moral, prudential, social, and civic. It seems clear that conflicts may arise between obligations of different sorts. For example, a person's moral obligation may conflict with his prudential obligation. Certain forms of obligation (such as civic) seem to admit of a sort of internal conflict. Relative to different social groups, a person may have incompatible civic obligations. Furthermore, even if we stick to absolute moral obligations, certain sorts of conflict seem to be possible. A person's moral obligation as of a certain time may conflict with his moral obligation as of another time. While admitting all this, I still maintain that a person's real moral obligations as of a time cannot conflict among themselves. In Chapter 9, I attempt to explain why someone might see things otherwise. I also attempt to sketch an answer to the question 'Why be moral?'

Throughout this whole book, I have tried to fit things into a very simple metaphysical and axiological scheme. I have tried to show that many different normative notions may be analyzed by appeal to a small number of concepts of value, together with a small number of concepts of possibility. One of the main points I want to defend here is that, for very many of the most important senses of 'obligatory', a statement to the effect that something is obligatory (in that sense) is equivalent to a statement to the effect that it is the best (in some sense) of the possibilities (in some sense).

It will be obvious to any reader that I am deeply indebted to Hector-Neri Castañeda and Roderick Chisholm. They discovered the problems, and suggested many of the answers, that I discuss here. I am also indebted to David Lewis, whose approach to absolute and conditional obligation is the basis for the one developed here. I am also grateful to many other philosophers. Over the years, Ed Gettier has consistently given me extremely valuable help. I have also benefitted enormously from the critical comments of Eva Bodanszky, Earl Conee, Judith DeCew, and Howard Sobel. Earlier versions of the manuscript were read by a number of people. Some of them made very useful suggestions. I would thank them all by name were it not for the fact that they were anonymous referees, and I don't know their names.

A preliminary version of some of the material in Chapters 2 and 4 appeared in 'Obligations: Absolute, Conditioned, and Conditional', *Philosophia* **12**, 3—4 (March, 1983), 257—272. A preliminary version of some of Chapter 7 appeared in 'The Principle of Moral Harmony', *The Journal of Philosophy* **LXXVII**, 3 (March, 1980), 166—179. I thank the editors of *Philosophia* and *The Journal of Philosophy* for permission to make further use of this material.

PART ONE

ABSOLUTE MORAL OBLIGATION

CHAPTER 1

UTILITARIAN FOUNDATIONS

There is a magnificent old idea according to which the concept of obligation can be understood by appeal to the concepts of possibility and goodness. Roughly, the idea is that something is obligatory if and only if it is the best of the possibilities. This idea appears in very simple guise in the popular maxim that "you ought to do the best you can". Classic act utilitarianism is perhaps the most famous theoretical development of the idea. On that view, the possibilities are taken to be the actions open to some person on some occasion, and the goodness of each is taken to be its "hedonic utility" — the amount of pleasure it would produce if performed, minus the amount of pain it would produce if performed. In standard terminology, the view is that a person morally ought to perform an act if and only if none of its alternatives has as great a hedonic utility as it has.

If we leave the general structure of the view as it is, but alter the way in which the goodness of the alternatives is to be measured, we arrive at other normative doctrines. For example, if we substitute "intrinsic goodness" for hedonic utility, we get Moore's "ideal utilitarianism". If we take "value for the agent", we get a sort of egoism.

In this book, I focus upon several normative concepts sharing this general structural feature. Each of them is a concept of obligation, and each of them is analyzed by appeal to some concept of goodness and some concept of possibility. Some of these concepts, such as the one asociated with hedonistic act utilitarianism, are pretty familiar. Others, I suspect, will turn out to be novelties. My view is that, when properly understood, these normative concepts are far more useful and important than is nowadays generally supposed. Indeed, it seems to me that many of our everyday "ought"-statements may best be understood as being rough approximations to statements involving one or another of these "doing-the-best-we-can" concepts of obligation.

It might be thought, then, that my thesis has been amply defended by many illustrious predecessors including Mill, Bentham, Moore, and Smart, among others. There is some truth to this suggestion. Mill and Bentham were the founders of the utilitarian movement. Moore, Smart and others have made significant contributions to our understanding of the doctrine.[1] Nevertheless, none of them has proposed or defended the views I want to propose and defend here. As I have already suggested, I want to consider a variety of concepts of obligation — not just moral obligation. Furthermore, I hold that there are deep formal problems with classic statements of utilitarianism. In my view, the doctrine discussed by Mill, Moore, and Smart is, strictly speaking, incoherent. Thus, it needs at least to be tidied-up before it can reasonably be defended (or fairly dismissed). Let us begin, then, with a brief consideration of classic hedonistic act utilitarianism and its formal problems.

1.1. FORMULATING TRADITIONAL ACT UTILITARIANISM

Utilitarianism is generally understood to be the view that an act is morally right if and only if it maximizes hedonic utility. In this form, it is a view about moral rightness, or permissibility. It can also be formulated as a doctrine about moral obligation. An obligatory act is one whose utility is higher than that of each alternative.

We assume that there is a suitable domain of possible acts, and we use '$a1$', '$a2$', '$a3$' '$b1$', '$b2$', etc. as variables for them. We also assume that there is some relation of alternativeness, and we use 'A$a1$, $a2$' to express the idea that some act, $a1$, is an alternative to some act, $a2$. We use 'U($a1$)' to name the hedonic utility of $a1$ — a number that represents the amount of pleasure $a1$ would produce if performed, minus the amount of pain $a1$ would produce if performed. Finally, we use 'O$a1$' to abbreviate '$a1$ is morally obligatory'. Then we can formulate our utilitarian doctrine as follows:

AUO: O$a1$ iff $(a2)$ (A$a1$, $a2$ → U($a1$) > U($a2$))

Associated doctrines about rightness and wrongness can be formulated in a variety of ways. We might say that an act is morally right iff it is not obligatory to refrain from performing it, and we might say that an act is wrong if it is not right. We can say just about the same thing in a somewhat more cumbersome way if we say that an act is morally right iff no alternative has higher hedonic utility than it has, and an act is morally wrong if some alternative has higher hedonic than it has. These doctrines may be stated, using the natural abbreviations, as follows:

AUR: R$a1$ iff ~ (E$a2$) (A$a1$, $a2$ & U($a2$) > U($a1$))
AUW: W$a1$ iff (E$a2$) (A$a1$, $a2$ & U($a2$) > U($a1$))

In simple cases, we may feel that AUO yields clear results. Suppose I'm looking forward to a Saturday morning, and I haven't yet made my plans for the day. I realize that I could work in the garden, or I could go to the dump, or I could set to work on painting the house. Let's suppose that I will not be able to do any two of these together, and that there is no other interesting option open to me. These three possibilities then seem to be my main alternatives. Suppose, futhermore, that each of these alternatives would produce some pleasure for me, as well as some pain. Each of them would also affect others — my wife, my children, perhaps even my neighbors. Having carefully calculated all the pleasures and pains that would be produced by each choice, we arrive at the Table 1.1.

TABLE 1.1

$a1$:	work in garden	$U(a1) = +12$
$a2$:	go to dump	$U(a2) = +8$
$a3$:	start painting house	$U(a3) = -15$

We may think that the implications of hedonic act utilitarianism are clear enough, even if mistaken. In this case, if the utilities have been properly calculated, AUO seems to imply that I ought to work in the garden, and AUW seems to imply that it would be wrong either to go the the dump or to start painting the house. Furthermore, according to AUR, it seems to follow that it would be morally right to work in the garden. Our formulations thus seem to be suitable expressions of the doctrine intended by the well-known utilitarian thinkers of the past.

1.2. A PUZZLE ABOUT PREREQUISITES

However, there are problems lurking in even this simple case. One problem has to do with some actions that have not yet been mentioned. Notice, first of all, that each of the acts mentioned above would require some preparations. I can't work in the garden unless I first gather my tools. I can't go to the dump unless I first get my truck loaded and started. I can't begin to paint the house unless I first mix the paint. Each of these acts seems to be open to me, and each of them has a utility. What does utilitarianism have to say about them?

Although I don't much enjoy travelling to the dump, I do enjoy loading and starting my truck. This causes pleasure for me, and pain for no one. On the other hand, although I do enjoy working in the garden, I dislike the preparatory efforts. I usually have to search around for my hoe and spade, and I often find them rusty and muddy in the grass. Let's suppose that the utilities of the preparatory acts are as in Table 1.2.

TABLE 1.2

$a4$:	gather garden tools	$U(a4) = -1$
$a5$:	load and start truck	$U(a5) = +1$
$a6$:	mix paint	$U(a6) = -2$

Now the first puzzle is beginning to emerge. Intuitively, we might think that where an act is obligatory, and some other act is a necessary prerequisite to it, that other act is obligatory, too. This seems to me to be a sort of deontic axiom. In the present case, it explains why I should get my hoe. Since, as we have already seen, I ought to work in the garden, and I cannot work in the garden unless I first get my hoe, it seems to follow that I ought to get my hoe. However, the example illustrates the fact that the property of maximizing utility is, in this respect, unlike the property of being obligatory. Although gardening maximizes utility, and gathering tools is a necessary prerequisite to gardening, gathering tools does not maximize utility. It simply is not the case that gathering tools will produce a greater balance of pleasure over pain than each of its alternatives.

The upshot is that our standard version of act utilitarianism seems to conflict with a perfectly reasonable general principle about obligation. Some acts are obligatory because they are necessary prerequisites to other acts that are obligatory. Nevertheless, these necessary prerequisites may fail to maximize utility. According to AUO, no such act is obligatory. Hence, AUO seems to be inadequate.[2]

It may be important to notice that gathering tools will not cause me to work in the garden, and will not cause any of the good that working in the garden will cause. Gathering tools is, at best, only something that helps to make it possible for me to work in the garden. Thus, it would be a mistake to insist that the utility of gathering tools must have been underestimated in the gardening example summarized in Table 1.1 and 1.2. Unless we significantly alter our intuitive concept of hedonic utility, we must accept the fact that there can be cases in which some act with low utility vis-à-vis its alternatives is a necessary prerequisite to another act that has maximal utility vis-à-vis its alternatives.

It might be thought that amalgamation would be the cure here. That is, we might insist that the alternatives in the example be viewed as in Table 1.3.

TABLE 1.3

a7:	gather tools and then work in garden	U(a7) = +11
a8:	load and start truck and then go to dump	U(a8) = + 9
a9:	mix paint and then paint house	U(a9) = −17

This approach, however, leads to problems that are no less serious. These have been explained by Hector-Neri Castañeda in his brilliant paper, 'A Problem for Utilitarianism'.[3] Notice that a7 here is, in effect, a compound act composed of a1 and a4. We can represent this by saying that a7 is the same as (a1 + a4). It might appear that this compound act is obligatory on AUO. As compared to its alternatives, it has the highest utility. But notice that it is not the case that both of its parts are obligatory according to the same standard. As compared to its alternatives, one of them, a4, fails to maximize utility. Hence, AUO seems to imply that a4 would be wrong. In this case, we have a violation of another intuitively plausible principle about obligation — the principle that obligation distributes through conjunction, or:

DC: $O(a1 + a2) \rightarrow Oa1$

In the present example, we have $O(a1 + a4)$, but we don't have $Oa4$. In fact, we seem to have $Wa4$. This shows that we do not solve our original problem merely be combining the various bits and pieces of each course of action. If we try, we discover that a whole course of action may be obligatory, but various of its parts forbidden.

1.2.1. *A Problem about Action Descriptions*

A more complex puzzle can be considered if we permit ourselves to indulge in a bit of whimsey.[4] Suppose there is a devilish machine on which there are four buttons, arranged as in Figure 1.1.

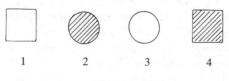

1   2   3   4

Fig. 1.1.

Suppose that the machine is so wired that, at a certain moment, only
one button can be pressed. Suppose also that, depending upon which
button is pressed, the machine will produce various amounts of pleasure and pain in some innocent people. Table 1 lists the utilities of the
various acts of button pushing.

TABLE 1.4

$a1$:	push button number 1	$U(a1) = +10$
$a2$:	push button number 2	$U(a2) = +5$
$a3$:	push button number 3	$U(a3) = -5$
$a4$:	push button number 4	$U(a4) = -10$
$a5$:	push no button	$U(a5) = 0$

Suppose, furthermore, that the operator of this machine has had
some experience with it, and has developed some propensities with
regard to button selection. Although he can press any of the four
buttons, some buttons are more likely than others. Thus, if he were to
press any button, it would be number 3. Also, although he could press
either striped button, he would select number 2 rather than number 4 if
he were to press either striped button. If he were to press an unstriped
button, it would be number 3. If he were to press a square button, it
would be number 4. If he were to press a round one, it would be 3.

The utility of an action is the amount of pleasure it would produce if
it were performed, minus the amount of pain it would produce if it
were performed. Thus, to determine the utility of an action, we have to
consider what would happen if it were performed. Of any set of
alternatives, at most one member will actually be performed. Thus, for
all the rest, the determination of utility remains unalterably counterfactual. It depends on things that *would* happen, if it *were* performed.

Consider that act of pushing a round button. Given the information
so far supplied, we can see that there are two different ways in which
this act might be performed. It might be performed by pushing 2, and it

might be performed by pushing 3. However, we have also seen that the machine operator has certain propensities concerning the selection of buttons. Given this further information, we can see that if he were to push a round button, he would do so by pushing button number 3. Thus, the utility of pushing a round button is the same as the utility of pushing button number 3. In other words, it is −5.

Let us now list some further acts and their alternatives. Each of these acts is also open to the machine operator, and the utility of each is determined by appeal to the information in Table 1.4 and the assumptions mentioned in the preceding paragraphs.

TABLE 1.5

a6:	push a round button	U(a6) = −5
a7:	push a square button	U(a7) = −10
a8:	push a striped button	U(a8) = +5
a9:	push an unstriped button	U(a9) = −5
a10:	push a button	U(a10) = −5

If we say that the machine operator's alternatives include all the acts from a1 to a10, then we must say that it is obligatory for him to push button number 1 (because it has the highest utility) but wrong for him to push a square button, and wrong for him to push an unstriped button (because each of these acts has less than maximal utility). Reflection on the shape and pattern of button number 1 shows how hard it will be for him to do what he ought to do while avoiding what's wrong.

On the other hand, we might take up the idea that alternatives come in sets.[5] Within each set, we might suppose, the acts must be exclusive and exhaustive. No two can be performed together, but at least one must be performed. If we adopt this proposal, we will find that there are several such "alternative sets" in this example. Table 1.6 shows some of them:

TABLE 1.6

A1:	(a1, a2, a3, a4, a5)
A2:	(a5, a6, a7)
A3:	(a5, a8, a9)
A4:	(a5, a10)

In each case, underlining indicates the act with the highest utility of all those in the alternative set. Thus, *a*1 has the highest utility in *A*1, while *a*5 has the highest utility in *A*4. The upshot of all this is that if we take *A*1 to be the relevant alternative set, we seem to get the result that button number 1 ought be be pushed. However, if we take any other set to be relevant, we get some result incompatible with this. For example, if we take *A*3 to be the appropriate set to consider, we seem to be driven to the conclusion that a striped button ought to be pushed. If we take *A*4 to be relevant, then our conclusion is that no button ought to be pushed.

Some people, upon first hearing of this puzzle, are inclined to dismiss it, supposing that the collection of assumptions about the operator is internally inconsistent. They may think, for instance, that it just can't be the case both that he can push any of the four buttons, and also that if he were to push a button, it would be number 3. It may appear that the second claim implies that he can't push any of the other buttons. If this objection is well-founded, then we have no need to investigate solutions to the puzzle. It simply does not arise.

It seems to me, however, that the puzzle is genuine, and that the assumptions about the operator are consistent. I think we may be able to see more clearly how they can be consistent, if we make use of a concept that will be developed in detail in Chapter 2. This is the concept of an "accessible" possible world. The statement that someone can perform a certain act at a certain time, as I see it, is equivalent to the statement that there is a possible world then accessible to him in which he does it. So, in the case described above, I would say that there are several possible worlds accessible to the man at the machine. For each button on the machine, there is at least one accessible world wherein he presses it. There are also worlds accessible in which he presses no button.

From the fact that all these worlds are accessible to him, it does not follow that all of them are equally likely. To use the often misunderstood analogy, we can say that these worlds are not all equally "near" the actual world. It may be that, of all the worlds accessible to this man, the nearest one in which a button is pressed is one in which button number 3 is pressed. Thus, the subjunctive conditional, 'if he were to press a button, it would be number 3' is true.[6] My assumptions, then, amount to little more than this: from nearest to farthest, the accessible worlds are ordered as follows: a world in which button number 3 is pressed; a world in which number 2 is pressed; a world in which number 4 is pressed; a world in which number 1 is pressed; a world in which no button is pressed. Even though these worlds differ in "nearness", each of them is accessible to the operator of the machine from the real world. I think this helps to show how the assumptions can be consistent.

1.2.2. *A Puzzle about Time*

A third puzzle is based on an example that I shall employ for several purposes in this book. It involves a doctor and a patient. The patient has some terrible disease. There are two ways in which the doctor can cure the disease. He can give two successive doses of medicine A, or he can give two successive doses of medicine B. Two doses of A would produce a speedy, safe cure. Two doses of B would produce a somewhat less satisfactory cure. Any mixture of medicines, or failure to administer medicine, will be fatal. Let's agree that the utilities of these various courses of treatment are as catalogued in Table 1.7.

TABLE 1.7

a1:	A on Monday, A on Tuesday	U(a1) = +100
a2:	B on Monday, B on Tuesday	U(a2) = +75
a3:	A on Monday, B on Tuesday	U(a3) = −100
a4:	B on Monday, A on Tuesday	U(a4) = −100
a5:	anything else	U(a5) = −100

If we view the alternatives listed in Table 1.7 from the perspective of utilitarianism, we seem driven to the conclusion that the doctor ought to give two doses of medicine A. That is, he ought to give A on Monday, and then again on Tuesday. After all, this course of treatment has higher utility than any other open to him. So it appears that the doctor ought to give medicine A on Tuesday — that's part of the course of action with highest utility.

Now, to make the puzzle complete, we must add one further assumption about the case. That assumption is that the doctor in fact gives medicine B on Monday. It now appears that a good case can be made for the view that he ought to give B on Tuesday. If he follows up the B on Monday with A on Tuesday, he will kill his patient. So utilitarianism seems to imply that this should be avoided. Similarly, if he follows up the B on Monday with no medicine on Tuesday, he will kill his patient. In order to get the best result still open to him, he must follow up the B on Monday with more B on Tuesday. This will produce a satisfactory cure, and 75 units of utility — clearly a better result than the miserable −100 that would be produced in either of the other available ways.

Thus, it seems that a good case can be made for each of two incompatible conclusions about what the doctor should do on Tuesday. On the hand, we may want to say that the doctor ought to give A on Tuesday. After all, this is part of the the optimal treatment, and it is open to him. On the other hand, we may also want to say that he ought to give B on Tuesday, and not A, since if he gives A he will in fact create a situation in which his patient gets a fatal regimen of B followed by A.[7]

This example shows, I think, that we must be more sensitive to the passage of time. One way in which we can do this involves the temporal relativization of our normative concepts. Instead of formulating necessary and sufficient conditions for an action's (timeless) obligatoriness, we can try to formulate necessary and sufficient conditions for its obligatoriness *as of some time.* Then, if this is handled properly, we can say that, as of Sunday, the doctor had an obligation to give A on Tuesday — because it was part of the best course of action then open to him. As of Monday night, when the first dose of B had already been given, he had an obligation to give B on Tuesday, rather than A. The change in obligations over time is to be explained by appeal to the change in the range of alternatives open to the doctor over the same time.

This gives a hint of the way in which I would deal with this puzzle about time, but it is no better than a hint. In order to determine whether or not the approach will work, we need to see it developed in detail.

1.2.3. *Axiological Problems*

In addition to these formal problems, utilitarianism faces some well known axiological problems. Traditionally, utilitarianism has been linked with a hedonistic theory of value. According to this theory, the value of the consequences of an act is to be determined exclusively by consideration the amounts of pleasure and pain in those consequences. Because of its association with this axiology, utilitarianism has been subjected to a variety of familiar objections. It has been said, for example, that it fails to account for some important intuitions about justice, promises, and rights. Mill struggled with this hedonistic axiology, and (according to standard interpretations) brought forth the doctrine of "qualified hedonism".

In my view, qualified hedonism goes a long way toward answering some of the standard objections to simple hedonism. However, many moral philosophers don't share my enthusiasm for Mill's aproach. Some have argued that qualified hedonism is internally inconsistent.[8] In any case, I intend to avoid these problems with hedonism by rising to higher ground. Following Moore, I shall rather assume that some states of affairs have "intrinsic value", and that it is this sort of value that's important here. Like Moore, I want to understand utilitarianism as the view that we ought to maximize intrinsic value.[9]

If some form of hedonism is true, then my view, stated in terms of intrinsic value, is extensionally equivalent to a corresponding view stated in terms of hedonic utility. However, I suspect that no form of hedonism is entirely satisfactory.

1.3. A SOLUTION TO THE PUZZLES

As I see it, the utilitarian insight may be understood to be the view that what a person ought to do as of a time is what he does in the intrinsically best worlds accessible to him as of that time. This is a preliminary formulation of the view I shall develop and defend in much greater detail in Chapter 2. It differs from classic hedonistic act utilitarianism in several important ways. Three differences seem to me to be most crucial. (1) Instead of trying to identify a person's "alternatives", we consider all the possible worlds still accessible to him as of the time. Thus, we avoid all the problems about the nature of actions and their alternatives. (2) Instead of trying to identify the "consequences" of each alternative, we consider the total intrinsic value of the worlds accessible to the person at the time. (3) Instead of focussing exclusively on pleasure and pain, we reflect upon anything of intrinsic value that occurs in any of the accessible worlds. In this way we avoid the axiological difficulties that trouble hedonistic forms of utilitarianism.

Moral obligation is to be understood by appeal to a concept of possibility and a concept of goodness. Possibility here is accessibility. Goodness is intrinsic value. Nevertheless, the basic moral intuition — that we ought to do the best we can — is retained. This fundamental intuition is at the core of old-fashioned versions of utilitarianism, and it is at the core of my neo-utilitarian view, too.

The three puzzles mentioned above may now be dealt with rather straightforwardly. The first puzzle had to do with prerequisites. We saw, in the gardening example, that an act with relatively low utility might be a necessary prerequisite to an act with maximal utility. When this happens, we come to have incompatible intuitions about the normative status of the act. In the example, the act of gathering my gardening tools seemed to be both obligatory and wrong. It seemed obligatory because it was a necessary prerequisite to gardening, which was itself obligatory. It seemed wrong because it had lower utility than some of its alternatives.

On the new theory, however, we ignore the utility of individual acts. Thus, it doesn't matter whether the act of gathering tools will cause any pleasure. Rather, what matters is a more global feature of the worlds accessible to me as of that Saturday morning. If the best of them is a world in which I toil in the garden, then it must also be one in which I gather my tools beforehand. Everything I do in that world is obligatory, whether it has high utility or not. This approach to the problem thus validates the intuitively plausible view that if an act is obligatory, then every necessary prerequisite to it is obligatory, too.

The puzzle involving the devilish machine is also readily solved. In the best accessible world, the operator of the machine evidently presses button number 1. Since button number 1 is square and unstriped, it follows that in the best accessible world he presses a square, unstriped button. Hence, my view yields the correct results. He ought to press a square button. He ought to press an unstriped button. He ought to press button number 1. The utilities of these acts have no bearing on the operator's obligations. What counts is that he performs these acts in the best accessible world. So we can see that if an act is obligatory, then it is obligatory "under all descriptions".

The medical puzzle is also quite easily handled. As of Sunday, the best world accessible to the doctor is one in which he gives two successive doses of medicine A. So, as of Sunday, he ought to give A on Monday, and he ought to give A on Tuesday. On Monday night, after he has given a dose of B, there is no longer any accessible world in which he gives A on Monday. All such worlds have by then been "bypassed". The remaining worlds are all worlds in which he has already given B on Monday. The best of these is, *ex hypothesi,* one in which he gives a second dose of B on Tuesday, thereby curing his patient in the best way still open to him. Hence, as of Monday night, he ought to give B on Tuesday. (I shall have more to say about this case in Chapter 4, Section 5.)

The account of moral obligation that I have suggested is, so far, rather sketchy. All I have said is that what a person ought to do, as of a time, is what he does in the intrinsically best worlds accessible to him as of that time. I haven't said nearly enough about accessibility, and I haven't said nearly enough about intrinsic value. Nor have I given a fully accurate statement of the normative thesis itself. In Chapter 2, I attempt to make good these deficiencies.

CHAPTER 2

A THEORY OF MORAL OBLIGATION

The fundamental insight behind utilitarianism is that we ought to do the best we can. I think the intuition is worthy of serious attention, but its traditional formulations are unacceptable. In order to formulate this insight adequately, we must have a suitable concept of possibility to account for the meaning of 'can' and a suitable concept of value to account for the meaning of 'best'. In Section 1 of this chapter, I explain my concept of possibility, which I call 'accessibility'. Then, in Section 2, I try to give an account of some of the main features of the concept of intrinsic value, which is the concept of value that is used in the formulation of the theory of moral obligation proposed here. Finally, in Section 3, I state the theory itself, and point out a few of its most fundamental logical features.

2.1. ACCESSIBILITY

Although others have used the term to express other relations, I use 'accessible' to express a relation that holds among a person, a time, and two possible worlds. That is, a world, w', will be said to be accessible to an agent, s, at a time, t, from a world, w. This can be abbreviated as As, t, w', w. Roughly, a world is accessible to a person at a time if and only if it is still possible, at that time, for the person to see to it that the world occurs, or is actual.

In a most simple case, accesibility is relatively easy to understand. Suppose s is the only person in the world, and suppose his only remaining interesting choice as of some time, t, is a choice between some state of affairs, p, and its negation. Suppose all the other facts are already settled, as far as possible. Now we can consider two possible worlds, quite alike up to t, and pretty much alike after t. They differ in that in one of them, p occurs, whereas in the other, $\sim p$ occurs. Of course, they differ in countless other ways, too, since the occurrence of p has all sorts of causal and logical consequences.

Since it is still up to s to determine whether p will occur or not, we can say that at least one possible world in which p occurs is accessible

16

to s at t, and at least one possible world in which $\sim p$ occurs is also accessible to s at t. If there are several different ways in which s can bring about p, then, for each of them, there is an accessible world in which s brings about p in that way.

If some state of affairs, q, is impossible for s as of t, then no q-world is accessible to s at t. For example, if q is metaphysically impossible, then it occurs in no accessible world. Furthermore, if q's impossibility is merely physical, then q still occurs in no world accessible to s. Finally, if q is something that is impossible for s in virtue of the fact that s simply lacks the ability, or skill, or capacity to see to the occurrence of q, then, once again, q occurs in no world accessible to s.

In the typical sort of case, involving real people in the real world, each agent has open to him an enormous variety of options. For each compossible system of options open to him, there is at least one accessible world. In each such world, the agent adopts one of these systems of compossible options. I used to think that accessibility could be defined by appeal to considerations about these systems of compossible options.[1] More exactly, I used to think that we could say that a world, w', is accessible to an agent, s, at a time, t, from a world, w, if and only if there is some "life history" still open to s at t in w such that, if s were to live out that life history, then w' would be actual. The problem with this approach, impressed upon me by David Lewis, is that it isn't clear that there always is a unique possible world that is the one that would exist if s were to live out his life in the specified way. Maybe two worlds would be equally likely on that assumption. In this case, neither world would be accessible on the proposed definition.

I have a second reason for preferring not to define accessibility in the suggested way. Notice that the proposed definition makes use of the notion of a life history being "open" to an agent at a time. To say that a life history is "open" is to say that the agent still can live it out — it is still one of his possibilities. Thus, on the suggested definition, we define accessibility by appeal to the concept of "being something s can do". As I now see it, this gets things in the wrong order. The concept of being something someone can do is an obscure one. It is preferable, I think, to avoid making use of it in the attempt to define so important a notion as accessibility. Rather, I prefer to take accessibility as a conceptual primitive, and elucidate its meaning as best I can in various informal ways, and then go on to define the concept of openness, or power, in terms of it.

So accessibility remains undefined here. Loosely, and informally, we may say that a world is accessible to an agent at a time if and only if he still can see to it that that world occurs, or is actual. An accessible world is one that is still open to the agent. It remains among his live options.

2.1.1. *Indiscernibility with Respect to the Past*

If a world, w', is accessible to an agent, s, at a time, t, from a world, w, then w' must be quite like w up to t. Indeed, there is a natural inclination to suppose that w and w' must be exactly alike up to t. To suppose otherwise is to suppose that, as of t, s has it in his power to change the past. For if w and w' differ with respect to their pasts as of t, and s still has the power to determine which of them will occur, then s has it in his power to affect how things will have been before t. It is reasonable to suppose that no one ever is able to do any such thing, and so it is reasonable to suppose that accessible worlds must be "past-wise indiscernible".

I think this natural inclination is mistaken. In order to see why, let us consider an example. Suppose I now have my choice among three options for tomorrow morning. I can work in the garden, I can go to the dump, or I can start painting the house. In this case, among the worlds currently accessible to me, there is at least one in which I garden tomorrow, at least one in which I go to the dump tomorrow, and at least one in which I start painting tomorrow. So the accessible worlds differ with respect to their futures.

It seems to me that these worlds must also differ with respect to their pasts. For example, suppose that last week I promised my wife that I would start painting tomorrow. Some of the worlds currently accessible to me are worlds in which I break that promise, and at least one of them is a world in which I keep it. It seems to me to follow that some of the worlds accessible to me now are worlds in which last week I made a promise that would be broken, and at least one of them is a world in which last week I made a promise that would be kept. This difference among the worlds is admittedly very trivial, but it seems to me that it is a difference nevertheless. Furthermore, it is a difference about the pasts of these accessible worlds. Thus, in this example, there are accessible worlds which differ with repect to their pasts.

In general, I think it can be shown that if anyone ever has accessible to him two worlds that differ with respect to their futures, then he then has accessible to him worlds that differ with respect to their pasts. For suppose s now has his choice between p and $\sim p$ tomorrow. Then there is a p-world accessible to s now, and there is a $\sim p$-world accessible to s now. In the p-world, it was already true yesterday that s will bring about p tomorrow. In the $\sim p$-world, no such thing was true yesterday. Hence, the worlds differ with respect to their pasts.

Perhaps another example will help to clarify this point. Suppose I smoked up until yesterday, but have not smoked for the past 24 hours. I now consider whether I shall take up smoking again. A world in which I resume smoking is accessible, and a world in which I never smoke again is accessible. These worlds differ with respect to their futures, but they also differ with respect to their pasts. In one of them, a certain cigarette that I smoked yesterday then had the property of being the last cigarette ever smoked by me. In the other world, that cigarette did not have that property. Yesterday, when I smoked it, it had the property a being such that I would smoke many cigarettes after it.

It should be clear that, in the examples just cited, the pasts of the accessible worlds differ only in certain very trivial ways. In the smoking example, the difference has to do with the question whether a certain cigarette was my last. In one world, 'this is Feldman's final cigarette' was true. In the other world, it was false. Such a fact as this is deeply "future infected". That is, its truth depends crucially upon what will happen later on. Once we see this, we immediately recognize that there are many such facts: facts about the truth values of various predictions; facts about whether or not some belief about the future constitutes knowledge; facts about whether or not some soldier has died in vain; facts about whether or not some promise will be fulfilled. In each such case, whether or not the future-infected state of affairs is a fact depends crucially upon how things turn out in the future. I think it is pretty clear, then, that if, among the worlds accessible to some one at some time there are some that differ with respect to their futures, then, among those worlds, there are some that differ with respect to the future-infected aspects of their pasts.

I think we may want to go beyond this fairly trivial point about past-wise indiscernibility. It is interesting to notice that if causal determinism is true, and we have power over the future, then we have a far less trivial sort of power over the past. To see this, suppose that determinism is true, and suppose also that I now have my choice of coffee, tea, or milk. Since falsifying determinism is not within my power, every accessible world must be deterministic. So in the accessible coffee-world, I must be caused to choose coffee. Hence, in that world, I must have had some property yesterday that is causally sufficient for coffee today. Similarly for the tea-world and the milk-world. These worlds must differ with respect to their yesterdays, since in each of them, I must have had a property yesterday that would be sufficient for my drinking whatever it is I turn out to drink in that world today. So if determinism is true, and worlds that differ in interesting ways with respect to their futures are accessible, then worlds that differ in interesting ways with respect to their pasts are also accessible.

In light of these facts, we cannot say that all the worlds accessible to an agent at a time are past-wise indiscernible. However, if we are realistic about it, we must acknowledge that our power over the past is somehow derivative from our power over the future. Most of our significant choices are apparently choices with respect to the future. Since some facts about the past are future-infected, we have a sort of derived power over the past. The exact extent and nature of this power is a matter of some controversy, and I shall not attempt to determine it here.[2]

2.1.2. *Some Formal Features of Accessibility*

Now let us consider some of the more formal features of accessibility. For one things, whatever world you are in is accessible to you from there. We can call this "reflexivity", and we can formulate the relevant principle as an axiom about accessibility:

Al: $(s)(t)(w')(w)(As, t, w', w \rightarrow As, t, w, w)$

In other words, if any world is accessible to s at t from w, then w itself is. For us, this means that the real world is always accessible to us from here. In light of this, we can say that anything that in fact is going to happen is something that can happen.

Suppose that w' is accessible to s at t from w. Then the past of w' is sufficiently like that of w so that nothing that has yet happened in w' rules out w'. It is still, at t, in s's power to choose between these worlds. In a way, then, we can view this as a case in which s is still living in both w and w, and hasn't yet done anything to filter out either of them. So we have to say that w is also accessible to s at t from w'. For this reason, accessibility is "symmetric":

A2: $(s)\,(t)\,(w')\,(w)\,(A s,\,t,\,w',\,w \rightarrow A s,\,t,\,w,\,w')$

As I see it, accessibility is also "transitive", in this sense:

A3: $(s)\,(t)\,(w)\,(w')\,(w'')\,(A s,\,t,\,w,\,w'\,\&\,A s,\,t,\,w''w' \rightarrow A s,\,t,\,w'',\,w)$

The transitivity axiom may easily be misunderstood. It is important to recognize that it does not imply, for example, that if s can work in his garden, and if he were to work in his garden, then he would be able to harvest his crop, that he can *already* harvest his crop. What A3 does mean is that if a world in which he gardens is accessible to s from here now, and if a world in which he harvests is accessible to him from there now, then the world in which he harvests is also accessible to him from here now. Undoubtedly, even in that harvest-world, he must garden diligently all summer long before he can bring in the harvest. No world is accessible in which he harvests without gardening.

There is only one interesting axiom about accessibility and time. This one says, roughly, that the set of accessible worlds never grows. More exactly, the axiom is this:

A4: $(w)\,(w')\,(s)\,(t)\,(t')\,(A s,\,t,\,w',\,w\,\&\,t' < t\,\&\,s$ exists at t' in $w \rightarrow A s,\,t',\,w',\,w)$

In other words, if a world is accessible to you from here now, then that world always has been accessible to you from here. Although you may lose certain opportunities as time goes by, you will never gain any wholly new ones.

My own view is that the truth is somewhat bleaker than A4 implies. As I see it, the set of accessible worlds is constantly shrinking. With every passing choice we have accessible to us only a proper subset of the set of worlds accessible to us before it. We begin our lives with an enormous set of accessible worlds. As time goes by, we filter out world after world. As we near death, the set becomes smaller and smaller. At the end, when no choices remain, nothing is accessible to us from the real world except the real world itself.

There are no interesting axioms relating what's accessible to one agent to what's accessible to another agent at the same time. A world may be accessible to s at t from w, but not to s' at t from w even though *s* and *s'* are as close as you like. For example, suppose that *s* and *s'* are neighbors, and each has a garden. Suppose *s* has choice between working in his garden one morning and not. Suppose that there's nothing *s'* can do either to make *s* work in the garden, or to prevent him from doing so. Suppose, finally, that *s* is not going to work in his garden that day. Then there is a world accessible to *s* in which he works in his garden, but no world in which *s* works in his garden is accessible to *s'*. Intuitively, the point is that *s* can see to it that *s* works in his garden, but *s'* can't see to it that *s* works in his garden.

In general, I want to treat the behavior of others in just the way I treat any event in the natural world. If *s* can't affect the behavior of another person, *s'*, and *s'* is going to behave in a certain way, then *s'* behaves in that way in every world accessible to *s*. If *s* can influence *s'*s behavior, then there are worlds accessible to *s* in which *s'* behaves in one way, and other worlds accessible to *s* in which *s'* behaves in the other way. In my view, our knowlege (or the lack of it) concerning the behavior of others is irrelevant here. Suppose *s'* has good reason to believe that *s* is going to work in his garden. *s'* might be willing to bet extravagant sums of money on this question. But if in fact *s* is not going to work in his garden, and *s'* can't make him do it, then no world in which *s* gardens is accessible to *s'*. Accessibility is not an epistemic notion.

2.1.3. *Unalterability, Power, and Openness*

Three important technical terms can be defined by appeal to our undefined concept of accessibility. These technical terms will prove to be quite useful later on. The first of these is 'unalterable'. When I say that a state of affairs is unalterable for a person at a time, I mean that it occurs in every world that is accessible to him as of that time. I use U*s, t, p* to express this notion. The official definition is this:

U: U*s, t, p* is true at *w* iff (w') (A*s, t, w', w* → *p* is true at *w'*)

If a state of affairs is unalterable for a person as of a time, then, no matter what he does (of all he can do) that state of affairs occurs.

Substantial facts already in the past are, in this sense, unalterable. Things in the future, but which *s* can't prevent, such as tomorrow's sunrise, are also unalterable for *s*. Things other people will do, and which are outside of *s*'s influence, are also unalterable for *s*, although they are not always unalterable for their own agents. Logical and causal necessities, no matter when they occur, are also unalterable for all of us at all times.

If someone has been brainwashed, or hypnotized, he may find that he has no choice with respect to some bit of behavior. For example, suppose I've been given a post-hypnotic suggestion. I will tend my garden tomorrow morning. When morning rolls around, I will be the one who makes this happen. I will gather my hoe and spade. I will put them in the wheelbarrow, and head for the garden. So I clearly have a certain sort of power over my tending of the garden. It is something I make happen. Yet, in my sense, it is unalterable for me. It is something I do in every world accessible to me.

When I say, using it as a technical term, that some state of affairs is "in my power" as of some time, I mean that this state of affairs occurs in some possible world accessible to me as of that time. I formerly thought of this as the "can do", and so I used, and still use Ks, t, p to express it. I define it as follows:

K: Ks, t, p is true at w iff $(Ew')(As, t, w', w \& p$ is true at $w')$

It now seems to me that it is somewhat misleading to think of this as the "can do", since many things that are in someone's power in this sense are not things that he can do. For example, tomorrow's sunrise is, in my sense, in your power today. It occurs in a world now accessible to you. (In fact, it occurs in all of them.) But you don't make the sun rise. The sunrise is not something that you "do" at all. Thus, Ks, t, p does not express the idea that as of t, s can do p. Rather, it expresses the idea that, as of t, s can see to the occurrence of p.

Among the things within a person's power as of a time are all the things that are unalterable for him then. He can see to the occurrence of such things merely by biding his time. No matter what he does, such things will happen — or already have happened. Furthermore, among things that are not unalterable, the agent's own possible future actions are within his power. If I can freely choose to work in my garden tomorrow, then there is a world accessible to me now in which I do so. In that case, according to K, working in my garden tomorrow is now within my power. Similarly, causal and other consequences of things that are in my power are also in my power. For example, suppose that my planting them today would cause my peas to sprout next Monday, and suppose that I now have the planting of the peas today in my power. Then I have it in my power to see to it that my peas sprout Monday. Finally, if I can get you to do something, perhaps by asking you to do it, or by issuing a threat, then your action may be in my power.

A final interesting concept is the concept of "openness". A state of affairs is open for a person as of a time iff it is in his power then, but not unalterable. It happens in some of the worlds accessible to him, but not all.

2.1.4. *The Epistemology of Accessibility*

It should be clear, in light what I've already said, that most of us, most of the time, don't have very extensive knowledge about which worlds are accessible to us. I'm pretty sure that there is a world accessible to me in which I work in the garden tomorrow morning, and I'm also pretty sure that there is a world accessible to me in which I go to the dump. However, I really don't know for sure whether there is any world accessible to me in which I harvest a good crop of peas at harvest time this summer, and I really don't know whether there is a world accessible to me in which I finally get the garage and shed cleaned out. These things take time, and, for all I know, something quite outside of my control may be coming along — something that will make it impossible for me to perform these tasks at the requisite time.

It mustn't be assumed that our ignorance about accessible worlds is restricted to cases involving the distant future. Here is a striking example concerning the very near future. Suppose I am holding a pair of dice in my hands. I am certain that there is a world accessible to me in which I roll the dice, but I simply do not know whether there is a world accessible to me in which I roll snake eyes on the first try. Perhaps such a world is accessible to me. If I roll the dice, and snake eyes turn up, then I will have determined that such a world was accessible all along. If I don't roll the dice, I will probably never know whether such a world was accessible to me.

There is a very important, but slightly different sort of epistemological problem about accessibility. This problem has to do with "knowing how", rather than with "knowing that". Suppose there is a safe with a combination lock right before me. Suppose I know that the lock is in good working order, and that the combination consists of three numbers. I realize that my fingers are in pretty good working order, and so I am capable of dialing any of the thousands of possible combi-nations. Thus, I know that for each combination, there is a world now accessible to me in which I dial that combination. Furthermore, since I know these things about the lock and my fingers, I also know that there is a world accessible to me in which I open the safe on the very first try. Nevertheless, I don't know how to "access" that world. Since I don't know which of the thousands of possible combinations will open the lock, I don't know how to make actual the world in which I dial the correct combination, and thereby open the safe.

If I were to try to open the safe, it is virtually certain that I would not succeed — surely not on the first try in any case. Thus, there is an important sense in which it would be correct to say, in a case such as this one, that I lack the ability to open the safe. I have no analysis of the concept expressed by 'ability' here. It is clearly not expressed by my 'K'. If we let f name me, and t name now, and we let p stand for the state of affairs *Feldman opening the safe*, then (given our assumptions) Kf, t, p must be judged to be true. There is a world accessible to me in which I open the safe. This seems to me to be a desirable result, since there is pretty clearly a sense in which I can open the safe. All I have to do is dial the correct combination. Since I can dial any combination, surely I can dial the correct one. The problem is that I don't know which one is the correct one, and so, in some as yet unexplained sense, I lack the ability to open the safe.

My general point here is a point about the epistemology of accessi-bility. I want to emphasize that most of us, most of the time, do not know which worlds are accessible to us. We don't know, in any great detail, what is within our power. Furthermore, even if we know that a certain sort of world is accessible, we may not know how to make any such world actual. Thus, even if I know that a certain state of affairs is in my power, I may nevertheless not know precisely what I have to do in order to see to its occurrence.

Moral obligation, as I see it, is to be explained by appeal to a concept of possibility and and concept of value. So far, I have been talking primarily about the relevant concept of possibility, which I call 'accessibility'. We now must turn to the relevant value concept — intrinsic value.

2.2. INTRINSIC VALUE

In order to assure a sort of uniformity and coherence, it will be useful to suppose that every bearer of value is a state of affairs. Thus, instead of saying that pleasure is good, I will say that the state of affairs of *someone's being pleased* is good; instead of saying that a certain person is good, I will say that the state of affairs of his existing is good. I believe that every attribution of value with which we will have to deal can thus be recast as an attribution of value to some state of affairs.

2.2.1. *Identifying Intrinsic Value*

A state of affairs may have a variety of sorts of value. It may be good as a means, as is, for example, the existence of plastic. It may be beautiful, as the existence of plastic apparently is not. It may be good as a sign. We sometimes hear a doctor say, 'that's good', when looking at an X-ray photograph. Perhaps he sees something that he takes to be a sign of good health. There may be other kinds of good and evil, too. However, what's most important here is "intrinsic" good and evil. Philosophers have used a lot of vague expressions in the attempt to get us to focus on intrinsic good and evil. They have said that this is the value a thing has "in itself", "in virtue of its own nature", "independently", "per se", etc. But I fear that if someone doesn't understand what intrinsic value is supposed to be, this sort of talk won't help.

Perhaps the most natural way to get someone to focus on the concept of intrinsic value is the Socratic way. We ask the person to mention something he takes to be good. Perhaps he will say that warm, sunny weather is good. Then we ask him why he thinks such weather is good. Perhaps he will reply by saying that, under standard conditions, such weather will help to make the fruits and vegetables grow more successfully. Pursuing the same line of questioning, we ask him whether he thinks it is a good thing that the fruits and vegetables grow successfully, and if so, why. If we follow out this Socratic line long enough, and if our respondent is willing to give honest and thoughtful answers, he will eventually come to a stop. He will come to something (perhaps the pleasure one gets from eating tasty fruits and vegetables) that he takes to be good, but whose goodness is not to be explained by appeal to any of its effects, or consequences, or accompaniments. When our respondent has reached such a point in the exchange, he has made a judgment about intrinsic value. He is saying that a certain sort of pleasure is intrinsically good. Or, to put the point in more official terminology, he is saying that the state of affairs of *someone's getting pleasure as a result of eating tasty fruits and vegetables* is intrinsically good.

Unfortunately, the Socratic line doesn't always work. Some respondents are unable or unwilling to participate. Others may be too willing. They can't find a place to stop. In any case, it would be good to have a more precise account of our concept of intrinsic value. Is there any clear principle that serves to distinguish intrinsic value from value of all other sorts?

2.2.2. *The Isolation Test*

Moore suggested that the intrinsic value of a thing is the value it would have if it existed in complete isolation.[3] When applied to states of affairs, this has no clear sense. An ordinary state of affairs, such as my being quite happy, simply can't occur in isolation. If it occurs, it occurs in some possible world. All of its entailments occur there, too. Furthermore, lots of other things occur there. In fact, for every state of affairs, either it or its negation occurs there. So it is hard to see just what it could mean to say that such a state of affairs occurs in isolation.

2.2.3. *Intrinsic Value as Necessary Value*

There is another traditional approach according to which intrinsic value, unlike all other sorts of value, is value that is had necessarily by the things that have it. Chisholm once stated this view rather neatly. He said:

And what do we mean when we say that a state of affairs is *intrinsically* good, or *intrinsically* bad — as distinguished from being merely *instrumentally* good or *instrumentally* bad? I suggest this: A state of affairs is *intrinsically* good if it is necessarily good — if it is good in every possible world in which it occurs.[4]

As should be obvious upon reflection, this approach is based on the idea that there is some more fundamental sort of value — we can call it "overall value". Some things have this sort of value necessarily, and others have it contingently. Chisholm's suggestion here, as I see it, is that if a state of affairs has this overall value only contingently, then its value is all extrinsic (non-intrinsic). On the other hand, if a thing has some overall value necessarily, then at least part of its value is intrinsic.

Before we attempt to deal with this suggestion, it will be useful to state it more exactly. Assuming that intrinsic values can be represented by numbers, we use IV(p) as a convenient way of naming the intrinsic value of the state of affairs, p. Thus, I assume that there is an intrinsic value function that takes us from states of affairs to numbers. Similarly, we can use V(p) to name the overall value of p. V(p) depends in some as yet unexplained way on p's intrinsic, extrinsic, signatory, and other values. We assume, quite naturally, that where IV(p) is greater than 0, p is intrinsically good; where IV(p) is less than 0, p is intrinsically bad; where IV(p) = 0, p is intrinsically neutral; and we make corresponding assumptions about V(p) and p's overall value.

The present proposal is that 'a state of affairs is intrinsically good if it is necessarily good'. The most natural way of formulating this proposal, making use of the suggested abbreviations, would be:

(1) $IV(p) > 0$ iff $N(V(p) > 0)$

In other words, a state of affairs, p, is intrinsically good if and only if it is necessary that it is overall good.

A moment's reflection reveals that this won't do. An intrinsically good state of affairs may be so bad extrinsically that its overall value falls below zero. My happiness might cause everyone else to be very sad. Then, even though my happiness would still be intrinsically good, it would be overall bad.

Chisholm has affirmed a different, but very closely related thesis about intrinsic value. In 'The Defeat of Good and Evil' he said that ". . . propositions about intrinsic value may be said to hold in every possible world and therefore they may be thought of as being necessary."[5] Obviously, Chisholm did not mean to affirm that *every* proposition about intrinsic value is a necessary truth. (Consider, for example, the proposition that *Chisholm has written about intrinsic value*.) Rather, his point was that if a certain state of affairs has a certain intrinsic value, then it has that value necessarily. In other words:

(2) $(n)(p)(IV(p) = n \rightarrow N(IV(p) = n))$

I think (2) is true. If happiness is intrinsically good, then it is necessary that happiness is intrinsically good. It can't just be an accident that something is good in itself. Since its intrinsic goodness derives from its own nature — from what it is per se — and this can't change, its intrinsic goodness can't change, either.

Notice that the corresponding thesis concerning extrinsic value is not correct. We cannot say:

$$(3) \qquad (n)\,(p)\,(V(p) = n \rightarrow N(V(p) = n))$$

This doctrine is false because a state of affairs that is useful in one possible world may be counterproductive in another. Thus, it might be overall good in the first world, but overall neutral in the second. Overall value is had only contingently, whereas intrinsic value is had necessarily.

While intrinsic value seems to differ in this way from overall value, it isn't clear that this difference provides a way of identifying intrinsic value. Perhaps there are other sorts of value that things have necessarily if at all. Evidential value might be an example. In any case, I think we can say that a kind of value is intrinsic only if things that have it, have it necessarily.

2.2.4. *Intrinsic Value of Possible Worlds*

Some of the most important views I want to discuss here are formulated in terms of the intrinsic values of various possible worlds. Thus, it will be useful to say a few words about the way in which the intrinsic value of a world relates to the intrinsic values of the things that occur in it.

One thing that we surely do not want to say is that the intrinsic value of a world is equal to the sum of the intrinsic values of the things that occur in it. One trouble with this view is that it would have us count the same things over and over again too many times. Suppose, for example, that there is a world, w, in which nothing intrinsically bad happens, and in which "just one" intrinsically good thing happens. Suppose the intrinsically good thing that happens there is this:

p: Jones is pleased at Noon, January 1.

Suppose that the intrinsic value of this state of affairs is exactly +10. It would be reasonable to suppose, in light of all this, that the intrinsic value of the world as a whole would also be +10.

Notice that if p is true at a world, then many other states of affairs related to *p* are also true there. For example, consider any conjunction of *p* with something else true at the world, such as:

q: Jones is pleased at Noon, January 1, and grass is green.

Consider the existential generalization of *p*:

r: Someone is pleased at Noon, January 1.

Consider the disjunction of *p* and some equally valuable falsehood:

s: Either Jones is pleased at Noon, January 1, or Smith is pleased at Noon, January 1.

Each of these things seems to have the same intrinsic value as *p*, and each of them occurs in worlds in which *p* occurs. Suppose they all occur in *w*. If this is right, then it is clear that there are indefinitely many intrinsically good states of affairs occurring along with *p* in *w*. If the intrinsic value of *w* is the sum of the intrinsic values of the things occurring there, we will have to say that the value of *w* is extremely high — much higher than +10. This is obviously wrong.

2.2.5. *Basic Intrinsic Value States*

Some intrinsically good states of affairs seem to have their intrinsic value in a more basic way than others. To see this, it may be useful to reconsider some of the examples that were just mentioned.

p: Jones is pleased at Noon, January 1.
q: Jones is pleased at Noon, January 1, and grass is green.
r: Someone is pleased at Noon, January 1.
s: Either Jones is pleased at Noon, January 1, or Smith is pleased at Noon, January 1.

It seems to me that while each of these is intrinsically good, *p* has its intrinsic goodness in a more fundamental way than any of the others. Part of the difference is that *p* seems to focus on the core of the good thing. It gives us no extraneous information, and it gives us all the essential information. The others contain either too much information or too little. For example, *q* tells us that grass is green — and that has no bearing on the intrinsic value of *q*. *r*, on the other hand, leaves out an important fact. It doesn't tell us *who* is pleased at Noon.

The general idea should be clear. A basic intrinsic value state is one that includes neither more than nor less than the part that is of value. It focusses exclusively on the thing of value. If we choose our basics correctly, it will turn out that the intrinsic value of a possible world is equal to the sum of the intrinsic values of the basic intrinsic value states that occur there. So it will be important to be able to identify the basics.

Unfortunately, it is not easy to say precisely what 'basic' means, and it is not easy to say precisely which states of affairs are the basics. One problem is that different axiologies imply different views about what's basic. For example, let's consider the simplest form of hedonism. On this view, pleasure is intrinsically good, and pain is intrinsically bad. Nothing else has any intrinsic value. More pleasure is always intrinsically better than less, and more pain is always intrinsically worse than less. No consideration is paid to such questions as whether the pleasure is of "high quality"; whether it is deserved; whether it is properly distributed; whether it is pleasure taken in a fitting object; etc.

If we adopt this axiological stance, we will have to say that a basic intrinsic value state is one that is about a certain individual, to the effect that he or she (or it) feels pleasure or pain to some specified degree at some specified time. Thus:

u: Jones is pleased to degree 5 at Noon, January 1, 2000.

might be basic, but none of the states of affairs mentioned a few paragraphs back would be basic. In order for u to be basic, 'Jones' would have to be an unambiguous and contentless name for some individual, and 'Noon, January 1, 2000' would have to be an unambiguous and contentless name for some suitable moment of time.

In general, we can say that, according to the simplest form of hedonism, the basics are all and only the states of affairs relevantly like u. Such things as p, q, r, and s would not be basics, since they either leave out some crucial information, or contain too much information. Thus, simple hedonism would be associated with this view about basics:

B/SH: p is a basic intrinsic value state iff $(Es)(En)(Et)$ (p is the state of affairs of s being pleased (pained) exactly to degree n at t).

Even in this simplest of cases, there are serious complications. One of these has to do with times. To see the difficulty, suppose that Jones enjoys some pleasure of uniform intensity throughout a one-minute long period of time. In this case, Jones also enjoys that pleasure throughout each of six different ten-second periods of time, and throughout each of ten different six-second periods of time, and throughout each of 60 different one-second periods of time. Indeed, if we slice the minute in other ways, we will be able to come up with indefinitely many intervals during which Jones enjoys pleasure. Since we want the value of the world to be equal to the sum of the values of the basics, we do not want there to be a different basic intrinsic value state for each of these periods of time. If we do so, we permit the same episode of pleasure to be counted over and over again. Thus, we must see to it that our basics are temporally discrete.

Let us assume, then, that time can be split up into an exhaustive and exclusive set of intervals of minimal duration. Let us furthermore assume that these intervals are just long enough so that it makes sense to say that someone feels pleasure or pain during one. Any episode of pleasure that takes up a longer period of time will be seen as being a collection of episodes, each of which is one unit in duration. Now we can insist that the 't' in B/SH be viewed as ranging over these minimal intervals. In this way we assure ourselves that no two basics will overlap temporally in an unsuitable way. I have to admit that these assumptions are controversial. However, they help to simplify our current project, and it does not seem to me that they are clearly wrong.

Another problem here has to do with the assumption that pleasure and pain are magnitudes susceptible of measurement. We needn't assume that these are in practice open to measurement, but merely that they are things that come in amounts having the features necessary to make measurement a conceptual possibility. I hereby make the necessary assumption.

If a person is experiencing pleasure, we can say that he is pleased to some degree, n, where n is positive. If he is experiencing pain, we can say that he is pleased to some degree, n, where n is negative. The more intense the pleasure (pain), the higher (lower) n will be. If the person is experiencing neither pleasure nor pain, we will say that he is pleased to degree 0.

If the simplest form of hedonism is true, then the intrinsic value of a basic intrinsic value state is directly proportional to the number, n, that records the intensity of the pleasure or pain experienced in that state. More intense pleasures are intrinsically better than less intense ones. More intense pains are worse than less intense ones. Any pleasure is better than any pain. Any pleasure is better than no pleasure. Any pain is worse than no pain.

Now we are in position to affirm a general principle concerning the values of worlds. It is this: if simple hedonism is true, then the intrinsic value of a possible world is equal to the sum of the intrinsic values of all the basic intrinsic value states, as determined by B/SH, that occur there. This principle would be of considerable interest if anyone believed in simple hedonism. I suspect that few do.

It should be noted that this approach does not assign intrinsic values to states of affairs other than basics and worlds. Thus, nothing I have said here would enable us to determine the intrinsic values of such things as p, q, r, and s (mentioned a few paragraphs back), even if we agreed that simple hedonism is true. This seems to me to be no defect in the approach, although it might be nice to have more to say about the intrinsic values of non-basic intrinsic value states.[6]

2.2.6. *More Complex Axiologies*

If we think that the "quality" of a pleasure or a pain has some bearing on the intrinsic value of that pleasure or pain, then we will have to reject simple hedonism. We will have to say that a state of affairs such as:

u: Jones is pleased to degree 5 at Noon, January 1, 2000.

is too indeterminate in value to serve as a basic intrinsic value state. For if the pleasure Jones feels is of very high quality, then the intrinsic value associated with u is very high, whereas if that pleasure is of low quality, then u itself is of low intrinsic value. The intrinsic value of a basic intrinsic value state must be perfectly determinate, and it must be unalterable — no further information about the circumstances of its occurrence should move us to think that it might be worth more or less than we originally thought.

If we assume that pleasures and pains come in different qualities, and that these qualities can be represented by suitable numbers, then we can formulate a coherent version of qualified hedonism. Let us suppose, therefore, that pleasures and pains can be ranked for quality on a scale from 0 to 1, with the lowest quality pleasures and pains getting a 0 and the highest quality ones getting a 1. I shall not venture to say just what makes for high or low quality. Perhaps the interested reader should consult the relevant passages in Mill for that. My point is more formal.

As I see it, qualified hedonism requires that basic intrinsic value states look more like this:

v: Jones is pleased to degree 5 and quality .6 at Noon, January 1, 2000.

Once again, if v is to be a basic intrinsic value state, then 'Jones' must be an unambiguous contentless name of some individual, and 'Noon, January 1, 2000' must be an unambiguous contentless name for some suitable time.

In general, the qualified hedonist will say that basic intrinsic value states are all ones relevantly like v. So the fundamental thesis can be put in this way:

B/QH: p is a basic intrinsic value state if and only if $(Es)(En)$ $(Em)(Et)$ (p is the state of affairs of s feeling pleasure (pain) of quantity n and quality m at time t).

Once again, we have to make the necessary proviso concerning the times. We must assume that time can be discretized, and that the 't' in B/QH ranges over the set of discretized minimal intervals.

The qualified hedonist may now affirm that the intrinsic value of a basic intrinsic value state is a function of the quantity and quality of the pleasure or pain involved in that state. The simplest principle here would identify the intrinsic value of the state with the product of the quality and quantity of the pleasure or pain. In this case, basic intrinsic value states with high quality pleasure would get relatively high intrinsic values, whereas those with low quality pleasure would get low intrinsic values, even if they involved pleasures of equal intensity. In the limiting case of a pleasure of quality 0, the intrinsic value would be 0, no matter how intense the pleasure might be. Such pleasure could literally be said to be (intrinsically) worthless.

It should be clear now that the principle defining the intrinsic value of worlds may be carried over from simple hedonism to this version of qualified hedonism. We can still say that the intrinsic value of a world is equal to the sum of the intrinsic values of the basic intrinsic value states that occur there. However, when we say this now, we will have in mind a whole new set of basics, and so we may arrive at radically different conclusions concerning the intrinsic values of various specified possible worlds. Ones that were quite good according to simple hedonism might turn out to be utterly worthless, or even rather bad according to qualified hedonism. It all depends upon the quality ratings of the pleasures and pains that occur in the worlds.

This sketch of two forms of hedonism should suggest the general features required of an axiological system. For each such system, there are states of affairs of some special sort that are taken as basic intrinsic value states. Thus, there is a general principle (or a set of principles) specifying the basic intrinsic value states. For each type of state, there is also a principle explaining how to assign intrinsic values to states of that kind. Finally, there is the grand principle stating that the intrinsic value of a possible world is equal to the sum of the intrinsic values of the basics that occur there.

In order to state my own normative view in a truly adequate form, I would have to present a complete axiological system. I would have to say which states of affairs have significant amounts of intrinsic value, and I would have to say which of them are the basics. I would also have to explain how the value of each such state is to be determined. Moore attempted to do something quite like this in Chapter VI of *Principia Ethica*. Unfortunately, I find that I am not able to provide anything as rich and detailed as Moore's axiology.

One problem for me is that my intuitions about what has intrinsic value are not sufficiently firm. Freedom, for example, is a source of puzzlement. Sometimes I think that freedom is good only as a means, and then at other times I become convinced that it is good in itself, even when it produces nothing else of value. Similar puzzlement arises in the case of knowledge. A second problem is of a rather different nature. I want to lay out the formal structure of a normative doctrine that will be acceptable to as wide as possible a range of moral philosophers. While I cannot compromise on the fundamental thesis that we ought to do the best we can, I can compromise on the question of what should count as "best". For present purposes, I am simply not all that interested in defending any specific doctrines about the internal content of axiology. Therefore, I want to leave the details of the axiological component open. I hope that you will be content to evaluate worlds by appeal to your own best axiological intuitions. I shall not burden you with a catalogue of mine.

For present purposes, then, we need only agree on some relatively formal doctrines about the intrinsic values of possible worlds. The most fundamental of these is that for every possible world, there is some number — positive, negative, or zero — that represents the intrinsic value of that world. I will use 'IV(w)' to abbreviate 'the intrinsic value of world w'. We must also agree that these numbers are assigned in such a way that a world, w, is intrinsically better than a world, w', iff IV(w) > IV(w'); w is intrinsically neutral, or worthless, iff IV(w) = 0; w is intrinsically good iff IV(w) > 0; w is intrinsically bad iff IV(w) < 0.

I see no reason to suppose that there is any upper or lower limit to the intrinsic value a world might have. So, for any value, there is one higher, and there is one lower, than it. Furthermore, I see no reason to suppose that the values of worlds move along in tidy increments. Thus, it seems to me that for any two values, there may be one in between. Finally, I think the whole project would be pretty pointless unless there are possible worlds that differ from each other in intrinsic value. I assume that there is such variation among possible worlds, and I hope the reader will do so, too.

2.3. THE FUNDAMENTAL NORMATIVE PRINCIPLE

My view is that we ought to do the best we can. More exactly, it is that our moral obligation is always to do what we do in the intrinsically best of the possible worlds accessible to us. I have attempted to clarify my concepts of of accessibility and intrinsic value. I will now be able to state and explain the normative principle itself.

We may think that doing the best we can requires doing what we do in the intrinsically best accessible world. Let us try to develop this idea. We can say that a world is a "best" for a person at a time iff it is accessible to him then, and no other world then accessible to him is as good as it is. In other words:

B: w' is a best for s at t from w = df. As, t, w', w & (w'') (As, t, w'', w & ~[w'' = w'] → IV(w') > IV(w''))

Making use of this concept of a best, we can say that a person ought to see to the occurrence of a state of affairs iff that state of affairs occurs in his current best. This account of moral obligation can be stated somewhat more accurately as follows:

MO1:   MOs, t, p is true at w iff p is true at the best for s at t from w.

MO1 is intended to be a statement of truth conditions for a certain sort of proposition. Where 's' names a person, 't' a time, and 'p' a state of affairs, this proposition can be expressed by 'MOs, t, p'. We can read this as 's morally ought, as of t, to see to the occurrence of p'. Since our obligations depend upon what's currently asscessible to us, and what's accessible to us at a time varies from world to world, 'MOs, t, p' will have different truth values at different worlds. So MO1 and succeeding doctrines give world-relativized truth conditions for the propositions expressed by 'MOs, t, p'.

MO1 is not a satisfactory formulation of the notion that we ought to do the best we can. The main trouble is that it entails that if anything is morally obligatory for s at t, then there is exactly one best world then accessible to s. But this is an indefensible view. In typical cases, there are several trivially different ways for us to do the best we can. For each of them, there is an accessible world in which we do it in that way. Since they differ only trivially, these worlds are equally good. Hence, in this sort of case, none of these worlds would be a best, and nothing would be obligatory. This calls for some alterations to our account of a best, and to our fundamental principle.

Instead of saying that a best is an accessible world better than every other accessible world, let us say that a best is an accessible world than which there is none better. In other words:

B′: w' is a best for s at t from w = df. As, t, w', w & $\sim (Ew'')(As, t, w'', w \,\&\, \mathrm{IV}(w'') > \mathrm{IV}(w'))$

Now we can say that a person has a moral obligation to do a thing iff he does it in all of his current bests. That is:

MO2:   MOs, t, p is true at w iff p is true at every best for s at t from w.

It is not clear to me that there is anything wrong with MO2. Nevertheless, I want to point out a possible source of difficulty, and show how it can be avoided. The problem here would arise if there were a case in which an agent had "limitless possibilities". That is, suppose that for every world accessible to s at t, there is a better one accessible, too. If there is no upper bound on the values of the worlds accessible to s at t, then there will be no bests, and everything will be obligatory. Although it seems extremely unlikely that human beings ever face such a bonanza of possible worlds, it may be better to formulate our doctrine in such a way as to be adequate even to this most delightful of cases.

In light of all this, I propose that we understand the principle that we ought to do the best we can in the following way:

MO: MO$s, t, p$ is true at w iff $(Ew')\,[As, t, w', w\ \&\ p$ is true at w'
         $\&\ \sim(Ew'')\,\{As, t, w'', w\ \&\ \sim p$ is true at $w''\ \&\ \ IV(w'')\geqslant$
         $IV(w')\}]$

On this formulation, which is the official one, s morally ought, as of a time, t, to see to the occurrence of a state of affairs, p, iff p occurs in some world accessible to s at t, and it is not the case that $\sim p$ occurs in any accessible world as good as (or better than) that one. So, if we consider the worlds accessible to s at t, we will find one in which p occurs. That one will be so good that we won't find any other as good as it (or better than it) in which p fails to occur. If there are better worlds accessible to s at t, p will be true in all of them.[7]

2.3.1. *MO and Ideal Utilitarianism*

In order to come to a clearer understanding of the neo-utilitarian concept of moral obligation defined by MO, let us see how this concept compares with the concept defended by Moore in *Principia Ethica* and *Ethics*.

It should be clear that in the simplest sort of case, MO yields the same results as Moore's ideal utilitarianism. That is, it tells us to do what maximizes intrinsic value. To see why this is so, let us consider an example. Suppose that I have my choice between tending my garden today (g) and not doing so. Suppose g has some good consequences, whereas $\sim g$ has none. Suppose, finally that the occurrence of g will not rule out any important things I might otherwise be able to do either today or at any later time. Then my choice between g and $\sim g$ is pretty much "isolated". Each has its consequences, but, aside from that, each is consistent with virtually anything I might want to do later. In this case, Moore's ideal utilitarianism says that I ought to tend my garden, since the consequences of doing so excel the consequences of each alternative. MO yields the same result, but the reasoning is a bit different. Consider some time, t, such that I still have my choice between g and $\sim g$ at t. There is a world, w, accessible to me at t in which g occurs, and in which I go on to do all the best things still open to me. Let's say that the intrinsic value of w is n. The best accessible $\sim g$-world, w', must have a slightly lower intrinsic value than w has, since in it, I evidently do all those other marvelous things, but I don't tend my garden, and don't bring about whatever valuable consequences garden-tending has in w. Hence, MO also yields that result that, as of t, I ought to tend my garden today.

In other cases, MO and ideal utilitarianism diverge. Consider my act of picking up my hoe today (h). In order to tend my garden properly, I must first pick up my hoe. There is no good world accessible to me in which g occurs, but h doesn't. Yet h does not have any valuable consequences. No *result* of h has any intrinsic value. The consequences of not picking up my hoe might be just as good as the consequences of picking it up. So ideal utilitarianism says that I have no obligation to pick up the hoe, even though I do have an obligation to tend the garden, and I can't tend the garden in the appropriate way unless I first pick up the hoe. This seems to me to be a defect in ideal utilitarianism. MO yields what I take to be the correct result. Since g occurs in some accessible world than which there is no better $\sim g$-world, and h occurs in any reasonably good g-world, h occurs in some accessible world than which there is no better $\sim h$-world. Thus, according to MO, I ought to get my hoe. That seems to me to be the correct result.

It might be thought that MO would be equivalent to ideal utilitarianism if we were to understand 'consequences' in the latter doctrine in a fairly generous way. Let us consider this idea. Suppose we define 'consequences' in such a broad way that the consequences of an act include everything that would happen if that act were to occur, whether before, during, or after the act. In this case, my act of gardening tomorrow gains all sorts of consequences. Among these will be all of its causal results — the things it would "make happen", and there is nothing odd about any of that. However, such things as next Tuesday's sunrise, and last Thursday's sunrise are also now to be treated as consequences of my gardening today.

If we assume that there is a certain possible world that would exist if I were to tend my garden today, and we stick to this broad conception of consequences, we will be led to the conclusion that the intrinsic value of the consequences of g are equal to the intrinsic value of the world that would exist if I were to tend my garden. Just for this example, let us make the necessary assumptions. Here's the question: is there any difference between ideal utilitarianism, thus interpreted, and the view formulated as MO?

It seems to me that there is an important difference between the doctrines. The difference has to do with subjunctive conditionals. To see it, we need to recognize, first, that most of our actions are capable of being performed in a variety of different ways. Tending my garden is no exception. I could do it in some careful, productive way, and I could do it in various sloppy ways. I could also do it and then go on to live my life in the best way possible, and I could do it and then go on to live my life in the worst way possible. Each of these constitutes a "way of tending my garden".

Some of these ways may be more likely than others. For example, it might be far more likely that if I were to tend my garden, I would do it in a sloppy, unproductive way rather than in the best way open to me. In this case, on any standard interpretation of subjunctive conditionals, it turns out that it is not the case that the world that would exist if I were to tend my garden is a good one. Our modified version of ideal utilitarianism requires that we assign a value to g by appeal to the intrinsic value of the possible world that would exist, if g were to occur. Hence, on this construal of ideal utilitarianism, g gets a low value, and is morally prohibited.

However, since we have been assuming that g also occurs in the best of the worlds accessible to me, MO yields the opposite result. It says that I ought to tend my garden today — and that I ought to do it in the best way possible. The value of the *nearest* world in which I garden is not relevant on MO, as it is on this form of ideal utilitarianism. What's relevant on MO is the question whether I tend my garden in the *best* of the worlds accessible to me. If so, I ought to tend my garden.[8]

2.3.2. *Some Deontic Principles*

One of the great defects of standard forms of act utilitarianism, as I see it, is that they do not generate any interesting set of deontic principles. Indeed, some of them generate seemingly absurd results for deontic logic. MO, on the other hand, yields a number of interesting and plausible principles about the logic of obligation. Let us consider some of these principles.

One of the most fundamental principles here is the doctrine that a given person never has incompatible obligations.

NC/MO: MO$s, t, p$ & MO$s, t, q$ → Ks, t, p & q

It is easy to see why NC/MO is true. Imagine the worlds accessible to s

at t lined up according to intrinsic value. At some point in the ranking, p starts being true, and remains true from there on up. Similarly for q. Thus, the upper reaches of the ranking consist entirely of p & q-worlds. Definition K tells us that Ks, t, p & q must therefore be true. Other "no conflicts" principles are also true. For example, no one ever has metaphysically or logically or physically incompatible obligations.

Of course, if we vary the agents or the times, conflicts of various sorts become possible. So we may have cases in which a person has a moral obligation, as of some time, to see to the occurrence of p, but the same person has a moral obligation, as of some other time, to see to the occurrence of $\sim p$. Similarly, we may have cases in which one person has a moral obligation, as of some time, to see to the occurence of p, but some other person has a moral obligation, as of that same time, to see to the occurrence of $\sim p$. What we can't have is a case in which a given agent, as of a given time, both must and must not bring about a given state of affairs.

Later, I will introduce a variety of other sorts of obligation. Among these will be prudential, civic, social, and etiquettical. Any case of conflict of obligations, I will maintain, can be understood either as a case of conflict between the requirements of two different sorts of obligation, or else as a case in which it just isn't clear which of two courses of action is really obligatory. At any rate, this is an issue to which I will return.[9]

Another principle validated by MO is a principle about doing the consequences of what you ought to do. If MOs, t, p is true, and q is a causal or logical consequence of p, then MOs, t, q is true, too. More generally, if s can't see to the occurrence of p without seeing to the occurrence of q, then q will be obligatory for s if p is. In order to state this principle neatly, notice that if, at some time, t, in some world, w, s can't see to the occurrence of p without also seeing to the occurrence of q then one thing that is unalterable for s at t in w is the material conditional $p \rightarrow q$. In light of this, we can formulate our deontic principle as follows:

MO/MO: (MOs, t, p & Us, t, $p \rightarrow q$) $\rightarrow$ MOs, t, q

If MOs, t, p is true, then there is some accessible p-world such that there is no as good accessible $\sim p$-world. Us, t, $p \rightarrow q$ means that every accessible world is a $p \rightarrow q$-world. So the best accessible p-worlds are all $p \rightarrow q$-worlds, and so each of them is a q-world, too. There can't be an even better $\sim q$-world, for if there were, it would be either a p-world or a $\sim p$-world. If it were a $\sim p$-world, then MOs, t, p wouldn't be true to start with. If it were a p-world, then we apparently didn't begin with a best accessible world.

Principle MO/MO is of some moral sigificance. It stands behind the point made earlier about one of the differences between ideal utilitarianism and MO. Even if the consequences or results of some act, q, are worthless, q may be obligatory on MO because q is a necessary condition for p, and p is obligatory. So if p entails q, or if p can't occur without q, or if s can't see to the occurrence of p without seeing to the occurrence of q, and MOs, t, p, then MOs, t, q. My moral intuition tells me that it is a good thing that MO/MO turns out to be true.

MO also validates a version of the principle, usually ascribed to Kant, that "ought" implies "can".[10] If we allow our K to express the relevant sort of possibility, we can formulate a valid version of this doctrine as follows:

MO/K: MOs, t, p → Ks, t, p

The explanation of this is straightforward. MOs, t, p means that there's an accessible p-world such that there's no as good accessible $\sim p$-world. So there's an accessible p-world. According to K, this means that Ks, t, p is true, too.

We should note that MO/K is much weaker than the view that we can "make happen" anything that's obligatory. For Ks, t, p does not mean that s can, as of t, make p happen. It only means that p happens in some world accessible to s as of t. s can see to the occurrence of p. Loosely, we may say that there is some course of action open to s such that, if he were to follow it out, p would happen. Nevertheless, the importance of MO/K is clear. If there is no way that I can see to the occurrence of p, then p does not occur in any world accessible to me. In this case, I can have no moral obligation, according to MO, to see to the occurrence of p. This seems to me to be true, and so I am happy that MO and K have this result.

MO also validates some fairly trivial principles, which may deserve mention. They are:

MO/&: (MOs, t, p & MOs, t, q) → MOs, t, p & q
MO/∨: (MOs, t, p ∨ MOs, t, q) → MOs, t, p ∨ q

One feature that some may find odd here is this: if p occurs in every world accessible to s at t, then MOs, t, p is true. In other words, this is valid:

U/MO: Us, t, $p \rightarrow$ MOs, t, p

The explanation of this is simple enough. If p occurs in every world accessible to s at t, then it occurs in some accessible world such that there is no as good accessible world where it fails to occur.

It must be admitted that U/MO records a somewhat surprising fact about this concept of obligation. It shows that virtually everything in the past is, from the perspective of today, obligatory. Similarly, everything that is going to happen "no matter what" is allegedly obligatory. The behavior of others, no matter how atrocious, is obligatory relative to you provided that you can't do anything about it. Some critics have suggested that this is unacceptable.

For my part, however, I am willing to swallow this oddity. I admit, of course, that we don't often tell someone that he ought to do what's already done, or what can't be helped in any case. This fact, as I see it, has no direct bearing on the question whether, if we were to say such things, we would be saying something false. In my view, we would be speaking truly. There are lots of things that we never say, but which, if we were to say them, would be correct. Nevertheless, I also want to point out that, if we decide that it is important, we may introduce a concept of obligation for which the analogue of U/MO fails. This concept may be defined as follows:

MO3:   MO*s, t, p is true at w iff MOs, t, p and Ks, t, $\sim p$ are both true at w.

It should be clear that the unalterability of p for s at t does not entail the obligatoriness, in the sense of MO3, of p for s at t. Furthermore, it should be clear that the sort of obligation defined in MO3 entails "can avoid" — thus we have a sort of improved version of the Kantian principle. Not only can we always obey the commands of morality, we can always disobey them. I leave it to the interested reader to determine which, if either, of these concepts of obligation is closer to "the ordinary concept of obligation". I shall stick with the concept intro-duced in MO. It is simpler, and it seems to me to be adequate.

A good part of deontic logic is devoted to the study of various combinations of deontic operators and conditionals. MO mixes with various conditionals to produce all sorts of interesting principles, and it might be thought that this would be the place to discuss them. However, it seems to me that it is preferable to reflect, first, on some moral objections to the concept of absolute obligation defined by MO. Once these have been answered, and the concept of absolute obligation is thus somewhat clearer, we can go on in Part Two to consider some of the forms of conditioned and conditional obligation associated with MO.

CHAPTER 3

MORAL OBJECTIONS TO MO

The sort of neo-utilitarian approach that I advocate has been subjected of a fair amount of criticism. I think it will be useful to spend some time considering and evaluating some of this criticism. I want to do this for two different reasons. In the first place, by explaining how I would reply to these objections, I hope to show that my approach is rationally defensible. The second reason for considering the objections seems to me to be more important. It is this: the presentation of the objections and replies will enable the reader to gain a deeper understanding of the nature and purpose of the theory.

3.1. AN EPISTEMIC OBJECTION

The first objection has to do with the epistemology of ethics.[1] It may be pointed out that if MO specifies our real moral obligations, one may have an obligation to perform an action even though he has no reason to believe that any good would come of it. Indeed, one may have an obligation to perform an action even though he is thoroughly justified in believing that that action would have horrible consequences, and would be the worst possible choice.

In order to make the objection more vivid, let us consider an example. Suppose that a certain doctor is responsible for the medical treatment of a patient. Suppose that the patient is an entirely delightful person who is, unfortunately, suffering from a rare and painful disease. There is some good news and some bad news. The good news is that the disease can be cured instantly and safely by the administration of one dose of Medicine A — a medicine readily available to the doctor. The bad news is that all the evidence suggests that the patient has some other disease, one that would be exacerbated by Medicine A. If, after observing the symptoms of the patient, the doctor were to give Medicine A, he would be taken to be an incompetent, reckless fool. (Of course, he would also be considered to be a remarkably *lucky* fool, since the patient would be cured.)

The objection now runs as follows: if MO specified the doctor's real

45

moral obligations, then the doctor would have a real moral obligation to give Medicine A. In fact, in a case such as this, the doctor has no obligation to give medicine A. Given what he knows about the case, he has an obligation to avoid giving A. Therefore, MO does not specify the doctor's real moral obligations.

In order to deal adequately with this objection, we must distinguish between what is often called "objective moral obligation" and what is often called "subjective moral obligation". Let us agree that a person has a subjective moral obligation, relative to a certain time, to bring about some state of affairs, p, provided that it would be most reasonable, given the evidence he has at that time, for him to hold that he morally ought to bring about p. Clearly, if we are interested in a person's subjective moral obligations, we may have to take account of what he knows, and what he is justified in believing would happen if he were to do this or that. I think that something like this concept of subjective moral obligation may be expressed by 'ought' in ordinary English.

However, I am convinced that there is also a concept of objective moral obligation. Indeed, the fundamental character of this concept is brought out by the fact that we can identify the other, subjective, concept by appeal to the latter, objective one. We do this when we say that a person has a subjective obligation if and only if he is justified in thinking that he has an objective one.

Even if we put aside questions of priority, I think we have to recognize that the concept of objective obligation exists, and is of preanalytic interest. Suppose the doctor in the example plays it safe, and refuses to give medicine A. The patient suffers for a long time, and then gradually recovers. Only then does the doctor discover that the patient in fact could have been cured easily by the administration of a readily-available drug. The doctor may then be disappointed. Realizing that he could have cured the patient, and thus could have relieved a considerable amount of needless suffering, he may say to himself, 'I should have given Medicine A — if only I had known!' In my view, the 'should' here may express objective moral obligation. If so, the doctor's imagined statement would be true. He indeed should have given medicine A. After all, that's precisely what he does in the best worlds then accessible to him.

Of course, there would be no point in blaming the doctor for his decision, or "holding it against him". He didn't know that he was failing to do something that he ought to have been doing. No good would come from blaming him for his mistake. Nevertheless, if we consider what he in fact did, and what he could have done instead, we can conclude that he should have given medicine A. Our conclusion, in this case, would be a conclusion about the doctor's *objective* moral obligation. This concept of objective moral obligation, freed as it is from the notions of blameworthiness and praiseworthiness, is the one I'm interested in. The defined concept MO is intended to be equivalent to it, not to the concept of subjective moral obligation.

With the distinction between objective and subjective obligation at hand, we may dispose of the epistemic objection. Recall that the objection goes as follows:

1.   If MO is true, the doctor ought to give medicine A.
2.   It's not the case that the doctor ought to give medicine A.
3.   Therefore, MO is not true.

If we take the 'ought' in lines (1) and (2) to express *objective* moral obligation, then (1) is true and (2) is false. If we take it to express *subjective* moral obligation, then (2) may be true, but (1) is false. If we take it to express objective obligation in (1), and subjective obligation in (2), then both lines are true, but the argument is no longer valid. Thus, as I see it, the epistemic objection suffers from the fallacy of equivocation.

Before turning to the second line of criticism, I want to consider a further point about the epistemology of obligation. Suppose again that our doctor faces a very tough decision, and doesn't have much good evidence to go on. Suppose morality is important to him. He wants to do what's right. He may expend a fair amount of time and energy in the effort to discover that would happen if he were to give Medicine A, and what would happen if he were to withhold Medicine A. Indeed, we may feel that, as a responsible person, he had some duty to engage in such enquiries. Yet, if the doctor's *subjective* obligations were of paramount importance, there would be no need to look for more evidence. He would only have to determine what, *on the evidence he already has*, seems to be his obligation. After all, his subjective obligation has been defined to be the act that, on his evidence, appears to be his obligation. Surely, however, the doctor is right to try to expand his evidence. I take this to suggest that he is not satisfied to perform his subjective obligation. He is looking for evidence concerning what he objectively ought to do. As I see it, it is far more important for him to do what he objectively ought to do than it is for him simply to go ahead and do what he subjectively ought to do.

I have to acknowledge that if my view is correct, then most of us, most of the time, really don't know what we ought to do. After all, who among us has genuinely adequate information concerning the worlds that are accessible? And even if we somehow come to know which worlds are accessible, we still are in the dark about their values. So, since we don't know which worlds are in our power, and we don't know what each is worth, we don't know for sure what we objectively ought to do. This is indeed unfortunate for us. However, it does not reveal any defect in the approach I advocate. The theory isolates and identifies the sorts of things we would have to know in order to know our objective moral obligations. In practice, we rarely know these things, and we rarely know our objective moral obligations. If the theory represented the epistemology of ethics as being any easier, that would show the theory to be wrong. In fact, it is quite hard to know what you ought to do.

3.2. AN OBJECTION BASED ON MORAL RIGOR

A second line of objection has to do with moral rigor. An objector might insist that the present concept of moral obligation is far too demanding. We are required, according to MO, always to do the very best we can. Shall we then leave our friends and families, devote the rest of our lives to charity, become servants to humanity? Do I violate my moral duty whenever I spend a quiet evening at home with my wife and children? Any theory that says so, according to this objection, asks more than morality really requires.

Kurt Baier presented a particularly vigorous version of this objection. He said that normative theories such as mine

... would have the absurd result that we are doing wrong whenever we are relaxing, since on those occasions there will always be opportunities to produce greater good then we can by relaxing. For the relief of suffering is always a greater good than mere enjoyment. Yet it is quite plain that the worker who, after a tiring day, puts on his slippers and listens to the radio is not doing anything he ought not to, is not neglecting any of his duties, even though it may be perfectly true that there are things he might do which produce more good in the world, even for himself, than merely relaxing by the fireside.[2]

I think this sort of objection may be based on either or both of two misconceptions. In the first place, I think it may overestimate our capacity for good. Most decent people can't do very much better than they are already doing. There may be possible worlds in which Baier's tired worker becomes saintly, or works devotedly among the needy. But given the sort of character that man probably has, and his talents and opportunities, such worlds probably are not accessible to him. If he were to try his hand at saintliness, he would probably botch it, and make things even worse. His greatest possible contribution to human welfare is probably not very much greater than the contribution, meager as it is, that he is already making. He goes to work each day, earns some money to keep his family clothed, fed and housed, and perhaps gives a bit of the excess to charity. So it isn't clear that he would be required by MO to do much more than he already does.

In the second place, the objection may be based on a too-lax view of morality. If the tired worker in fact can rid the world of famine or war, then, in my view, he morally ought to do it. More precisely, I am convinced that morality does require us to do the best we can, and if it's not much fun, or if it makes our friends think we've gone daffy, that's simply too bad. The demands of morality are inescapable. It doesn't become inoperative on holidays and weekends. So while I think that most of us really can't do very much better than we are already doing, I also think that if we can, we should.

I should also point out a certain misleading feature of Baier's argument. He seems to be attacking a view according to which one must always perform the best of his alternatives. Old-fashioned act utilitarianism is apparently a view of this sort. My own neo-utilitarian doctrine is different. It requires a person to do what he does in the best accessible worlds. Instead of focussing on some set of current alternatives, and insisting that the best of them be performed, it focusses on whole lives open to the agent. It requires him to live out the best of them. Thus, it may permit the tired worker to relax by the fireside each night so as to have the energy to return to modest saintliness on the following day. So there is a sense in which my own view allows a person a bypass certain opportunities for doing good. He may bypass any such opportunity if bypassing it is consistent with living the best life still open to him.

Another somewhat more controversial point should perhaps be made here. Some moral philosophers maintain that asking a person to

do the best he can is asking too much of him. Morality, they say, just
isn't that demanding.[3] However, it seems to me that if certain axiological assumptions can be granted, my approach can be made to
accommodate this view. We can say that freedom and privacy are
intrinsic goods, too. We can say that it's a bad thing to force a person,
against his inclinations, to do more than his fair share of good deeds. It
may be especially bad to force someone to do good deeds when the
cost to himself is high. Perhaps some will want to phrase this axiological
view in terms of the alleged instrinsic value of "respect for rights". At
any rate, if these things are bad in themselves, then their badness may
serve to counterbalance the good that might otherwise be produced by
grudging acts of saintliness. Thus, it isn't entirely clear that MO has the
serious counterintuitive consequences some have alleged.

3.3 AN OBJECTION BASED ON JUSTICE

A third line of objection has to do with justice. Traditional forms of
utilitarianism are often accused of requiring us to maximize utility,
no matter how many innocent toes get stepped upon. My own neo-
utilitarian view, I believe, does not have the offensive feature in
question.

If justice is good, as I believe it is, then two worlds with equal
hedonic utility may yet differ in intrinsic value because the distribution
of pleasure and pain in one of them is fairer than the distribution of
pleasure and pain in the other. Indeed, we may hold that justice is so
important that a world with a very low hedonic utility may yet have a
greater intrinsic value than another world in which the pain is vastly
outbalanced by the pleasure.

A particularly persuasive version of this sort of objection has to do
with utilitarianism's alleged impact on criminal justice. The objection is
usually based on some outlandish example in which the punishment of
an innocent person is required in order to secure a large bonus of
hedonic utility.[4] The examples are designed to show that utilitarianism
violates some of our most secure and legitimate moral intuitions.
Specifically, it is alleged that utilitarianism would permit punishment of
the innocent. Can such an argument be mounted against MO?

Consider the typical case. A community is in an uproar because of a
string of unsolved murders. The police can't catch the perpetrators. A
riot will break out, and the populace will fall into a panic, unless their

fears can be allayed. Should the chief select an innocent person, frame a case against him, and publicize his capture and conviction? If MO says that the chief should do these things, then MO is wrong.

To answer the question about the chief's obligations under MO, we need to know more about the situation. For one thing, we need to know more about the worlds accessible to the chief. Is there one in which the frame-up succeeds? Is there one in which the riot is avoided at lower cost? We also need to know much more about the values of the accessible worlds. How bad is the best accessible world in which the innocent person is framed? How bad is the best accessible world in which the chief refuses to engage in any such frame-up, but searches diligently for the real criminals? Until we know such things as these, we don't know whether MO has counterintuitive results in this sort of case.

The most important thing here, however, is a fact about the axiology associated with MO. That axiology is not naive hedonism. It is a more complicated form of pluralism, according to which basic intrinsic value states come in a variety of fundamental forms. Among these basic intrinsic value states, some are states of affairs recording the degree of justice or injustice prevailing at a time. Injustice is intrinsically evil. The badness of injustice explains why it is generally wrong to bring it about. Thus, the intrinsic values of possible worlds in which the chief frames an innocent person will be significantly reduced by the occurrence in those worlds of a great injustice. If the injustice is great enough, it will be sufficient to make the frame-up morally forbidden.

An objector might insist that the objection can still be raised. Suppose the frightened crowd is larger, or that the riot would be more destructive. No matter how evil the injustice, imagine a case in which the evil of avoiding it would be greater. On MO, the chief would be morally obliged to frame an innocent man.

My own view, for what it's worth, is that injustice is intrinsically bad. But injustice is not the only evil, nor is it so evil as to be morally wrong in absolutely every instance. If enough good would come of it, or if enough evil can be avoided by it, then it may be permissible, or even obligatory, to select a possible world in which a serious injustice is committed. So if the chief's very best accessible world is one in which he commits an injustice, then, while he may curse fate for putting him in such an unfortunate situation, he ought to commit the injustice.

If you disagree with me about this, I wonder how you would answer these questions: Why should we avoid injustice? Isn't it because injustice is bad? But surely injustice is not the only bad thing. Then can't the evil of injustice be counterbalanced by some other great good, securable in no other way? When the evil of injustice is outweighed by a great good securable in no other way, then, it seems to me, we must endure the injustice.

3.4. AN OBJECTION BASED UPON MORAL IMPERFECTION

In 'Dated Rightness and Moral Imperfection', Holly Goldman presented a striking and provocative objection to any theory of absolute moral obligation relevantly like mine.[5] Substantially the same point was made independently by Howard Sobel at about the same time.[6] We can simplify the point, and modify the example slightly so as to make it bear directly on what has been said here. I hope, of course, that the modifications do not introduce any serious distortion of the central critical point.

Suppose a doctor is charged with the treatment of a patient — one who deserves to be treated properly. Suppose the doctor has his choice of several main courses of treatment, the relative values of which are as follows:

	Monday	Tuesday
Best treatment	A	A
Good treatment	B	B
Horrible treatment	A	B
Horrible treatment	B	A

Although, as of Sunday, the doctor *can* adopt the best course of treatment (A-A), he in fact would not do so. If he were to give A on Monday, he would give B on Tuesday. Perhaps he has some character defect, or is otherwise predisposed to fail to carry through on the ideal course of treatment. In any case, if he were to set out to give two doses of A, he would end up giving a mixed treatment (A-B) with the stipulated horrible results.

However, let us also stipulate that if the doctor were to give B on Monday, he would follow through with another dose of B on Tuesday, thereby achieving a reasonably good cure. An objector, following Goldman and Sobel, would hold, with Iris Murdoch, that the doctor morally ought to choose the lower course that can be sustained and carried through, rather than the higher course that he will bungle. In the case at hand, since the doctor would not carry through the ideal course of treatment with two doses of A, he should not begin it. He should set out, on Monday, on the lower course that he can sustain and carry through. That is, he should give B on Monday. This plausible result is in apparent conflict with my view that the doctor should always do the best he can. For, on that view, as developed in MO, the doctor's absolute moral obligation is to give A on Monday, since that is part of the best course of action still open as of Sunday.[7]

One problem with this objection is that it isn't entirely clear that the case, as described, is genuinely possible. Is the allegedly ideal course of treatment really open to the doctor? We are told that, if he were to give A on Monday, he wouldn't give A on Tuesday. In this case, it isn't clear that it is possible for him to give A on Monday and then again on Tuesday. If this course of action is not among the doctor's alternatives, then, obviously, MO does not imply that it's the one he ought to perform.

It seems to me that Goldman and Sobel have an adequate reply to this point. They can remind us that there is a big difference between saying (a) that the doctor *would* give B on Tuesday if he gave A on Monday and saying (b) that the doctor *has to* give B on Tuesday if he gives A on Monday. I take both of these statements to be about the worlds accessible to the doctor. Furthermore, I take them to be restricted to worlds in which he gives A on Monday. Statement (a) means that in the *nearest* of those worlds, he gives B on Tuesday. Statement (b) means that in *all* of those worlds, he gives B on Tuesday. The puzzle arises because (a) is stipulated to be true. There is no reason for the objector to affirm (b) as well.

Clearly, then, the situation described by Goldman and Sobel is possible. There are several worlds accessible to the doctor in which he gives A on Monday. In some of these, he goes on to give A on Tuesday. In others, he goes on to give B on Tuesday. However, in the *nearest* of the accessible worlds in which he gives A on Monday, he gives B on Tuesday. Thus, there is no conflict between the claim (a) that he *can* adopt the best course of treatment, and the claim (b) that he *would not do so*.

A far deeper problem with the objection is that it is not clear that the objectors' view of the situation is really incompatible with mine. They would say that, since the doctor won't give A on Tuesday, he shouldn't give A on Monday. I say that he should give A Monday. It appears that my view is incompatible with theirs. However, there may be no disagreement here.

Consider the statement:

(1)   Since he won't give A on Tuesday, the doctor shouldn't give A on Monday.

This is at the heart of the objection. The objectors would take it to be true, and they may assume that I have to take it to be false, since I affirm:

(2)   The doctor should give A on Monday.

However, it seems to me that (1) is ambiguous. On one reading it is true. On that reading, (1) is basically a statement of conditional obligation. It means, roughly, that in the best accessible worlds in which he does not give A on Tuesday, the doctor does not give A on Monday.[8] Reflection on the list of alternatives open to the doctor reveals that this is correct in the example. Worlds in which he fails to give A on Tuesday come in two main varieties. Some are worlds where he gives A on Monday. Others are worlds in which he fails to give A on Monday. The latter (B-B) worlds are better than the former (A-B) worlds since in the latter, the patient gets good treatment, and in the former the patient gets horrible treatment. Thus, if he isn't going to give A on Tuesday, he shouldn't give A on Monday.

Clearly, however, all this is compatible with the claim that the doctor absolutely ought to give A on Monday. That claim, as I see it, amounts to the claim that in the best accessible worlds, he gives A on Monday. Thus, if (1) is taken to be a statement of conditional obligation, it is compatible with (2). There is no conflict between what I want to say about the case and what the objectors want to say about it.

The case has been described in such a way that something stronger than the mere statement of conditional obligation is true. It's not just that *if* he is going to give B on Tuesday, he ought to give B on Monday. Rather, we are told that *since* he is going to give B on Tuesday, he ought to give B on Monday. It might be thought that this difference between 'if' and 'since' rules out my reply.

As I see it, the 'since' statement is really a conjunction. It means (a) that in fact he is going to give B on Tuesday, and (b) if he is going to give B on Tuesday, then he ought to give B on Monday. The 'since' statement can therefore be seen as the conjunction of the statement of conditional obligation and its factual "antecedent". It might very naturally be thought that this 'since' statement, so understood, conflicts with my claim that the doctor absolutely ought to give A on Monday.

In Chapter 4, Section 5, I will introduce and explain two principles concerning the detachment of statements of absolute obligation from statements of conditional obligation. One of these principles tells us that if p is true, and q is conditionally obligatory on p, then q is absolutely obligatory. This is the so-called principle of "factual detachment". If this principle were true, it could be used to derive the conclusion that the doctor in the example absolutely ought to give B on Monday. That would cause serious difficulties for my approach. However, as I show in Chapter 4, the factual detachment rule is not valid — at least, it is not valid for what I call conditional obligation.

The second detachment principle is a principle permitting the detachment of statements of absolute obligation from statements of conditional obligation together with the *unalterability* of their antecedents. This so-called "unalterability detachment" rule is valid. In the present case, it would permit us to infer that the doctor absolutely ought to give B on Monday, from the statement of conditional obligation together with the premise that he unalterably is going to give B on Tuesday. It is important to recognize that, in the case at hand, unalterability detachment is unavailable. It is stipulated that there are worlds accessible to the doctor in which he gives A on Tuesday. Thus, as of Sunday, it is not the case that it is unalterable that he gives B on Tuesday. (I realize that my treatment of this example depends crucially on my account of conditional obligation, which has not yet been presented. I hope the interested reader will come back, and reconsider what I say about this case after reading the relevant parts of Chapter 4.)

The objectors may want to understand (1) in some stronger way. They may take it in such a way that it entails that the doctor absolutely ought to avoid giving A on Monday. In that case, however, my moral intuition conflicts with theirs. I am willing to accept (1), but only so long as it is understood as a statement of conditional obligation. As I will show in Chapter 4, such statements do not entail the absolute obligatoriness of their "consequents" — not even together with the truth of their "antecedents". So long as the doctor still can give his patient the best course of treatment, he ought to do so.

Support for the Goldman-Sobel position may be derived from some facts about moral advice.[9] Suppose the doctor comes to us for advice about how to treat his patient. Knowing as we do that if he gives A on Monday, he'll botch things up by giving B on Tuesday, we would undoubtedly advise him to start out on the lower course. We would tell the doctor to give B on Monday. Indeed, if the bad outcomes were really horrible, as suggested above, it could plausibly be argued that we would have a moral obligation to tell the doctor that the ought to give B on Monday. Thus, it may seem that there is support for the Goldman-Sobel moral intuition.

I agree that we, as advisors, ought to tell the doctor to give B on Monday — assuming that what we tell him will have some influence on his behavior. We can see why this is so if we consider the worlds that are accessible to us. Among these worlds are some in which we advise two doses of A — but in these the doctor does not follow our advice. He gives A on Monday, but then bungles and gives B on Tuesday. These are not very good worlds. There are also some worlds in which we advise two doses of B. In these, assuming that we can influence the doctor with our advice, he indeed gives two doses of B. These worlds are pretty good. It is reasonable to assume that of the worlds accessible to us (the advisors) there are none better than than the best in which we advise two doses of B, and he follows our advice. So, making use of the concept defined in MO, we have the result that we ought to tell the doctor that he ought to give two doses of B.

However, from the fact that we ought to tell him that he has this obligation, it does not follow that he in fact does have the obligation. On my view, when we tell him that he ought to give two doses of B, we will be doing what we ought to do, but we won't be saying something true. In this case, morality requires us to speak falsely in order to spare an innocent patient some needless suffering.

The crucial fact about this sort of case is that an important world accessible to a certain agent is not accessible to his moral advisors. Specifically, in this case, there is a world accessible to the doctor in which he gives two doses of A. This is a very good world — the best open to the doctor. This fact explains why the doctor absolutely ought to give A on Monday and then again on Tuesday. However, we as advisors cannot see to it that the doctor realizes this world. No matter what we say to him, he will not give two doses of A. Thus, there is no world accessible to us in which we advise him to give two doses of A, and he follows our advice. If we tell him to give two doses of A, he will begin to follow our advice, but then will bungle. This explains why we should not tell him to give two doses of A. In the best worlds accessible to us, we advise him to give two doses of B, and he follows our advice. That's why we ought to tell him (falsely) that he ought to give B.

The general conclusion to be drawn here is that, when we give moral advice, we morally ought to advise in the best way we can. That is, we should advise in the way we advise in the best world open to us. When things go smoothly, our advice will be true (or at least it will be advice we believe). But when things go awry, we may find that to advise in the best possible way, we must give false advice. Reflection on a more extreme case should make this clear. Suppose an ornery child always does the opposite of what we tell him to do. Suppose we know that he ought to turn right, and that hundreds of lives depend upon it. Should we tell him to turn right? Obviously not.

3.5. AN OBJECTION BASED ON THE CASE OF JIM AND THE INDIANS

In his contribution to *Utilitarianism: For and Against*,[10] Bernard Williams expressed serious dissatisfaction with utilitarianism. Although Williams did not explicitly address himself to neo-utilitarian views such as my own, it would be quite natural to suppose that his remarks have some relevance to my view as well as to more traditional forms of utilitarianism. Thus, I want to devote some attention to some of the main themes of the Williams paper. In particular, I want to consider whether anything said in that paper reveals any serious defect in the normative view I have presented.[11]

Williams illustrates his discussion by appeal to two examples. The more interesting of these involves Jim, a botanist. While on an expedition in South America, Jim finds himself in the central square of a small town. Twenty Indians are tied up against a wall, and some soldiers are preparing to execute them as a warning against political protest. After some conversation, the Captain offers Jim the opportunity to kill one of the innocent Indians. If Jim accepts this invitation, the Captain will let the other nineteen go free. On the other hand, if Jim chooses not to kill an Indian, one of the soldiers ("Pedro") will kill all twenty of them. Williams goes on to make clear that Jim really has no interesting third choice. Either Jim kills one, and nineteen live, or Jim kills none, and they all die. 'The men against the wall, and other villagers, understand the situation, and are obviously begging him to accept. What should he do?"[12]

A few pages later, Williams seems to be summing up his discussion of these cases, when he says:

> It is absurd to demand of such a man, when the sums come of from the utility network which the projects of others have in part determined, that he should just step aside from his own project and decision and acknowledge the decision which utilitarian calculation requires.[13]

The story is simple, but it illustrates a number of different themes. Different readers, perhaps focussing on different aspects of the essay, have understood Williams in a wide variety of different ways. In order to do justice to this most important critical work, it will be necessary to consider several main possibilities.

Some commentators apparently think that Williams meant to present the case of Jim as a straightforward counterexample to utilitarianism. That is, they take Williams' objection to be representable as follow:

Argument A

1.   If utilitarianism were true, it would be morally obligatory for Jim to kill an Indian.
2.   In fact, it is not morally obligatory for Jim to kill an Indian.
3.   Therefore, utilitarianism is not true.

Though many readers would accept Argument A as a fair representation of Williams' objection, I suspect that there would be considerable disagreement about the way in which Williams is supposed to defend line (2). Why, according to Williams, doesn't Jim have an obligation to kill one Indian? Among the answers I have heard, the following are the most common:

(i) Since Jim is a botanist, not a political activist, the affairs of the Indians do not concern him. His projects and commitments are all botanical — not political. To force him to take sides in a local political dispute would be to violate his integrity. The Indian's problems, though profoundly troubling, are none of his business. He has no moral obligation to intervene.

(ii) Jim is no murderer. He finds murder morally repugnant. To force Jim to murder an innocent Indian is therefore an attack on his integrity.

Thus, even if killing would be for the best, he has no moral obligation to murder.

(iii) Jim can only be held responsible for his own acts — not for the acts of sadistic monsters such as Pedro and the Captain. Thus, Jim cannot be held responsible for the evil that would result from his refusal to murder. If Jim refuses to murder, twenty innocent Indians will die. However, their blood will not be on his hands. His hands will be clean. Thus, he has no obligation to murder.

Each of these themes emerges in the essay, and a careless reader could easily assume that Williams might appeal to one or another of them in an attempt to defend line (2) of Argument A. However, a closer look at the text of Williams' paper reveals that none of these provides the basis for a satisfactory interpretation of the argument. In a later discussion of Jim's case, Williams acknowledges that 'the utilitarian is probably right in this case.'[14] So it appears that Williams' view here is that, if there were a case such the one he has described, then the utilitarian conclusion concerning it would be correct. Jim would have a moral obligation to kill an Indian. So Williams would join the utilitarians in rejecting line (2) of Argument A.

3.5.1. *Obviousness*

In the paragraph following the one in which he presents the example, Williams points out that utilitarianism implies that Jim should kill one of the Indians. He goes on to say:

> If the situation [is] essentially as described and there are no further special factors, [utilitarianism] regards [this] . . . as obviously the right answer. But even one who came to think that perhaps that was the answer, might well wonder whether it was obviously the answer.[15]

This passage suggests a rather different interpretation of Williams' argument. More specifically, it suggests that the argument turns on an epistemological point — that alleged "obviousness" of Jim's obligation according to utilitarianism. Williams seems to be saying that while utilitarianism yields the correct normative conclusion in this case, it makes the decision too simple — it overlooks some complexities that deserve notice. Perhaps I can facilitate discussion of this point by recasting the argument. On one interpretation, it is this:

Argument B

1.   If utilitarianism were true, then it would be obvious that Jim
       ought to kill an Indian.
2.   It isn't obvious that Jim ought to kill an Indian.
3.   Therefore, utilitarianism isn't true.

It is important to recognize that, by itself, the truth of utilitarianism
implies nothing about the obviousness of any particular normative
conclusion. There's no contradiction in the supposition that utilitarianism is true, but that its truth is obvious to no one. In this case, even if
we knew ever so much about Jim's case, we might still be in doubt
about what he ought to do. Even if we knew the utilities of his
alternatives (or the intrinsic values of the worlds accessible to him) we
still would not know his moral obligation. Thus, the mere truth of
utilitarianism doesn't make anything more obvious. Line (1) is false.
Thus, this cannot be a satisfactory reading of Williams' remark about
utilitarianism regarding this as "obviously the right answer".
     By changing the scope of the epistemic operator in (1) we can
convert it into something far more plausible. What I have in mind is:

1′.   It is obvious that, if utilitarianism is true and Jim's situation
       is exactly as described, then Jim ought to kill an Indian.

The substitution of (1′) for (1) in Argument B leaves the argument as a
whole invalid. Indeed, I see no way to combine (1′) with other plausible
premises so as to yield the desired conclusion.
     In case it isn't clear that the revised argument is invalid, consider this
analogy:

Argument C

1.   It is obvious that, if there is life on Mars, then there is life on
       the Red Planet.
2.   It isn't obvious that there is life on the Red Planet.
3.   Therefore, there is no life no Mars.

Lines (1) and (2) here are in fact true, but they provide not the
slightest reason to accept (3).
     It is possible to produce a valid argument having to do with the
obviousness of Jim's obligation. We can do so as follows:

Argument B'

1.   If it were obvious that utilitarianism is true and that killing an Indian would maximize utility, then it would be obvious that Jim ought to kill an Indian.
2.   It isn't obvious that Jim ought to kill an Indian.
3.   Therefore, it isn't obvious that utilitarianism is true and that killing an Indian would maximize utility.

I am inclined to accept Argument B'. I cannot imagine how anyone could mistake it for an objection to utilitarianism of any sort. I certainly do not maintain thay my own neo-utilitarian view is *obviously* true.

The moral to be drawn from this is that the truth of utilitarianism would not, by itself, render anything more obvious. I think that my version of utilitarianism is true. Yet particular moral judgments are almost never obvious to me. The reasons are clear: I rarely know what worlds are accessible, and I never know their intrinsic values. Even if I knew these things, moral judgments would still lack obviousness. After all, it isn't *obvious* (even to me) that the normative theory I have proposed is correct.

One fairly interesting thing about the arguments so far discussed is that neither of them makes any essential appeal to claims about integrity. Yet it is pretty clear that Williams' dissatisfaction with utilitarianism does have something to do with integrity. Let us consider that Williams says on this topic.

3.5.2. *Projects and Commitments*

A substantial part of Williams' discussion of integrity has to do with "projects and commitments". Williams distinguishes between very general projects, such as seeking to maximize utility, and "lower order" projects, such as those associated with "desires for things for oneself, one's family, one's friends, including basic necessities of life, and, in more relaxed circumstances, objects of taste."[16] Williams suggests that a person's life is given meaning and structure by the pattern of these commitments, and that reflection upon them may reveal what a person's life "is about".[17]

Perhaps Williams would say that a person's integrity is somehow tied to the pattern of his projects and commitments. We can develop this idea by proposing that one's integrity is a measure of the extent to which his behavior accords with the pattern of his projects and commitments. If a person regularly acts in furtherance of his most important projects, his integrity rating is high. On the other hand, if a person has projects and commitments, but rarely does anything to bring them to fruition, then his integrity rating is low. We violate someone's integrity when we prevent him from pursuing an important project.

In a passage toward the end of the section on integrity,[18] Williams raises an important question. He asks us to consider what happens when there is a conflict between acting for the best and acting in furtherance of one's most important commitments. Of course, utilitarianism of any sort implies (roughly) that one must always act for the best. Hence, in this sort of situation, utilitarianism implies that one must sacrifice one's integrity. Williams evidently finds something unacceptable about this. It is in this context that he claims that it is "absurd" to demand that one 'step aside from his own projects'. To ask him to do so, he says:

> . . . is to alienate him in a real sense from his actions and the source of his actions in his own convictions. . . . It is thus, in the most literal sense, an attack on his integrity.[19]

The bearing of all this on Jim should be pretty clear. If we ask Jim to step aside from his botanical project so as to save nineteen lives, we may violate his integrity. He didn't go to South America to save lives — or to take any either. He went there to look for flowers. If we force him to accept the Captain's offer, we "alienate him from his actions". It therefore may appear that Williams is arguing that utilitarianism is to be rejected because it yields an absurdly wrong normative result in Jim's case, or in any case in which one is required to sacrifice his own integrity in order to maximize utility.

However, as I have already pointed out, Williams did not mean to use Jim's case as a counterexample to utilitarianism. Thus, we cannot assume that, in the passages under consideration, Williams was trying to back up the claim that utilitarianism is to be rejected because it has incorrect normative consequences in cases such as Jim's. A more plausible interpretation of Williams' point would be this: utilitarianism goes wrong, not because it yields the wrong normative conclusion in Jim's case, but because it takes no account whatever of Jim's integrity. Perhaps Williams means to insist that even if Jim's integrity is ultimately found to be less important than the lives of nineteen Indians, it is still worth something. It should somehow figure in the determination of

Jim's obligations. Perhaps Williams' complaint is that utilitarianism fails to take any account of Jim's integrity.

Let us say that integrity is "normatively irrelevant" provided that considerations of integrity play no role in the determination of moral obligations. We can then summarize this version of the objection as follows:

Argument D

1. If utilitarianism were true, integrity would be normatively irrelevant.
2. In fact, integrity is not normatively irrelevant.
3. Therefore, utilitarianism is not true.

If we understand integrity in the suggested way, then it is easy enough to understand why someone might say that integrity has some relevance to morality. Surely, we can sympathize with the view that there's something objectionable about violating a person's integrity. Wrenching someone away from his projects and commitments can be cruel and demoralizing. Sensitive people recognize that it is important to allow others to "go on with their lives". So, with integrity understood in accordance with the current proposal, we may want to accept line (2) of Argument D.

The problem is that it is not clear that line (1) is true. Perhaps some old-fashioned hedonistic forms of utilitarianism are guilty as charged. However, the criticism applies entirely to the hedonistic axiology — not to the normative doctrine itself. This can be seen most readily if we consider whether the objection would apply to the sort of view I have proposed.

According to my view, the normative status of each act is determined by the intrinsic values of the worlds accessible to the agent. My view is consistent with the idea that the intrinsic value of a world is determined, at least in part, by the extent to which the integrity of its inhabitants is violated or respected. One could maintain that possible worlds in which integrity takes a beating are much worse than otherwise similar ones in which integrity is respected. Since moral obligations, according to this view, depend upon the intrinsic values of the accessible worlds, we must conclude that integrity may very well be a most important factor in the determination of moral obligations. Hence, if we take Argument D to be an attack on my own neo-utilitarian doctrine, we must say that it fails. Line (1) is indefensible.

3.5.3. *Neo-Utilitarian Agents*

In a number of places in his essay, Williams alludes to something he calls "the utilitarian agent". A utilitarian agent seems to be a person who makes his moral decisions by consideration of the utilities of his alternatives. As an extension of this usage, let us say that a "neo-utilitarian agent" is a person who makes his moral decisions by consideration of the intrinsic values of the accessible possible worlds. He always aims to do what he does in the best of these worlds.

There appears to be a conflict between maintaining one's integrity and becoming a neo-utilitarian agent. If I am to behave as a neo-utilitarian agent, then I must focus on the intrinsic values of the accessible worlds. Even if integrity is normatively relevant, I must not pay any special attention to my own integrity-level in those worlds. Each other person's integrity is as important as mine. As a result, I may find that morality requires that my own projects and commitments often fail to come to fruition. In a mad scramble to do the best I can, I may lose the opportunity to engage in the projects that matter most to me. Thus, I may pay a very high price as I try to maximize intrinsic value. Indeed, the price may be so high that no ordinary person will be able to pay it.

It is hard to see precisely how all this is supposed to bear on the truth of utilitarianism. Some have suggested that the point is that utilitarianism presents an inaccurate model of moral decision-making. We do not reach our moral decisions in anything like the way utilitarianism says we do. We are are not neo-utilitarian agents. Taken in this way, the argument would be:

Argument E

1.   If MO were true, we would be neo-utilitarian agents.
2.   We aren't neo-utilitarian agents.
3.   Therefore, MO is not true.

The trouble with this argument is that utilitarianism does not even purport to present a moral decision making procedure. My own neo-utilitarian doctrine is not intended to be an empirical account of the

way in which people in fact reach their moral decisions. Line (1) of
Argument E is utterly indefensible.

A slightly more plausible line of reasoning would be based on the
idea that utilitarianism tells us how we ought to reach our moral
decisions. By extension, the idea would be that MO implies that we
ought to become neo-utilitarian agents. However, it might be insisted, it
is impossible for ordinary humans beings to behave in such a cold and
calculating way, and so we cannot have any such obligation. Maybe this
is what Williams meant when he spoke of the "absurd demand" of
utilitarianism. In other words, the argument might be this:

Argument F

1. If MO is true, we have a moral obligation to become
   neo-utilitarian agents.
2. We cannot become neo-utilitarian agents.
3. If we cannot become neo-utilitarian agents, then we have no
   moral obligation to become neo-utilitarian agents.
4. Therefore, MO is not true.

It should be pretty clear that this argument fails. My view implies
that I morally ought to do what I do in the intrinsically best worlds
accessible to me. If there is no world accessible to me in which I
become a neo-utilitarian agent, then, no matter how good such worlds
might be, I have no moral obligation to become such an agent. Thus, if
line (2) is true, line (1) is false.

On a slightly different interpretation, we could take Williams to be
claiming that utilitarianism's demand is absurd not because unfulfillable,
but because it exceeds the actual demands of morality. That is, we
could take Williams' point to be that morality in fact does not require
me to become a mere channel for the production of best outcomes. On
this interpretation, the argument might look like this:

Argument G

1. If MO is true, I have a moral obligation to become a
   neo-utilitarian agent.
2. In fact, I do not have a moral obligation to become a
   neo-utilitarian agent (because doing so would violate my
   integrity).
3. Therefore, MO is not true.

My own view is that some of us might be able to become neo-utilitarian agents. Sufficient propagandizing and training might turn some of us into cold and calculating individuals who always try to maximize intrinsic value. However, I do not think that MO implies that we have an obligation to undergo any such transformation, even if it is within our power to do so. As I see it, neo-utilitarian agents would be unattractive characters. Furthermore, there's no reason to suppose that their chances of realizing the best of the accessible worlds are any better than ours. After all, they have no special intellectual capacities. They can't tell with any assurance what worlds are accessible, or how much each is worth. Thus, it seems to me that, even if there are accessible worlds in which I become a neo-utilitarian agent, those worlds are probably not among the best accessible to me. Hence, line (1) of the argument strikes me as being false.

The reader may then wonder about the point of my neo-utilitarian doctrine. If it is not intended to tell us how to make our moral decisions, then what is its point? Why formulate a normative theory unless others are to be guided by it as they try to determine what to do?

G. E. Moore once said that 'the direct object of ethics is knowledge, not practice.'[20] I take this to be a claim about the central purpose of normative theories such as the one I propose in this book. Such a theory is intended to provide a certain sort of philosophical enlightenment. It is supposed to explain certain conceptual connections. In the case of the view I defend in this book, the idea is to display some of the important connections among the normative notions of *right, wrong,* and *obligatory*, the axiological notions of *good* and *evil*, and the metaphysical notions of *possibility* and *impossibility*.

While I hope that moral philosophers will find my view attractive in various ways, I do not hope that they will be moved to become neo-utilitarian agents. I do not intend to change the moral habits of my readers. Nor do I see any reason to suppose that they ought to become neo-utilitarian agents. Morality requires me to do the best I can. It does not require me to be motivated by considerations of what would be for the best. I see nothing paradoxical in this.[21]

3.5.4. *Moral Integrity and "Clean Hands"*

One of the most striking things about Jim's predicament concerns what we might call his "moral integrity". If Jim is a typical sort of fellow, he is wholeheartedly against murder. As he contemplates the Captain's cruel invitation, he feels overwhelming moral repugnance. He hates the thought of murdering an innocent man. Yet, in order to bring about the best of the available outcomes, he will have to kill an Indian. It has been suggested that this is the crucial feature of Williams' argument against utilitarianism — utilitarianism sometimes requires us to violate our most cherished moral convictions. It requires us to "dirty our hands".

I have to admit that if our moral obligations are the ones specified by MO, then my own favorite doctrine has this allegedly objectionable feature. There surely are cases in which, in order to do the best they can, people have to do things that seem morally repugnant to them. In extreme cases, MO may require someone to lie, cheat, break promises, or even murder. In virtue of this feature, we may say that MO some-times violates our moral integrity — it requires us to do things that seem to us to be morally repugnant.

Although it is reasonably clear that MO does in this way violate our moral integrity, it is not at all clear why anyone would think that this is a defect in MO. So long as people find certain act types morally repugnant, every normative theory runs the risk of violating someone's moral integrity. Suppose someone finds acts of type M (murder, for example) to be morally repugnant. Suppose this person now find himself in a horrible situation in which he must either murder A or murder B. Any normative theory that generates any prescription for this situation violates the moral integrity of this poor person.

Every normative doctrine has this same feature. As a most extreme example, consider what we may call "The Doctrine of Comfort" — the grotesque notion that "you ought to do what you feel most comfortable with". Now consider Jim's case in the jungle. His main choices are (a) killing an Indian, or (b) turning his back on the ugly scene, and walking away. We have already seen that (a) is morally repugant to Jim. Thus, if he feels more comfortable with (a), then the Doctrine of Comfort violates his moral integrity. On the other hand, suppose Jim feels more comfortable with (b). Then, according to the Doctrine of Comfort, that's what he ought to do. Nevertheless, if he does turn his back on the ugly scene, he will, by doing so, reject the impassioned entreaties of the innocent villagers. Surely, if Jim is a decent fellow, doing this will also violate his moral integrity. Thus, in a hard enough case, even the Doctrine of Comfort requires a person to do something that seems to him to be morally repugnant.

3.5.5. *Responsibility*

Some commentators have focussed on the fact that the badness of Jim's worst alternative is due entirely to something that someone else would do. Jim would not kill the twenty innocent Indians. The Captain would order the executions, and Pedro would carry out the order. The Captain could just as easily see to it that no one is murdered in that village. He could announce that the whole thing was just a big bluff, and he could march his men off to the next village, there to engage in some other sort of mischief. Thus, if Jim walks away, and allows twenty innocent Indians to be murdered, responsibility for the evil deed would fall not on Jim, but on the Captain and Pedro.

Can Jim be responsible for deaths that would be caused by someone else? Or is Jim only responsible for his own actions? Perhaps this is what Williams has in mind when he suggested that utilitarianism goes wrong because it isn't sensitive to the fact that 'each of us is specially responsible for what *he* does, rather than for what other people do'.[22]

A reader could very naturally suppose that Williams' point here is that utilitarianism goes wrong because it forces us to include too much in the utility calculations. Instead of considering absolutely everything that would happen if Jim were to walk away from the village with clean hands, we should only consider things that would happen as a direct result of Jim's action. The consequences of Pedro's actions ought not to be tallied up against anything Jim did.

We must not fall into the trap of supposing that these remarks are designed to back up the claim that Jim has no obligation to kill an Indian. Recall that Williams agrees with the utilitarian conclusion here. The story of Jim is not supposed to be a counterexample to utilitarianism.

For legal purposes, we must distinguish between the case in which Jim murders twenty innocent Indians, and the case in which he stands aside and permits Pedro to commit the atrocity. The distinction is important to the law because, for legal purposes, we want to punish the appropriate person. We want to punish the person who bears the responsibility for the crime. In the case at hand, it would be the Captain and Pedro, not Jim.

However, if we look at the issue from the moral perspective, and consider the options open to Jim, it seems to me that it doesn't make much difference who kills the Indians. In some worlds accessible to

him, twenty innocent Indians are shot. In other worlds accessible to
him, only one is shot. Given normal assumptions about the evil of
murder, we must conclude that the worlds with only one dead Indian
are less bad. (Williams suggests that the Indians in the story see things
this way, too. Why else would they beg Jim to accept the Captain's
offer?) So, while I wouldn't blame him for refusing to kill one Indian, I
think Jim ought to accept the Captain's invitation. Failure to do so, in
these horrible circumstances, would only make things worse.

In the end, I have to admit that it is far from clear that I have come
to grips with Williams' dissatisfaction. The central problem, as I see it,
is that it is very difficult to determine precisely what the objection is. I
have attempted, however, to present some of the more plausible interpretations of his point, and to explain how I would reply to each of
them. So far as I can tell, my replies are satisfactory.

With this, I conclude my consideration of objections to my view
about absolute moral obligation. In Part Two, I turn to the analysis of
statements containing both an 'ought' and an 'if'.

PART TWO

IFFY OUGHTS

CHAPTER 4

BASIC IFFY OUGHTS

Some of the most interesting and challenging puzzles concerning the logic of 'ought'-statements have to do with "iffy oughts" — sentences that contain an 'if' as well as an 'ought' (or appropriate equivalent terms). Each of these sentences is an iffy ought:

(1)   If it is his most stringent prima facie duty, then he ought to do it.

(2)   If she promised to come for lunch, then she should come for lunch.

(3)   If you want to gain a reputation for honesty, then you should give correct change.

(4)   If rain would make the flowers grow, then there ought to be rain.

The scope of the deontic operator in an iffy ought may be small, as it is in each of (1)—(4), or it may be large, as it is in 'It ought to be that if someone makes a promise, then he keeps it.' I mean to use 'iffy ought' in a fairly broad way, and so I'm also prepared to count a sentence as an iffy ought on some occasion of use if, as used on that occasion, it may properly be translated by something that's clearly an iffy ought. So this category includes some degenerate sentences of English, as well as some sentences of other languages.

The fundamental aim of Part Two is to give a clear account of the conditions under which iffy oughts are true. It would be quite natural to suppose that the account of iffy oughts is a direct consequence of the account of absolute 'ought'-statements, together with the standard accounts of the conditional. Since I have attempted to give an account of the truth conditions for absolute 'ought'-statements in my principle MO in Chapter 2, Section 3, and most of us are quite familiar with the standard explications of typical 'if, then' constructions, we might think there is no need to give special attention to iffy oughts.

The central theme of Part Two is that this supposition is wrong. In my view, there are many logically distinct sorts of iffy ought. Each of them requires independent treatment. Furthermore, it seems to me that

73

an understanding of some iffy oughts requires more than an understanding of the meaning of 'ought' and an understanding of the traditional conditional connectives. Indeed, it seems to me that examples (2),
(3), and (4) above illustrate sorts of iffy ought that go beyond MO and
the standard conditionals.

In this chapter, I try to distinguish four relatively simple sorts of iffy
ought. Each of these is somehow based on the concept of moral
obligation introduced in MO. One of them involves something other
than a standard conditional connective. In Chapters 5 and 6, I will
distinguish several further sorts of iffy ought. These are based on other
concepts of obligation, or on other sorts of conditional connective, or
both.

4.1. MATERIALLY CONDITIONED ABSOLUTE MORAL OBLIGATION

From the perspective of logical form, the simplest sort of iffy ought is
the one I call 'materially conditioned absolute moral obligation', or
"MCAMO". A sentence is of this sort just in case it is of the form: $p \rightarrow$
$MO s, t, q$. Such a sentence is true at a world iff either the antecedent
(p) is false there, or the consequent ($MO s, t, q$) is true there. So it is
just a sentence whose main connective is a material conditional, whose
consequent is a statement of absolute moral obligation, relativized to
some agent and time.

It is of course a well known fact that the material conditional does
not correspond very well to any conditional construction of ordinary
English. In virtue of this, we should not be surprised if we find that
there are very few ordinary language iffy oughts that are properly
representable as statements of materially conditioned absolute moral
obligation. Nevertheless, I want to discuss some of the logical features
of this sort of sentence, so as to illustrate some of the things we will be
looking for in the more complicated cases we will be considering later
on. This will also provide an opportunity to explain why MCAMO is a
relatively unimportant form of iffy ought.

One question we have to ask about any sort of iffy ought is the
question whether "factual detachment" is valid for it.[1] When I say
that factual detachment is valid for some sort of iffy ought, I mean that
the following inference pattern cannot have true premises and a false
conclusion when the iffy ought in it is of that sort:

FD: If A, then OB

A
_____
Therefore, OB

So factual detachment is a form of inference in which the first premise is an iffy ought of some sort, and the second premise is the factual "antecedent" of that iffy ought. The conclusion of the inference is a statement of absolute obligation based upon the "consequent" of the iffy ought in the first premise. FD is intended to display the general structure of this inference pattern. In some cases, the 'ought' in the iffy ought will turn out to have large scope, and in other cases it will turn out to have small scope. In yet other cases, the iffy ought will turn out not to be a genuine conditional at all. In light of this, we shouldn't make too much of the fact that the scope of the 'O' in the first premise seems to be small. 'If A, then OB' serves, in FD, merely to represent any sort of iffy ought, where the "antecedent" is A, and the "consequent" is B.

Since in this first case we are dealing with MCAMO, the relevant instance of FD would be this:

FD1: $p \rightarrow MOs, t, q$

p
_____
MOs, t, q

It should be obvious that FD1 is valid. This is guaranteed by the logic of the material conditional, ' $\rightarrow$ '. The fact that the consequent of the first premise, and the conclusion of the argument as a whole, is a statement of absolute moral obligation is irrelevant, as far as the logic is concerned.

A closely related form of inference may be called "deontic detachment". In this case, we attempt to derive a statement of absolute obligation from an iffy ought together with the obligatoriness of its antecedent. Schematically, this can be represented as follows:

DD: If A, then OB

OA
_____
Therefore, OB

For certain iffy oughts, deontic detachment may seem to be valid. We will consider some of these shortly. But for MCAMO, deontic detachment fails. That is, this inference pattern may have true premises and a false conclusion:

*DD1: $p \rightarrow MOs, t, q$

$$\frac{MOs, t, p}{MOs, t, q}$$

To see why *DD1 fails, we need only consider a case in which the statement of MCAMO is true because of a false but obligatory antecedent. For example, let p be the sentence 'Smith does the best he can', and let s and t represent Smith and some suitable time. Suppose that Smith in fact does not do the best he can. Then p is false here in the real world, and $p \rightarrow MOs, t, q$ is true no matter how we interpret q. Falsity of the antecedent alone assures truth of any statement of MCAMO. To generate the counterexample to *DD1, we must see to it that q is something forbidden. Let q be 'Smith sins remorselessly'. MOs, t, q is false at the real world. In this case, although both premises of *DD1 are true, the conclusion is false. So *DD1 is not valid.

The fact that $p \rightarrow MOs, t, q$ is true in the sort of case just considered reveals something of interest about MCAMO. Falsity of the antecedent is sufficient to assure truth of any such statement. The typical iffy oughts of ordinary English seem to lack this feature. Surely we would be somewhat perplexed if someone presented the following argument: 'you are not going to do the best you can. Therefore, if you do the best you can, you ought to sin remorselessly.' However, if the iffy ought in the conclusion is taken as an instance of MCAMO, such an argument would be valid. In virtue of this feature, which has been called a "paradox of derived obligation",[2] MCAMO apparently does not serve to explicate anything of interest from ordinary discourse. I will have more to say about this shortly.

Let us next consider a form of inference we can call "augmentation". In augmentation, we move from an iffy ought to another just like it except that something has been conjoined to the antecedent. Schematically, this may be represented as follows:

Aug: $$\frac{\text{If A, then OB}}{\text{Therefore, if A and C, then OB.}}$$

In the case of MCAMO, augmentation takes this form:

Aug1: $$\frac{p \rightarrow MOs, t, q}{(p \ \& \ r) \rightarrow MOs, t, q}$$

Aug1 is, of course, valid. If the original antecedent is false, then any conjunction of it with another statement will still be false. If the original consequent is true, then the augmented conditional will have to be true, too, regardless of the truth value of the augmented antecedent.

A closely related feature of some iffy oughts is "overridability". Moral philosophers use this term is a variety of ways, and so it is important to make clear just how I mean to use it.[3] I shall say that a type of iffy ought is overridable just in case it is possible, where that type of iffy ought is in question, to have a true sentence of this form:

Over: A & B & (if A, then OC) & (if A & B, then O ~C)

It might seem that no iffy ought could be overridable, in this sense. I believe, however, that many are. Consider the familiar story. You promised to meet him to lunch, and so you ought to meet him for lunch. Now you have come across an injured person on the highway. This person needs your medical attention. In order to give your medical attention, you must fail to keep your luncheon appointment. So, if we let p abbreviate 'you promised to go to lunch', and we let g abbreviate 'you go to lunch' and we let h abbreviate 'the stranger needs your medical help', than we seem to have: 'p & h & (if p, then Og) & (if p & h, then $O \sim g$)'. If we see this as being possibly true, and with two instances of the same sort of iffy ought, then we see it as containing iffy oughts of an overridable sort.

The question whether MCAMO is an overridable iffy ought is easily answered. We merely need to consider whether it is possible to have a true sentence of this form:

*Over1: p & q & ($p \rightarrow$ MOs, t, r) & (p & $q \rightarrow$ MOs, t, $\sim r$)

The logic of the material conditional generates MOs, t, r and MOs, t, $\sim r$ in this case. The account of MO rules out such incompatible obligations. Hence, *Over1 is impossible. MCAMO is not an overridable iffy ought.

In a 1954 paper in *Mind*, A. N. Prior called attention to some other logical features of some iffy oughts.[4] He called these the "paradoxes of derived obligation". For present purposes, I want to focus on three of these so-called paradoxes. We can say that an iffy ought is paradoxical in the first way iff this form of inference is valid for it:

~A
_____

Therefore, if A, then OB

The paradoxicalness of this form of inference should be pretty obvious. So far as I know, no iffy ought of ordinary English is paradoxical in this way.

We will say that an iffy ought is paradoxical in the second way iff this sort of inference is valid for it:

OB
_____
Therefore, if A, then OB

Perhaps it is not clear why there is anything paradoxical about this second argument form. Here is an example that may bring it out. As things in fact stand, you ought to cut open the patient. Shall we infer that, even if he isn't sick, you still ought to cut open the patient? Surely not. So it is clear that in some cases we would get terribly wrong results if every sort of iffy ought were paradoxical in the second way.

A third sort of paradox may be represented as follows:

O ~A
_____
Therefore, if A, then OB

In this case, we are allowed to derive a certain iffy ought from the doing of anything forbidden. If this sort of thing were in general valid, then we could derive 'if you break your promise, then you ought to go on a wild rampage of looting and plundering' from the relatively innocent 'you shouldn't break your promise'. It's as if the mere violation of one duty opens the floodgates of sin. If you do anything wrong, then everything would be obligatory.

MCAMO is paradoxical in the first two ways. This is a straight-forward consequence of the fact that the material conditional is the main connective here, and each of the following is valid: $\sim p \rightarrow (p \rightarrow q)$; $q \rightarrow (p \rightarrow q)$. The presence of an obligation operator in some of these sentences is quite irrelevant. MCAMO is not paradoxical in the third way. We can have cases in which MOs, t, $\sim p$ is true, but $p \rightarrow$ MOs, t, q is false.

I would be quite happy to find that the logic of some iffy ought of ordinary English is the same as that of MCAMO. However, it seems to me that this is not the case. My view is that this is an instance in which we have a technical locution that has the power to express something that none of us previously had much interest in saying. (At least, we had little interest in saying it with an iffy ought. Perhaps we said it with a 'not' and an 'or'.) The trouble seems to be that, when we use 'if . . . , then . . .', we just don't mean to express what's meant by the material conditional. It has been suggested that we may do this in the odd instance in which we use 'if . . . , then . . .' just to emphasize our belief in the negation of the antecedent. Suppose we have a flat tire. You consider yourself a real "can do" person. I wonder whether you will be able to fix it. You say, 'Well, if I can't fix it, I ought to move to the old folks' home.' It is not clear to me that this is properly represented as a case of MCAMO. But that's mainly because I don't know exactly what this statement is supposed to mean.

4.2. STRICTLY CONDITIONED ABSOLUTE MORAL OBLIGATION

Let us turn now to a conditional connective that is closer to one of ordinary laguage. I use '$\Rightarrow$' to express the necessity of the material conditional. That is, '$p \Rightarrow q$' means the same as '$N(p \rightarrow q)$'. In accordance with what I take to be standard current practice, I call '$\Rightarrow$' the "strict conditional". Let us say that any sentence that has a factual statement as antecedent, a strict conditional as major connective, and a statement of absolute moral obligation as consequent, is a case of "strictly conditioned absolute moral obligation", or "StCAMO". Although such sentences may have all sorts of internal structure, in their main outlines, they look like this: $p \Rightarrow MOs, t, q$.

In my view, StCAMO does explicate the logic of an ordinary language iffy ought. For example, consider some utilitarian who takes utilitarianism to be necessarily true. He might say, 'If it would maximize utility, then he ought to do it'. As I see it, this is a likely candidate for StCAMO. The utilitarian thinks that the fact that it would maximize utility entails (strictly implies) that it absolutely ought to be done. The connection between maximizing utility and being absolutely obligatory is utterly indefeasible, and is not a mere contingency. Similarly, those who think it is necessarily always absolutely wrong to take the life of an innocent person would hold that 'it would take the life of an innocent person' entails 'it ought to be avoided'. That provides the basis for another statement of StCAMO.

It should be obvious that factual detachment and augmentation are valid for this sort of iffy ought. We have:

FD2: $p \Rightarrow MOs, t, q$

   p
   _____

   Therefore, MOs, t, q

and

Aug2: $p \Rightarrow \text{MO}s, t, q$
─────────────────────────
     Therefore, $(p \& r) \Rightarrow \text{MO}s, t, q$

Once again, the validity of these patterns of inference is assured by the logic of the main connective alone, without any help from the fact that some of the components of these statements are statements of absolute moral obligation. You can see that FD2 is valid. If this is a world in which p is true, and every p-world is an $\text{MO}s$, t, q-world, then this is an $\text{MO}s$, t, q-world. Similarly, if every p-world is an $\text{MO}s$, t, q-world, then every $(p \& r)$-world is, too. So Aug2 is valid.

The case with regard to deontic detachment is somewhat more complicated. However, if we understand accessibility and intrinsic value in the ways I have suggested, then deontic detachment is valid for StCAMO. That is, I accept the validity of all inferences of this form:

DD2: $p \Rightarrow \text{MO}s, t, q$
       $\text{MO}s, t, p$
─────────────────────────
     Therefore, $\text{MO}s, t, q$

The second premise implies that, if we order the accessible worlds in terms of their intrinsic values, we'll reach a point at which p is true, and we'll find that p is true "from there on up". That is, p is true at that world, and is true in every accessible world as good as or better than that one. The first premise implies that $\text{MO}s$, t, q is true at all of those p-worlds. That means that, relative to those excellect p-worlds, the best accessible worlds are all q-worlds. Since accessibility is transitive, and betterness is absolute, it follows that the best worlds accessible from here are q-worlds, too. So $\text{MO}s$, t, q is true here.

Since the main connective in StCAMO is the strict conditional, this sort of construction is not overridable in the sense I have explained. That is, we have to say that nothing of this form is possibly true:

*Over2: $p \& q \& (p \Rightarrow \text{MO}s, t, r) \& ((p \& q) \Rightarrow \text{MO}s, t, \sim r)$

The impossibility of overriding should be obvious. If p entails $\text{MO}s$, t, r, and p is true here, then $\text{MO}s$, t, r is true here, too. Hence, $\text{MO}s$, t, $\sim r$ can't also be true here. This follows from A1. So we can't also have $(p \& q)$ and $((p \& q) \Rightarrow \text{MO}s, t, \sim r)$. I think it can be shown that any augmentable iffy ought cannot be overridden. Since StCAMO is augmentable, it is not overridable.

StCAMO is not subject to any of the paradoxes we have considered. None of these is a valid pattern of inference:

$$\frac{\sim p}{\text{Therefore, } p \Rightarrow \text{MO}s, t, q}$$

$$\frac{\text{MO}s, t, q}{\text{Therefore, } p \Rightarrow \text{MO}s, t, q}$$

$$\frac{\text{MO}s, t, \sim p}{\text{Therefore, } p \Rightarrow \text{MO}s, t, q.}$$

I leave it to the interested reader to verify the invalidity of these forms of inference.

It seems to me that there are some iffy oughts of ordinary language that may properly be represented as statements of StCAMO. An example was suggested just a few paragraphs back. It was:

(5)   If it would maximize utility, then he ought to do it.

Let us use m and d for 'it would maximize utility' and 'he does it' respectively, and let us assume that the two occurrences of 'it' pick out the same act. Then, allowing s and t to refer to him and some suitable time, we have:

(5a) $m \Rightarrow \text{MO}s, t, d.$

Although (5) could be used to express any of a variety of other things, I believe it could also be used to express what is more perspicuously expressed by (5a). Furthermore, I think that, for many contexts, (5a) provides the most plausible reading. If you take utilitarianism to be necessarily true, and you utter (5), you undoubtedly mean to assert something that is augmentable, non-overridable, and subject to factual detachment. Furthermore, you undoubtedly mean to assert something that is not paradoxical in any of the three ways discussed above. (5a) has the appropriate features.

Nevertheless, StCAMO would not provide a suitable interpretation for the vast majority of iffy oughts of ordinary English. For example, consider:

(6)   If the engine won't start, you ought to check the gas tank.

Using abbreviations in the natural way, we can interpret (6) as a statement of StCAMO as follows:

(6a) $\sim s \Rightarrow$ MO$y, t, c$.

The unsuitability of (6a) should be obvious. Surely, not *every* world in which the car fails to start is one in which you have an obligation to check the gas tank. In some possible worlds where the car fails to start, you don't even exist. In others, the engine runs on solar power, and has no gas tank. In every such world, $\sim s$ remains true, but MO$y, t, c$ is false. Hence, while (6) may be a fairly reasonable thing to say under certain circumstances here in the real world, (6a) is blatantly false. Reflections such as these may help to bring out the fact that StCAMO is a very strong construction. We don't often use iffy oughts to express anything quite that strong.

4.3. SUBJUNCTIVELY CONDITIONED ABSOLUTE MORAL OBLIGATION

Let us turn, next, to a more interesting conditional connective, the subjunctive conditional. We can use $\rightsquigarrow$ to represent this connective, and we can say that $p \rightsquigarrow q$ is true at a world iff q is true at the nearest p-world.[5] We should keep in mind, however, that "nearness" or "similarity" is not to be taken too literally. We do not assume that possible worlds stand in some objective, eternal relations of nearness, and that in every case just that sort of nearness in all that matters. Rather, different contexts of utterance will presuppose different orderings of worlds. What counts as near in one context may be not so near in another. I should also mention that, whenever I consider an argument form with more than one subjunctive conditional in it, I assume that for all of these conditionals, the relevant ordering is the same.

To say that factual detachment is valid for subjunctively conditioned absolute moral obligation (SuCAMO) is to say that an argument of this form cannot have true premises and a false conclusion:

FD3: $p \rightsquigarrow$ MO$s, t, q$

    $\dfrac{p}{\text{Therefore, MO}s, t, q}$

All such arguments are valid. If MO$s, t, q$ is true at the nearest p-world, and this is a p-world, then MO$s, t, q$ is true here. No world is as near to the real world as the real world is to itself.

Deontic detachment, on the other hand, is not valid for SuCAMO. So we don't have:

*DD3: $p \rightsquigarrow$ MO$s, t, q$
        $\underline{\text{MO}s, t, p}$
        MO$s, t, q$

In order to see why *DD3 fails, we can consider a case in which p can happen in two significantly different ways. One of these is obligatory for s at t. The other is much more likely, but not open to s at t. If p were to come about in this likely way, q would be obligatory for s at t. In fact, however, q isn't obligatory for s at t. So we have $p \rightsquigarrow$ MO$s, t, q$ and MO$s, t, p$, but we don't have MO$s, t, q$.

To see this in a more concrete case, consider the following example. Let p represent the state of affairs of *somebody takes the trash to the dump*. Suppose that neither of us is in fact going to take the trash to the dump, so in the real world p does not occur. Suppose that I really ought to do it, but that if anyone were to do it, it would probably be you. Suppose furthermore, that if the trash were taken to the dump, then I would have an obligation to thank you for having done it. (After all, it is assumed to be something I should have done myself.) Let q represent *I thank you for taking the trash to the dump*. We can see that, as things in fact stand, I have no absolute obligation to thank you for taking the trash to the dump, since, as things in fact stand, you don't do it. In this case, using s for me, and t for a suitable time, we have $p \rightsquigarrow$ MO$s, t, q$ and we have MO$s, t, p$, but we don't have MO$s, t, q$.

Since a number of people have expressed bewilderment about this sort of example, perhaps it will be useful to take a closer look. According to our assumptions, neither of us is in fact going to take the trash to the dump. So p is false here at the real world. In the best worlds accessible to me from here now, I see to the occurrence of p, and I do not thank you for doing it — that's because in those worlds I do it myself. Thus, from the perspective of the real world, I do have a moral obligation to see to the occurrence of p (MO$s, t, p$) but I don't have a moral obligation to thank you for it ($\sim$MO$s, t, q$). We have also assumed that it is more likely that you would take the trash to the dump. Hence, in the *nearest* world in which the trash is taken to the dump, you do it. In the best worlds accessible from there, I thank you for doing this odious task. So $p \leadsto MOs, t, q$ is true here at the real world. It should be clear, then, that there can be cases in which an argument of the form *DD3 has true premises, but a false conclusion.

Augmentation is not valid for SuCAMO. It might be true that at the nearest world in which Smith wins a million in the lottery, he has an absolute obligation to give generously to charity. It does not follow that at the nearest world at which Smith wins a million in the lottery, but has it all confiscated by the IRS, he still has an absolute obligation to give generously to charity. In that world, Smith might be a welfare case himself. So we have to reject:

*Aug3: $p \leadsto MOs, t, q$
———————————————
Therefore, $(p \& r) \leadsto MOs, t, q.$

Although augmentation is not valid here, SuCAMO is not an overridable construction. This may come as a bit of a surprise, but that may be due to some confusion about what 'overridable' means. As I'm using it, to say that SuCAMO is overridable is to say that this is possibly true:

*Over3: $p \& q \& (p \leadsto MOs, t, r) \& (p \& q \leadsto MOs, t, {\sim}r)$

There is no conflict between $p \leadsto MOs, t, r$ and $p \& q \leadsto MOs, t, {\sim}r$, taken just by themselves. The lottery-taxation example shows this. If Smith were to win, he would have an obligation to give to charity. But if Smith were to win and have his winnings confiscated, then he would have an obligation to avoid giving to charity. Notice that in this example, it cannot be the case that, here in the real world, Smith in fact does both win and have his winnings confiscated. For, if this were the case, then, here at the real world, Smith would have an obligation both to give to charity, and to avoid doing so. That's impossible.

So we can see that there is a conflict if we suppose that Smith wins; that his winnings are confiscated; that he would have an obligation to give to charity if he were to win; and that he would have an obligation to avoid charity if he were both to win and have his winnings confiscated. In general, then, we can see that *Over3 is impossible. Hence, SuCAMO is not overridable, in my sense.

This construction is not subject to any of the so-called paradoxes. Each of these is invalid:

$$\frac{\sim p}{\text{Therefore, } p \rightsquigarrow \text{MO}s, t, q}$$

$$\frac{\text{MO}s, t, q}{\text{Therefore, } p \rightsquigarrow \text{MO}s, t, q}$$

$$\frac{\text{MO}s, t, \sim p}{\text{Therefore, } p \rightsquigarrow \text{MO}s, t, q}$$

Once again, it seems to me that the failure of these inferences is pretty obvious, and needs no explanation.

I believe that SuCAMO provides an adequate explication for certain natural language iffy oughts. For example, consider this sentence:

(7)   If Smith were to win a million in the lottery, he would have an obligation to give generously to charity.

Under typical circumstances of utterance, (7) would probably be used to express the idea that in the nearest world in which he wins, Smith has an absolute obligation to give to charity. This does not presuppose that Smith has it in his power to win. It's not as if we think winning is somehow "up to him". Rather, it is that when we reflect on the most natural, most plausible way to suppose that things would stand if the world were changed only so much as to allow Smith to win, we seem to see that Smith has an absolute obligation to give to charity.

Notice that, so understood, (7) has the following features: (i) factual detachment is valid for it. If we suddenly find that Smith has in fact won a million in the lottery, we must either give up (7) or else accept the conclusion that Smith should give to charity. (ii) Deontic detachment is not valid for (7). Even if it were somehow obligatory for Smith to win, and he would have an obligation to give to charity if he were to win, it still does not follow. that, as things in fact stand, he already has an obligation to give to charity. (iii) Augmentation surely fails for (7). This was illustrated by the lottery-taxation example. Although (7) is true, it is not the case that if Smith were to win a million in the lottery, and have it all confiscated by the IRS, then he would still have an absolute obligation to give generously to charity. Finally, (iv) none of the paradoxical inferences seems to be valid for (7). (7) itself is not a consequence of the fact that Smith is not going to win. Nor is (7) a consequence of the statement that Smith ought to give to charity.

Finally, it should be clear that (7) does not follow from the statement
that Smith ought not to win.

In light of these facts about (7), I suggest that (7) may properly be
understood as a statement of SuCAMO. That is, with *w, s, t,* and *c*
understood in the expected ways, (7) is representable as:

(7a) $w \rightsquigarrow \text{MO}s, t, c.$

In my view, SuCAMO provides the appropriate rendering for a fairly
significant number of iffy oughts of ordinary language. However, it is
not universally adequate. There are many cases for which it simply
won't do. Some of these have already been discussed. For example,
some iffy oughts are used to express the idea that the antecedent *entails*
the conclusion. These are augmentable. For them, we need StCAMO,
SuCAMO is too weak. Other iffy oughts are still weaker than SuCAMO.
These don't even support factual detachment. For these, SuCAMO will
be inappropriate. For example, consider the iffy ought in 'If she
promised to meet him for lunch, then she ought to meet him for lunch.'
This is often used in such a way that it is genuinely doubtful whether
factual detachment is valid for it. Some philosophers would insist that,
even if we know that she did promise to meet him for lunch, we still
can't say for sure whether she ought to meet him. In order to make that
decision, they would say, we would have to know whether any other
"more stringent" or "demanding" obligation conflicts with the luncheon.
All of this notwithstanding, these philosophers would allow that 'if she
promised to meet him for lunch, then she ought to meet him for lunch'
is still true. Thus, the iffy ought in it cannot be SuCAMO. (Nor can it
be StCAMO or MCAMO.)

4.4. CONDITIONAL MORAL OBLIGATION

Now let us turn to conditional moral obligation, or "CMO". I take this
to be the most interesting sort of iffy ought to be dealt with here. My
leading idea throughout this book is that we ought to do the best we
can. In Part One I discussed the application of this idea to statements of
absolute moral obligation. There it means that we morally ought to do
what we do in the intrinsically best of the worlds accessible to us.
Statements of conditioned moral obligation are merely conditional
statements whose consequents are statements of absolute moral obliga-

tion. The idea that we morally ought to do the best we can therefore applies to such statements in a perfectly straightforward way.

The application of this leading idea to statements of conditional moral obligation is only a little more complicated. A statement of conditional moral obligation can be seen as being of the form: given that p occurs, s morally ought, as of t, to see to the occurrence of q. On my view, such statements mean, roughly, that if s does the best he still can consistent with p, he will see to the occurrence of q. So if we focus on worlds accessible to s as of t, we will find one in which p and q both occur, and we won't find any as good as or better than that one, but in which p and $\sim q$ occur. In this way, conditional moral obligation can be seen as another doing-the-best-we-can concept of obligation.[6]

We can use MOs, t, q/p to express conditional obligation. Notice that, as I use this expression, the 'q' in it represents the *consequent* and the 'p' represents the *antecedent* of the ordinary language iffy ought. Thus, MOs, t, q/p can be read as 's morally ought, as of t, to see to the occurrence of q, if p occurs' We can formulate truth conditions for this as follows:

CMO: MOs, t, q/p is true at w iff $(Ew')(As, t, w', w$ & p and q are true at w' & $\sim(Ew'')(As, t, w'', w$ & p and $\sim q$ are true at w'' & $IV(w'') \geqslant IV(w')))$

To see how this works in a typical example, consider again the case of the doctor mentioned above in Chapter 1. Suppose that this doctor is charged with the treatment of a patient. Two medicines are effective against this patient's disease. We can call these medicines A and B. Suppose that two doses of A would be the beat treatment for the disease, that two doses of B would be next best, and that any mixture of A and B would be fatal. These, and some other relevant assumptions, are codified in Table 4.1.

TABLE 4.1

	Monday	Tuesday
Best treatment	A	A
Good treatment	B	B
Bad treatment	A	B
Bad treatment	B	A
Bad treatment	(anything else)	

As of Sunday, the doctor's absolute moral obligation is to do what he does in the best worlds then accessible to him. Presumably, this means that he absolutely ought to give a course of treatment consisting of two successive doses of A. So he ought to give A on Monday, and he ought to give A again on Tuesday. However, just to be sure that all bases are covered, we may want to know what he should do if he gives B on Monday. The answer, I believe, is this:

(8)   If the doctor gives B on Monday, then he should give more B on Tuesday.

As I see it, (8) is a good example of an ordinary language iffy ought that is best understood as a case of conditional moral obligation. If it is so understood, then it can properly be represented as follows:

(8a)   MO d, s, d gives B on Tuesday/d gives B on Monday.

(8a) means just this: there is some world accessible to the doctor (d) as of Sunday (s) in which he gives B on Monday and then again on Tuesday, and there is no world as good as that one accessible to him as of Sunday in which he gives B on Monday but does not give B on Tuesday. Loosely, then, we can say that if he does the best he can consistent with giving B on Monday, he has to give B on Tuesday.

A number of philosophers have suggested that statements of conditional obligation are in some way tied down to the passage of time.[7] For example, it might be thought that the state of affairs expressed by the antecedent would have to be temporally prior to the state of affairs expressed by the consequent. Thus, the idea is that a statement of conditional obligation tells us what to do *next*, *after* we have done a certain thing. I think this suggestion is erroneous. In any case, it certainly does not apply to the analysis I have proposed.

Notice that the relevant time in the medical example is Sunday. This is a time before the doctor is stuck with either the antecedent or the consequent. He hasn't yet committed himself either to A or to B on either Monday or Tuesday. We can readily switch the temporal relation between antecedent and consequent, if we like. We may ask this: suppose he is going to give B on *Tuesday*. Then what should he do on *Monday*? The answer is this:

(9)   If he gives B on Tuesday, then, as of Sunday, he ought to give B on Monday.

This can be understood as:

(9a)   MO d, s, d gives B on Monday/ d gives B on Tuesday.

Reflection on this example will show, I believe, that the temporal order of antecedent and consequent is irrelevant. It doesn't matter whether the state of affairs mentioned in the antecedent occurs before, during, or after the one mentioned in the consequent. What matters is that the one mentioned in the consequent is something the agent would have to do in order to do the best he can consistent with the occurrence of the one mentioned in the antecent.

Let us now consider some of the formal features of *CMO*. One of the most important of these has to do with the connection between conditional and absolute moral obligation. From the fact that some state of affairs, q, is conditionally obligatory on some condition, p, we may not infer that q is absolutely obligatory. For while q may occur in the best accessible p-world, that p-world may not be the best of all the accessible worlds — and q may fail to occur in the worlds that are best. For example, we have seen that giving B on Tuesday is conditionally obligatory on the condition that B is given on Monday. However, giving B on Tuesday is not absolutely obligatory. Indeed, in our example, not giving B on Tuesday is absolutely obligatory for the doctor as of Sunday.

Equally, we cannot infer from the fact that something is absolutely obligatory, that it is conditionally obligatory on just any condition. For example, consider giving A on Tuesday. That is absolutely obligatory as of Sunday. Yet it is not conditionally obligatory on the condition that B is given on Monday. It would be wrong to give A on Tuesday, if B were given on Monday. So an absolutely obligatory state of affairs may fail to be conditionally obligatory, on certain conditions. However, it turns out that whatever is absolutely obligatory is conditionally obligatory on every necessary, inevitable, or obligatory condition.

The logic of CMO is different from that of each form of conditioned absolute obligation. This comes out clearly in the case of factual detachment. Factual detachment, as we have seen, is valid for each form of conditioned absolute obligation. It is not valid for CMO. That is, this form of inference can have true premises and a false conclusion:

*FD4:   MO s, t, q/p

     p
     ———————
     Therefore, MO s, t, q

We can see that this is invalid by reflecting further on our medical example. Suppose our doctor still has his choice, as of Sunday, of giving any combination of A and B on Monday and Tuesday. Given our assumptions about the values of these various courses of treatment, we have seen that he has a conditional obligation to give B on Tuesday if he gives B on Monday. We may suppose that, though he doesn't have to, he in fact is going to give B on Monday. In spite of all this, as of Sunday, he does not have an absolute obligation to give B on Tuesday. As of Sunday, his absolute moral obligation is to give A on Monday, and more A on Tuesday.

If we reflect on the proposed truth conditions given in CMO, we can see how this can be true. In the best worlds accessible to the doctor on Sunday, he gives two doses of A. So his absolute obligation is to give A on Monday, and then again on Tuesday. However, in the best worlds in which he gives B on Monday, he gives more B on Tuesday. Thus, his conditional obligation is to give B on Tuesday, if he gives B on Monday. Finally, consistent with all this, we can suppose that in the real world, he gives B on Monday. In this case, using the natural abbreviations, we have: MOd, s, d gives B on Tuesday/d gives B on Monday and d gives B on Monday, but we don't have MOd, s, d gives B on Tuesday. This shows how *FD4 can fail.

A modified version of the factual detachment rule is valid. If s has, as of t, a conditional obligation to see to q, given p, and s cannot avoid p, then s has, as of t, an absolute obligation to see to q. We can make use of our unalterability operator, U, which was introduced in Chapter 2, Section 1.3., to formulate this principle clearly. Inferences of the following form are all valid:

FD4′:   MOs, t, q/p
 Us, t, p
 $\overline{\text{Therefore, MO}s, t, q}$

If every accessible world is a p-world (as the second premise says), and the best accessible p-worlds are all q-worlds (as the first premise says), then the best accessible worlds are all q-worlds (as the conclusion says). We can modify the medical example slightly so as to make it illustrate this inference. Suppose that for some reason the doctor cannot avoid giving B on Monday. Perhaps there is no A left in the hospital, and the Chief of Staff insists that B be given. If the doctor still has a conditional obligation to give B on Tuesday, if B is given on Monday, then he already has an absolute obligation to give B on Tuesday.

Deontic detachment is also valid for CMO. That is, all inferences of this form are valid:

DD4:   MO$s, t, q/p$
      MO$s, t, p$
      ─────────────
      Therefore, MO$s, t, q$

If all of s's best p-worlds are q-worlds, and all of s's best worlds are p-worlds, then all of s's best worlds are q-worlds.

Augmentation is not valid for CMO. We can have inferences of the following form with true premises and false conclusions:

*Aug4:   MO$s, t, q/p$
      ─────────────
      Therefore, MO$s, t, q/(p \& r)$

The problem here is that, even if there are accessible $p \& r$-worlds (which of course is not guaranteed by the premise), the best of them may be worse than the best of the p-worlds. In the best of these (bad) $p \& r$-worlds, $\sim q$ may be a better choice than q. Once again, our medical example serves to illustrate the point. If the doctor gives a dose of medicine on Monday, then he ought to give A on Tuesday. However, it does not follow that if he gives a dose of medicine on Monday, *and what he gives is B*, then he still ought to give A on Tuesday. The augmented condition supports a new conditional obligation — on the argumented condition, he ought to give B on Tuesday.

Overridability, in the case of CMO, amounts to the possibility of there being truths of this form:

Over4: $p \& q \& $ MO$s, t, r/p \& $ MO$s, t, \sim r/p \& q$

CMO is an overridable construction. We can see that Over4 is possible if we consider another instance of our medical example. We interpret $p, q, r, d,$ as s as follow:

    p: The doctor gives medicine on Monday
    q: The doctor gives B on Monday.
    r: The doctor gives A on Tuesday.
    d: The doctor
    s: Sunday

We make the following assumptions: p and q are true at the real world; r is true at the best accessible p-world as of Sunday; $\sim r$ is true at the best accessible $p \& q$ world as of Sunday. In light of all these assumptions about the case, the following instance of CMO would have to be true:

(10) $p \& q \& \text{MO} d, s, r/p \& \text{MO} d, s, \sim r/p \& q$

CMO is not paradoxical in any of the three ways I mentioned above.

4.4.1. *CMO and SuCAMO*

It is very easy to confuse CMO with SuCAMO, and so it may be useful to investigate some of the ways in which these differ.[8] Among the most important, I think, is a difference involving inaccessible antecedents. Suppose Smith is not able, as of t, to win in the lottery. Perhaps all the tickets have been sold, and the winners have already been selected. He's not among them. Then, no matter what q is, Smith does not have a conditional obligation to see to q, given that the wins in the lottery. For the statement that he has such a conditional obligation entails that a world in which he wins is accessible to him, and we have assumed that that's not so. So this is a valid principle:

CMO/K: $\text{MO} s, t, q/p \rightarrow \text{K} s, t, p$

CMO/K is a version of the Kantian principle that "ought" implies "can". A glance at the relevant definitions will show that it is verified by my proposals.

However, the corresponding principle is not valid where SuCAMO is concerned. We must reject:

*SuCAMO/K: $(p \leadsto \text{MO} s, t, q) \rightarrow \text{K} s, t, p$.

The nearest p-world may be one in which $\text{MO} s, t, q$ is true, even though it is not one accessible to s at t. The lottery example illustrates this. Even though no world in which he wins is accessible to Smith, there are such worlds, and one of them is nearest. In that one, $\text{MO} s, t, q$ is true. This shows that there are some iffy oughts of English whose proper representation calls for SuCAMO, not CMO. Letting w, g, s, and t be interpreted as follows:

w: Smith wins a million in the lottery.
g: Smith gives generously to charity.
s: Smith
t: Now

we have an example. This iffy ought:

(11)   If he wins a million in the lottery, then Smith ought to give generously to charity.

can be understood as

(11a) $w \rightsquigarrow MOs, t, g$

but not as

(11b) $MOs, t, g/w$

Another difference between CMO and SuCAMO has to do with the way in which the temporal references may be juggled. With SuCAMO, we can readily express propositions about what a person's obligations would be afterwards, if he should do certain things. It isn't as easy to represent such propositions with CMO. To see this, consider the following case, which is another variant of the medical example. Suppose the doctor has his choice of giving two doses of A, or two doses of B, or mixing these medicines, or giving nothing at all. Suppose that two doses of A would be best, two doses of B would be good, and any other course of treatment horrible. Now (and here's the variation) suppose that he in fact is not going to give any medicine, but that, if he were to give medicine, it would be B. In other words, in the real world he gives no medicine, but in the nearest would where he does give medicine, it is B that he gives.

I think the following statement would have to be judged to be true:

(12)   If he were to give medicine on Monday, then he would have an obligation to give B on Tuesday.

I think (12) is true, given the stated assumptions, because according to those assumption, if he gives any medicine on Monday, it will be the less good medicine, B. Once he has given B, it will be better for him to follow up with more B, rather than to give a dose of A. A dose of A, under those circumstances, would be fatal to the patient.

Let us use the following abbreviations:

m: The doctor gives some medicine on Monday.
b: The doctor gives medicine B on Tuesday.
d: The doctor
s: Sunday
n: Monday night, after the time for giving medicine has passed.

Consider the following sentences:

(12a)   MO$d, s, b/m$
(12b)   MO$d, n, b/m$
(12c) $m \sim> $ MO$d, s, b$
(12d) $m \sim> $ MO$d, n, b$

Every one of these can be read as 'if the doctor gives medicine on Monday, then he ought to give B on Tuesday'. However, no two of them are equivalent. Only one of them is a suitable representation for the original sentence, (12). (12a) is not suitable, since, as of Sunday, the doctor's best accessible medicine world is not a b-world. If he did the best he could consistent with giving medicine on Monday, he would give A on Tuesday, not B. So (12a) is just false on our assumptions. (12b) is not suitable since it entails that, as of Monday night, there is a b & m-world accessible to the doctor. Since he is in fact not going to give any medicine on Monday, there will be no such world then accessible to him. So (12b) is false, too. (12c) asks us to consider the nearest world in which he gives medicine on Monday. What is the doctor's moral obligation there *as of Sunday*? Clearly, it is to give A on both Monday and Tuesday. (In that world, unfortunately, the doctor is going to fail to do what he should do.) Since (12c) says that the doctor's moral obligation there is to give B, rather than A, (12c) is false. Thus, it is not a suitable interpretation for the apparently true (12).

(12d) seems to me to say just the right thing. Consider the nearest world where the doctor gives some medicine on Monday. As of Monday night there, his best accessible-from-there worlds are b-worlds. That's because, in that world, he has already given one dose of B. So (12d) is true, and more neatly expresses what is rather ambiguously expressed by our original sentence, (12). This example shows, I think, that CMO and SuCAMO are significantly different constructions, and that some ordinary language iffy oughts require the latter representation.

CMO has a clear meaning, too, and is also useful for the representation of certain statements from English. For example, suppose we want to give directions for the treatment of a certain disease. We may give some absolute advice: 'you ought to give two doses of A.' We may also want to give some conditional advice: 'if you give B on the first day, then, by all means, you should give B on the second day, too.' As I see it, this last is a statement of conditional moral obligation, and its truth conditions are given in CMO.

4.4.2. *The Iffy Ought of Commitment*

It is extremely important to recognize that none of the constructions so far discussed will serve to express the iffy oughts associated with the concept of prima facie duty, or "commitment". These require special treatment, and are discussed in greater detail in Chapter 6. For now, however, it will be sufficient to indicate the sort of sentence I have in mind, and to explain why nothing yet introduced serves to analyze it.

Consider the statement that if you make a promise, you ought to keep it. This statement is sometimes understood to express a certain allegedly important connection between promise-making and promise-keeping. Promise-making is sometimes said to give rise to a prima facie obligation for promise-keeping. It is also sometimes said that promise-making "commits" you to promise-keeping. Whetever the precise nature of this connection may be, it is a deeply defeasible connection. Sometimes, having made a promise, a person may have an absolute moral obligation *not* to keep it. For example, suppose some gangster promises to commit a horrible crime. Though he has made the promise, and promise-making commits him to promise-keeping, still it would be absurd to suppose that he has an absolute moral obligation to commit the crime. The horror of the promised crime is so great that it "overrides" the prima facie obligation to keep the promise, and gives rise to an even more stringent obligation to break the promise. In light of this, we can see that no form of factual detachment is valid for the statement:

(13)   If you make a promise, then you ought to keep it.

However, we have seen that a straightforward version of factual detachment is valid for each form of conditioned absolute moral obligation, and that unalterability detachment is valid for conditional moral obligation. Therefore, none of the constructions so far introduced is adequate for the expression of statments of the sort illustrated by (13).

One of the most important general conclusions I want to emphasize here is that the iffy oughts of ordinary English are a very heterogeneous lot. For each such iffy ought, there are many different potential logical structures. In order to determine which of the logical structures best represents the logical structure of the original, we have to study the iffy ought in its natural setting, and we have to consider the main possibilities. Throughout all this, we must avoid falling into the trap of supposing that all iffy oughts are to be given the same analysis. A good part of the literature on conditional obligation is marred by this narrowness. So, for example, some philosophers write as if they take conditional obligation and commitment to be the same thing, and they offer sentences relevantly like (13) as instances of ordinary language sentences that should be treated as cases of conditional obligation. In my view, if these things are to be properly understood, they must first be distinguished from each other.

4.5. THE CHISHOLM PUZZLE

In 1963, Professor Chisholm's 'Contrary to Duty Imperatives and Deontic Logic' appeared in *Analysis.*[9] In that paper, Chisholm presented a set of sentence that provides a sort of test case for any view about iffy oughts. Subsequent discussion has established that Chisholm's original point was extremely penetrating.[10] We can abstract slightly from his example, and formulate four sentences which then will provide the basis for a version of the puzzle.

(14)   Jones ought to go to the aid of his neighors.
(15)   If Jones goes to the aid of his neighbors, he ought to tell them he is coming.
(16)   If Jones does not go to the aid of his neighbors, then he ought not to tell them he is coming.
(17)   Jones does not go to the aid of his neighbors.

We are asked to imagine a case in which each of (14)—(17) is true. That shouldn't be too hard. Notice that the set is not only consistent, it is also independent — no member entails any other.

In order to make discussion of the case easier, let us make use of some convenient abbreviations:

g: Jones goes to the aid of his neighbors.
n: Jones notifies them that he is coming.
j: Jones
t: some suitable time prior to the time at which he would either go or notify.

It should be obvious that we will run into lots of trouble if we attempt to represent the iffy oughts in (15) and (16) as instances of MCAMO. If we try, we will find that the four sentences get the following interpretation:

(14a) MOj, t, g
(15a) $g \rightarrow MOj, t, n$
(16a) $\sim g \rightarrow MOj, t, \sim n$
(17a) $\sim g$

One trouble with this proposal is that (17a) entails (15a), whereas the originals were independent. This shows that at least one of the proposed translations is inadequate. It is pretty clear that (15a) is unacceptable.

So long as we stick to material conditionals, a mere change of scope won't do much good. We can replace (15a) by:

(15b) $MOj, t, g \rightarrow n$

but since (14a) and (15b) entail MOj, t, n, and (16a) and (17a) entail $MOj, t, \sim n$, we'd get a violation of the "no-conflicts" principle.

Nor would it help to replace (16a) by:

(16b) $MOj, t, \sim g \rightarrow \sim n.$

For now (14a) entails (16b), whereas the originals were independent. The moral to be drawn here is that we cannot understand the iffy oughts in Chisholm's puzzle as statements of MCAMO, nor can we understand them as statements of absolute moral obligation, but with material conditionals in their objects. The material conditional simply has to go.

StCAMO is no more suitable. There is no plausibility to the view that (15) and (16) can be understood as:

(15c) $g \Rightarrow MOj, t, n$

and

(16c) $\sim g \Rightarrow MOj, t, \sim n$

These are just much too strong, as would be the sentences we'd get by changing the scope of the obligation operator, but retaining the strict conditional.

A number of philosophers have considered the idea of representing

Chisholm's sentence with the help of the subjunctive conditional.[11] This approach is somewhat more promising. Consider:

(14a) MOj, t, g
(15d) $g \sim> MOj, t, n$
(16d) $\sim g \sim> MOj, t, \sim n$
(17a) $\sim g$

(15d) says that in the nearest world in which he goes, he has, as of t, an absolute obligation to notify them. (16d) says that in the nearest world in which he doesn't go, he has, as of t, an absolute obligation not to notify them. There is no inconsistency here.

In my view, the proposed SuCAMO solution to Chisholm's puzzle is not entirely successful. The trouble arises because factual detachment is valid for SuCAMO. In light of this, we have to say that (17a) and (16d) together entail $MOj, t, \sim n$. In itself, this may seem acceptable. But, according to (14a), MOj, t, g is also true. These may be conjoined to yield $MOj, t, g \& \sim n$. This is simply false. If anything, Jones' conjunctive moral obligation, as of t, is to notify them that he is coming, and then go.[12]

I take Chisholm's sentences to be adequately representable as statements of conditional moral obligation.[13] We can put them as follows:

(14a) MOj, t, g
(15e) $MOj, t, n/g$
(16e) $MOj, t, \sim n/\sim g$
(17a) $\sim g$

These sentences have the logical features of the originals. None entails another. The set is consistent. Notice that since factual detachment is not valid for CMO, we cannot derive $MOj, t, \sim n$ from (17a) and (16e). That seems to me to be appropriate. Since deontic detachment is valid for CMO, we can derive MOj, t, n from (14a) and (15e). Once again, my intuition tells me that this is as it should be.

There are other ways to represent these sentences, and some of them may seem to some readers to be more attractive than the way I have proposed here. My main point here is just that, insofar as their logic is concerned, these sentences can be understood in the way suggested. No paradox or contradiction arises if we interpret them in this way.

CHAPTER 5

HYPOTHETICAL IMPERATIVES

The moral writings of Immanuel Kant have drawn attention to a class of interesting and puzzling iffy oughts. These are the so-called "hypothetical imperatives". While some philosophers[1] have apparently used the term 'hypothetical imperative' as little more than a stylistic variant for 'statement of conditional obligation', I think there is good reason to distinguish hypothetical imperatives from other iffy oughts, and to give them a separate analysis. Some of these reasons will emerge shortly. In this chapter, I try to identify the sort of statement Kant may have had in mind; I note a variety of puzzling features of these things; I explain why some proposed accounts seem to me to be inadequate; I give my own account of them; and I try to explain why they have the puzzling features noted.

5.1. HYPOTHETICAL IMPERATIVES

Since Kant apparently introduced the term 'hypothetical imperative' into the technical lexicon of moral philosophy, he would seem to be the leading authority on what counts as a hypothetical imperative. Accordingly, we should start by considering what he has to say. Kant's examples of hypothetical imperatives are familiar, although some of them are rather sketchy. As a general schema for hypothetical imperatives, Kant gives this: 'I ought to do something *because I will something else*.'[2] As an instance of this schema, he explicitly offers:

(1)   I ought not to lie if I want to maintain my reputation.[3]

There are several passages in which Kant suggests other examples. One of the most famous of these is the one in which he mentions the would-be poisoner. Kant tells us that some hypothetical imperatives give instructions concerning some merely possible end.

Here there is no question about the rationality or goodness of the end, but only about what must be done to attain it. A prescription required by a doctor in order to cure his man completely and one required by a poisoner in order to make sure of killing him are of equal value so far as each serves to effect its purpose perfectly.[4]

99

This suggests two statements in the pattern of (1):

(2)   If you want to cure him, you ought to use aspirin.
(3)   If you want to kill him, you ought to use arsenic.

Kant's remarks in the passage just quoted, and the fact that (3) seems to be a bona fide hypothetical imperative, should tip us off to the fact that these statements are not to be confused with statements of conditional moral obligation. We cannot plausibly interpret (3) as meaning that in the intrinsically best of the accessible worlds in which you want to kill him, you use arsenic. Undoubtedly, in the best accessible worlds in which you find yourself having that perverted desire, you do *not* use arsenic (or any other poison). Rather, in the best such worlds, you promptly seek psychiatric counselling, so as to avoid acting upon your murderous desire.

Some other examples that may be constructed on the basis of Kantian suggestions are these:

(4)   If I want to divide a line, I ought to draw two arcs.[5]
(5)   If I want to be happy, then I ought to be careful in my diet, frugal, polite, reserved, etc.[6]
(6)   You ought not to make a lying promise if you want to maintain your credit rating.[7]
(7)   If I want to be happy, then I ought to make others happy.[8]
(8)   If you want to avoid indigence in old age, then you ought to be industrious and thrifty in youth.[9]

It appears, on the basis of these examples, that Kantian hypothetical imperatives have a number of important features in common. Each of them is properly expressible by a sentence that is conditional in form. In each case, the antecedent of the conditional is a statement about someone's wish, will, want, or end. The content of the wish is apparently quite variable. Anything anyone might want seems to be fair game. The consequent of the hypothetical imperative seems to be some sort of "ought"-statement. It says, with respect to some course of action, that the person with the want mentioned in the antecedent ought to undertake that course of action.

It seems to me, however, that the possession of these features does not ensure that a statement is a genuine hypothetical imperative. As I see it, a statement having these characteristics might be an instance of any of a variety of other forms of iffy ought. For example, it might turn out to be a case of subjunctively conditioned absolute moral obligation.

Since Kant contrasts the moral ought with the ought of the hypothetical imperative, there must be some further feature that serves to distinguish hypothetical imperatives from these other sorts of iffy ought. In light of the fact that they are syntactically indistinguishable from iffy oughts of other kinds, this other feature must be a semantic feature, rather than a syntactic one.

5.2. SOME PUZZLES ABOUT HYPOTHETICAL IMPERATIVES

One of the most puzzling and controversial questions concerning these hypothetical imperatives is the question whether any form of factual detachment is valid for them. It surely seems that the most straightforward form of factual detachment cannot be valid here. This example, adapted from Prichard,[10] seems to drive this home in a striking manner:

(9)   If you want to kill him, you ought to use a double dose.
(10)   You do want to kill him.
(11)   Therefore, you (absolutely) ought to use a double dose.

If we take the 'ought' in (11) to express any familiar form of moral obligation, and we take (9) to be a hypothetical imperative, then it's easy enough to imagine case in which (9) and (10) are true, but (11) false. Suppose, for example, that "he" is a rather large fellow, and would probably survive if you gave him less than a double dose. However, a double dose would do the trick. Suppose, also, that you are very angry at him, and want to kill him, Suppose, finally, that a frank, open discussion of your differences, and a hearty handshake would lead to much better relations between you and him. In this case, it would appear that you shouldn't kill him. So (9) and (10) seem to be true, but (11) is false.

It appears, then, that factual detachment fails in this case. There are a number of ways in which we might attempt to explain this fact. One suggestion is that (9) really isn't a conditional. Another idea is that (11) would follow from (9) and (10) only if the 'ought' in (11) were understood in some special non-moral sense. Some have suggested that the failure of factual detachment here is to be explained by reference to (10). Perhaps something stronger than (10), such as:

(10a)   You unalterably want to kill him.

is required for the derivation of (11).

My own view is that, in the absence of a clear account of the meaning of the hypothetical imperative, it is pointless to debate the question about factual detachment. If we don't know precisely what (9) means, and we aren't entirely clear on the interpretation of the 'ought' in (11), then we are in no position to speculate on the question whether (9) and (10) entail (11).

If a satisfactory analysis of the meaning of the hypothetical imperative were at hand, we could answer further questions about the logic of these things. We could, for example, consider the analogues of deontic detachment, augmentation, and overridability. We could also investigate the question whether hypothetical imperatives are subject to versions of the paradoxes of derived obligation.

A second area of interest concerning hypothetical imperatives has to do with the 'want' (or 'wish' etc.) in sentences such as (1)–(9). It isn't clear that it has anything to do with desire, or craving. Indeed, Hare has gone so far as to say that it is just a "logical term".[11] Support for this view comes from the fact that a statement such as (1) is apparently interchangeable with a statement without 'want' or any equivalent term. It certainly seems that we can rewrite (1) as:

(1′)   If I'm to maintain my reputation, then I'll have to avoid lying.

So the second question has to do with the meaning and role of 'want', 'wish', 'will', etc. in the antecedents of hypothetical imperatives.

A closely related question, also suggested by Hare, is the question whether a hypothetical imperative says anything more than that a certain means is essential to the attainment of some end.[12] Hare's comment is based upon an example. Suppose that Grimbley Hughes is in fact the largest grocer in Oxford. Does it follow that if you want to see the largest grocer in Oxford, you ought to see Grimbley Hughes? If so, we seem to have a breach of Hume's dictum about 'ought' and 'is'. For this would be a case in which some sort of 'ought'-statement can validly be derived from a clearcut 'is'. Furthermore, the example suggests an even more radical thesis about hypothetical imperatives. It suggests (to use Hare's words) that such statements 'say no more than' that a certain means is essential to the attainment of some end. If Hare's suggestion is correct, then hypothetical imperatives are 'ought'-statements of a very degenerate sort indeed. Really, they are just 'is'-statements in disguise. In that case, it is no wonder that they can be derived from purely factual premises.

There are passages in Kant that suggest another source of puzzlement concerning hypothetical imperatives. Kant maintains that all hypothetical imperatives declare certain actions necessary for the attainment of things that someone wills, or might will. If the thing willed is a thing that one may fail to will, then the hypothetical imperative is "problematic". It is an imperative of skill. It tells someone how to go about securing some merely possible end. Examples (1), (2), (3), (4), (6), and (9) are pretty clearly of this sort. Not everyone wants to divide a line, or kill someone. On the other hand, if the thing willed is something that everyone must will, then Kant says the hypothetical imperative is "assertoric". It is an imperative of prudence. Since, according to Kant, everyone necessarily wills his own happiness, it would appear that examples (5) and (7) are examples of this second sort of hypothetical imperative.[13]

None of these examples, as Kant sees it, has anything to do with morality. The imperative of morality does not command hypothetically. It commands categorically. Thus, 'I ought not to lie whether or not lying would get me into trouble' seems to be categorical and moral, while things like (1)—(9) seem to be hypothetical and non-moral.[14] These Kantian claims give rise to a number of questions about the relationship between the hypothetical/categorical distinction and the non-moral/moral distinction. Among these questions are: is every hypothetical imperative non-moral? Is every moral imperative categorical? More generally, is there any interesting connection between the two distinctions? Although many philosophers (including, perhaps, Kant himself) have debated these questions with considerable fervor, it seems to me that none of them sufficiently clarified the issue. Before we can answer any such questions, we need to have a clear account of what's meant by 'hypothetical', 'categorical', 'imperative', and 'moral'.

In addition to particular hypothetical imperatives such as (1)—(9), there is another, far grander general principle that must be discussed here, too. This is the principle nowadays often called 'The Hypothetical Imperative'. Traditionally, this has been taken to be the doctrine that "he who wills the end, wills the means". In this aphoristic form, the doctrine is rather vague, but none too plausible. Kant provides several more interesting formulations: 'who wills the end, wills also (necessarily, if he accords with reason) the sole means which are in his power.'[15] 'If I fully will the effect, I also will the action required for it.'[16] These formulations suggest a number of restrictions on the principle. Apparently, it applies only to rational persons; it applies only in cases in which they "fully will" the end; and it applies only in cases in which some means is both necessary to that end, and within the person's power.

Kant introduces The Hypothetical Imperative in an attempt to explain how the various narrower hypothetical imperatives are "possible". He seems to claim that The Hypothetical Imperative is analytic, and that this fact explains why someone having a certain end (and, presumably, satisfying the other conditions) must take the means to that end. I find this question and its alleged answer somewhat difficult to understand, and so I shall have nothing further to say about them. Nevertheless, I intend to discuss a variety of questions concerning The Hypothetical Imperative. The first is the question about the proper formulation of the Kantian principle. Exactly what is The Hypothetical Imperative? Is it analytic? If not, is it true at all? If not, is there something relevently like it that is true? What is the connection between The Hypothetical Imperative and the various particular hypothetical imperatives we have already mentioned?

5.3. AN ACCOUNT OF HYPOTHETICAL IMPERATIVES

It is important that we recognize at the outset that hypothetical imperatives are not to be identified with any sort of statement of conditioned absolute obligation. I think this point can be established even if we disregard the interpretation of the 'ought' in the hypothetical imperative.

Let us consider, as a start, the suggestion that hypothetical imperatives are statements of materially conditioned absolute obligation. In this case, a statement such as:

(2)   If you want to cure him, then you ought to use aspirin.

would be equivalent to a statement such as:

(2′)   You want to cure him → you ought to use aspirin.

However, it is easy to see that (2) and (2′) are not equivalent. (2′) is entailed by 'you don't want to cure him' as well as by 'you ought to use aspirin'. (2), when understood as a hypothetical imperative, is entailed by neither of these. Hence, (2) and (2′) are not equivalent.

Nor is (2) equivalent to:

(2″)   You want to cure him ⇒ you ought to use aspirin.

For, given natural assumptions, (2″) would not be true even if (2) were. Surely, there are some possible worlds in which you do want to cure him, but in which you have no obligation to use aspirin. For example, consider any world in which his problem isn't headache, but is stomachache. Aspirin would only make that worse.

The question whether hypothetical imperatives might be equivalent to statements of subjunctively conditioned absolute obligation is a bit more difficult to answer. One especially serious difficulty here is that any ordinary sentence of English that can be used to express a hypothetical imperative can also be used to express a variety of other things. In my view, one of these "other" things is subjunctively conditioned absolute obligation. My reason for holding that these are distinct is that, as I see it, factual detachment fails for the hypothetical imperative, but not for any version of subjunctively conditioned absolute obligation. A good example was provided by Prichard.

(3)   If you want to kill him, you ought to use arsenic.

(3) may be imagined to be a true hypothetical imperative. Nevertheless, even if you were to have the horrible want mentioned in the antecedent, you would not have any absolute obligation (moral or otherwise) to use arsenic. In fact, it would still be wrong (in all relevant senses) to use arsenic. Thus, as I see it, (3) does not mean the same as:

(3′)   You want to kill him $\leadsto$ you ought to use arsenic.

I recognize that I have not shown my view to be true. I will attempt to explain its rationale a bit later. For the present. I ask readers with contrary intuitions to suspend disbelief temporarily.

Some philosophers, following Kant, have suggested that, in a true hypothetical imperative, the consequent points out "indispensably necessary" means to be satisfaction of the want mentioned in the antecedent.[7] If we take this as a doctrine about the sort of sentence illustrated here, it is clearly wrong. In many cases, there are several ways to satisfy the want mentioned in the antecedent. Any one of them would suffice, and so none of them is "indispensably necessary". The one specified in the consequent of the true hypothetical imperative is perhaps somehow preferable — but for all that it is not indispensable. Consider example (2) again. Even if (2) is true, there still may be other ways in which you could cure him. Another drug, such as Tylenol, might be almost as good as aspirin. (2) seems to be saying that giving aspirin is somehow involved in the best of the available ways. At any rate, (2) does not seem to be saying that giving aspirin is "indispensably necessary".

Philosophers have also suggested that in a true hypothetical imperative, the consequent specifies a "way of producing" the desired end.[18] "Production" evidently implies some sort of causal connection between what's prescribed and what's desired. For example, we might say that giving aspirin (is part of what) will cause him to be cured. The general thesis, then, is that a hypothetical imperative of the form 'if you want A, then you ought to do B' is true if and only if doing B will cause you to get A.

This general thesis will not stand scrutiny. Some statements that clearly belong in the same category with the typical hypothetical imperatives do not match cause to desired effect. For example, suppose the woods are full of mosquitoes. Camping without insect repellent would be unbearable. I might then say, 'if you want to go camping, you ought to get some insect repellent'. Surely, I'm not silly enough to suppose that buying insect repellent will cause you to go camping. Yet the statement itself seems relevantly like the standard hypothetical imperatives.

One of the examples suggested by Hare also refutes the causal thesis. Meeting Grimbly Hughes won't cause you to meet the biggest grocer in Oxford. In some way, meeting him *will be* meeting the biggest grocer in Oxford.

5.3.1. *Absolute Prudential Obligation*

In my view, hypothetical imperatives are a special case of "conditional prudential obligation". In order to explain this, I must first explain prudential obligation in its simpler, absolute form.

Suppose that at some moment, some grocer is considering whether to adopt the policy of giving correct change.[19] His main alternative here, we may suppose, is to adopt the policy of cheating where possible, but mounting a substantial advertising campaign. From the perspective of the grocer, this choice may be seen as a choice among the various possible worlds then accessible to him. He might try to imagine the relevant parts of the more interesting of these worlds in an effort to decide what to do. If the grocer is being rational and self-interested here, he will contemplate these accessible worlds primarily in order to determine how well he would fare if he were to realize one of them rather than another. So when he tries to imagine a world in which he adopts the policy of honesty, he focusses primarily on himself in that world. He tries to see how things turn out for himself there.

Let us assume that for every person and possible world there is a number that represents how well that person fares at that world. If the person is called 's' and the world is called 'w', then we can express this value as 'V(s, w)'. Hedonists may say that V(s, w) is a measure of how much pleasure and pain s feels in w. Others will say that V(s, w) should take into account nothing but the extent to which s's preferences are satisfied in w.[20] Pluralists will maintain that V(s, w) is a more complex measure, and that it takes into account not just pleasure or preference-satisfaction, but a variety of goods and evils that befall s in w. For my present purposes, however, it is not necessary to take sides on this issue. The essential point is that V(s, w) is a measure of the value of w *for s*. It tells us how well things go for s in w.

When we evaluate worlds in this way, our evaluation is "person-relative". However, it is a strictly objective measurement. We are not interested, here, in the value that s thinks that w has, or the value s would attribute to w if asked. Rather, we are interested in how well s actually fares in w. So s may think that w is of low value, and he may even think that he fares rather poorly there, even though V(s, w) is in fact quite high.

I understand absolute prudential obligation in such a way that it closely mirrors the concept of absolute moral obligation discussed in Part One. So I want to say that something, p, is absolutely prudentially obligatory for a person, s, at a time, t, if and only if there is a p-world accessible to s at t such that there is no ~p-world in which he fares as well then accessible to him. More strictly, this notion may be intro-duced as follows:

PO: PO s, t, p is true at w iff (E w') (A s, t, w', w & p is true at w'
        & ~(E w'') (A s, t, w'', w & ~p is true at w'' & V(s, w'') ⩾
        V(s, w')))

In order to see how this concept operates, let us briefly reconsider the Kantian grocer example. Suppose there is a fairly attractive world accessible to the grocer in which he adopts the policy of honesty. In that world his customers respect and trust him, and his business flourishes. Suppose he becomes wealthy and happy in that world. There may be no other accessible world in wich he fares as well. In this case, PO yields the result that, from the point of view of rational self-interest, or prudence, he ought to treat his customers honestly.

Unless we assume that the intrinsic value ranking of each world is the same as its value-for-s ranking, this concept of prudential obligation is not equivalent to the concept of absolute moral obligation. Some moral obligations may fail to be prudential obligations, and vice versa. So, for example, the grocer may find that there's a world accessible to him in which he gives up business entirely and devotes the rest of his life to charity. Maybe that world is intrinsically better than even the best of the accessible worlds in which he becomes an honest businessman. So, from the moral point of view, he ought to get out of business entirely. This is consistent with the view that, from the prudential point of view, he ought to stay in business and treat his customers honestly.

In ordinary parlance, 'prudence' has certain epistemic overtones. When we say that a certain course of action is most prudent, we suggest that the course of action minimizes *risk*. Given what the agent knows about likely outcomes, that one seems safest. It is important to recognize that my concept of prudential obligation does not have any such epistemic component. A course of action may be prudentially obligatory, in my sense, even if everyone has good reason to think it would be terribly risky. To say that it is prudentially obligatory, then, is not to say that it maximizes expected utility. Rather, what it maximizes is actual benefit to the agent.

In an interesting passage, Kant contrasts our capacity for knowledge of what is morally obligatory with our capacity for knowledge of what is most to our own advantage. He seems to maintain that it is always easy to know what is morally obligatory, but never possible to know what is most in our own interest. Kant says ". . . what is duty is by itself plain to everyone. But what will bring durable advantage extending to one's whole existence is always veiled in impenetrable obscurity."[21] Perhaps it could be said that Kant's position is somewhat overstated. As I see it, it is generally rather difficult to determine our moral obligations. Who among us knows with certainty which worlds are accessible, and how much each is worth? The same seems to me to be true of prudential obligation. We generally don't know, in any detail, which worlds are accessible to us, or precisely how well we fare in each. So, except in certain extreme cases, we know neither what we morally ought to do nor what we prudentially ought to do.

Prudential obligation can thus be seen as a second instance of a concept of obligation that may be explicated by appeal to a concept of possibility and a concept of goodness. Possibility here is accessibility, just as it was in the case of moral obligation. Intrinsic goodness, however, is here replaced by the person-relativized concept of "value-for-s", indicated by 'V(s, w)'. So, instead of asking how good the accessible worlds are in themselves, we ask how good they are *for s*. The resulting concept of obligation is formally very much like the concept of moral obligation introduced in MO, but, since it is tied to a different value concept, it is not equivalent to that concept.

5.3.2. *Iffy Prudential Oughts*

We found, in Chapter 4, that there are several main sorts of conditioned absolute moral obligation. These were MCAMO, StCAMO, and SuCAMO. There are corresponding structures for prudential obligation. In other words, there are sentences of the following forms:

MCAPO: $p \to \text{PO}s, t, q$
SuCAPO: $p \gg \text{PO}s, t, q$
StCAPO: $p \Rightarrow \text{PO}s, t, q$

The logical and semantic features of these things are relevantly like the corresponding features of the moral constructions already discussed.

Furthermore, associated with the notion of absolute prudential obligation introduced in PO, there is a notion of conditional prudential obligation. Following the pattern of CMO, we can introduce this as follows, letting POs, t, q/p abbreivate 'given that p occurs, s prudentially ought, as of t, to see to q':

CPO: POs, t, q/p is true at w iff $(\text{E}w')(\text{A}s, t, w', w \& p$ and q are true at w' & $\sim(\text{E}w'')(\text{A}s, t, w'', w \& p$ and $\sim q$ are true at w'' & $V(s, w') \geqslant V(s, w')))$

Consideration of a simple example may help to clarify the intent of CPO. Suppose that you really shouldn't (prudentially speaking) embark upon a career in crime. Nevertheless, you want to know what you would have to do if you were to choose such a life. In reply to your enquiry, I say:

(12)   If you're going in for crime, then you ought to buy a gun.

As I see it, (12), when so used, is best understood as a statement of conditional prudential obligation, rather than as a statement of MCAPO, SuCAPO, or StCAPO. These other things seem to me to have the wrong logic. The idea behind (12) is rather that of all the possible worlds currently accessible to you in which you go in for crime, there's one in which you take the precaution of buying a gun first. In all the accessible worlds in which you go in for crime, there is none in which you fare as well, but fail to buy a gun. Loosely, then we can say that among the accessible-to-you crime-worlds, you fare best in a gun-world.

The logical features of CPO are just the same as those of CMO. Factual detachment is invalid, but unalterability detachment and deontic detachment (suitably modified) are valid. Augmentation fails. The construction is, in the sense introduced above in Chapter 4, overridable. It is not subject to any of the paradoxes of derived obligation.

5.3.3. *CPO and Hypothetical Imperatives*

We might think that a hypothetical imperative is simply a statement of conditional prudential obligation in which the antecedent happens to be a want-statement. However plausible this suggestion may be, it is wrong. To see why, consider this example:

(13)   If Sam wants to smoke, then he ought to smoke filters.

We may assume that (13) is true, and is to be understood along the lines of the preceding examples of hypothetical imperatives. Letting s and t stand for Sam and a suitable time, we can try to formulate this as a straightforward statement of CPO:

(13a)   PO s, t, Sam smokes filters/Sam wants to smoke.

If we reflect on what (13a) means, we will discover that it is not a suitable translation for (13). (13) is true, but, given some natural assumption about Sam and smoking, (13a) is false. (13a) tells us that there is some world accessible to Sam in which he wants to smoke and smokes filters, and that Sam fares better in that world than he does in any world accessible to him in which he wants to smoke but doesn't smoke filters. The falsity of this claim is to be explained by appeal to the fact that, among accessible worlds in which he desires to smoke, Sam undoubtedly fares best in some in which he simply frustrates his desire to smoke altogether. That is, if we limit our attention to accessible worlds in which Sam wants to smoke, we will find that he doesn't fare best in one in which he smokes filters. Rather, he fares best in one in which he doesn't smoke at all. Perhaps there is an accessible world in which Sam desires cigarettes, but eats candy instead of smoking. Perhaps he fares better in this world than he does in even the best of the accessible worlds in which he smokes. Clearly, we are sometimes better off frustrating certain of our desires rather than giving in to them in even the least self-destructive of the available ways.

So, if we are interested in (13), we should not focus upon accessible worlds in which Sam desires cigarettes. Rather, we should think about accessible worlds in which he actually smokes. In the best-for-him of these, it is reasonable to suppose, he smokes filter cigarettes.

These reflections suggest a general translation procedure for hypothetical imperatives. We start with an iffy ought of English, assuming it to be relevantly like the typical hypothetical imperatives. For example, let's reconsider an example already discussed:

(2)   If you want to cure him, then you ought to use aspirin.

The first step is to get rid of the business about wanting. As we saw in the smoking example, that introduces an irrelevancy. So we have:

(2a)   If you are going to cure him, then you ought to use aspirin.

Now we can treat (2a) as a straightforward case of conditional prudential obligation. Letting y and t name you and a suitable time, we have:

(2b)   POy, t, you use aspirin/you cure him.

This means that, as we contemplate better- and better-for-you accessible worlds in which you cure him, we eventually find one in which you use aspirin. That one is such that there is no better-for-you accessible cure-world in which you effect this cure without aspirin. Simply put, things go best for you if you cure him with aspirin.

Another procedure here world involve the use of a special notation to represent hypothetical imperatives. Instead of moving from a sentence like (2) to one like (2a) and then to one like (2b), we could go directly from the ordinary language hypothetical imperative to a sentence using this new notation. This procedure, while not really necessary, may make it easier for us to concentrate on some oddities of hypothetical imperatives. In any case, I propose to use HIs, t, q/p to represent the hypothetical imperative, 'given that s wants p, s ought, as of t, to see to q'. This may be introduced, somewhat provisionally, as follows:

HI: HIs, t, q/p is true at w iff $(\mathrm{E}w')\,(\mathrm{A}s,\ t,\ w',\ w\ \&\ p$ and q are true at $w'\ \&\ \sim(\mathrm{E}w'')\,(\mathrm{A}s,\ t,\ w'',\ w\ \&\ p$ and $\sim q$ are true at $w''\ \&\ \mathrm{V}(s,\ w'')\geqslant\mathrm{V}(s,\ w')))$

One possible objection to the truth conditions proposed in HI is that where q is unalterable for s at t, and p is still open to him, HIs, t, q/p must be true. So if you are going to pay taxes no matter what, and can still become physically fit, then this is true:

(14)   HIy, t, you pay taxes/you become physically fit.

In English, this comes out as:

(14a)   If you want to become physically fit, you ought to pay taxes.

This misleadingly suggests some sort of connection between the payment of taxes and an improvement in your physical condition. Of course, there is none. It's just that in the best-for-you accessible world in which you become fit, you do pay your taxes. To deal with this problem, we could require that if a hypothetical imperative is true, then the obligation cannot be unalterable. More precisely, we could make use of the concept defined in HI*.

HI*:   HI*s, t, q/p is true at w iff HIs, t, q/p and Ks, t, $\sim q$ are both true at w.

It seems to me that the concept introduced in HI* bears a somewhat closer resemblance to what we ordinarily mean when we utter a hypothetical imperative than does the concept introduced in HI. Thus, in what follows, when I speak of the truth conditions for hypothetical imperatives, I have in mind the truth conditions formulated in HI* rather than the ones formulated in HI.

5.4. SOLUTIONS TO THE PUZZLES

Now that we have a proposed account of the truth conditions for hypothetical imperatives, we can return to the puzzles introduced earlier in Section 2. The first of these, suggested by Prichard's example about the double dose of poison, had to do with the validity of factual detachment for the hypothetical imperative. It should be clear that the question is really quite ambiguous. There are several different things that might be meant by 'factual detachment' here. I can think of eight reasonably plausible candidates, and I suspect that further reflection would generate still more. We can formulate these as follows:

FDHI*1: $(\text{HI}^*s, t, q/p \& p) \rightarrow \text{MO}s, t, q$
FDHI*2: $(\text{HI}^*s, t, q/p \& p) \rightarrow \text{PO}s, t, q$
FDHI*3: $(\text{HI}^*s, t, q/p \& s \text{ wants } p) \rightarrow \text{MO}s, t, q$
FDHI*4: $(\text{HI}^*s, t, q/p \& s \text{ wants } p) \rightarrow \text{PO}s, t, q$
FDHI*5: $(\text{HI}^*s, t, q/p \& \text{U}s, t, p) \rightarrow \text{MO}s, t, q$
FDHI*6: $(\text{HI}^*s, t, q/p \& \text{U}s, t, p) \rightarrow \text{PO}s, t, q$
FDHI*7: $(\text{HI}^*s, t, q/p \& \text{U}s, t, (s \text{ wants } p)) \rightarrow \text{MO}s, t, q$
FDHI*8: $(\text{HI}^*s, t, q/p \& \text{U}s, t, (s \text{ wants } p)) \rightarrow \text{PO}s, t, q$

Reflection on the proposed truth conditions for hypothetical imperatives will reveal, I believe, that only FDHI*6 is a fully satisfactory version of the factual detachment rule. The problems with the others are fairly obvious. The odd-numbered rules purport to derive an absolute *moral* obligation from a hypothetical imperative and its factual "antecedent". Since hypothetical imperatives are a special case of *prudential* obligation, it should be clear that no such principle can be valid. The relevant rankings of the worlds have no direct bearing on one another.

FDHI*2 is relevantly like the simplest form of factual detachment for conditional moral obligation,[22] and is invalid for the same reason. The antecedent of FDHI*2 merely tells us (i) that in the best-for-s accessible p-world, q is true, and that (ii) p is true in the real world.[23] Clearly enough, this does not give us reason to conclude that in the best-for-s accessible world, q is true.

FDHI*4 fails for a different reason. It focusses too narrowly on the fact that s wants p. Given my account of the meaning of the hypo-thetical imperative, the word 'want' is really quite irrelevant to the meaning of the hypothetical imperative. As I see it, we can simply delete the business about wanting from the sentence without any change of meaning. The case involving the desire for cigarettes was intended to help clarify this point. Hence, the fact that s wants p is irrelevant to the derivation of an absolute prudential obligation for q. Needless to say, the unalterability of the want is also irrelevant, and so FDHI*8 is also invalid.

Of the principles listed, only FDHI*6 is a satisfactory version of the factual detachment rule. We can see that it is valid if we reflect upon what it means. Suppose every accessible world is a p-world. (That's what Us, t, p means.) Suppose there is some accessible p & q-world such that there is no as-good-for-s accessible p & $\sim q$-world. (That, roughly, is what HI*$s, t, q/p$ means.) Then there's some accessible q-world than which there is no better-for-s accessible $\sim q$-world. (And that's what PO$s, t, q$ means.)

It should be pretty clear that this factual detachment rule for hypothetical imperatives is very closely related to the unalterability detachment rule for conditional moral obligation, discussed above in Chapter 4, Section 5. The crucial differences are, first, that we have replaced the intrinsic value ranking relevant to MO with the value-for-s ranking relevant to PO, and, second, that we have introduced the added clause indicating that the negation of the conditional obligation is still open.

These various possible factual detachment rules are easily confused, and so it's no wonder that moral philosophers have sometimes expressed puzzlement over the "detachability" of the ought-statement in hypothetical imperatives. Let's reconsider the example from Prichard:

(9)   If you want to kill him, you ought to use a double dose.
(10)   You do want to kill him.
(11)   Therefore, you (absolutely) ought to use a double dose.

It is easy enough to imagine a case in which (9) and (10) are true, but in which (11) seems to be false. Imagine, for example, that he weighs over 300 pounds, and thus would easily survive the administration of a single dose of the poison. A double dose, however, would be quite effective. Imagine also that he has done you some wrong, and so you do want to kill him. Then (9) and (10) would be true. However, if we also suppose that killing him would be both morally wrong and seriously contrary to your own self-interest (you'd end up in jail for the rest of your life), then we can see that no matter how we take the 'ought' in (11), it is false.

If we assume that (9) is meant as a hypothetical imperative, and we make use of the proposed analysis of such statements, we can see why the inference fails. (9), on this account, means (roughly) that among the worlds accessible to you in which you kill him, the best-for-you is one in which you give him a double dose. (10) is taken to mean that here in the real world you do want to kill him. Obviously, we cannot conclude (as (11) does) that in the best (or best-for-you) accessible worlds you use a double dose. It is far more likely that in the best (and best-for-you) accessible worlds, you don't kill him at all, and don't give poison to anyone. Thus, the inference from (9) and (10) to (11) is invalid whether (11) is interpreted as a statement of moral or as a statement of prudential obligation.

Of course, if you are unalterably going to kill him, so that every accessible world is one in which this deed is performed, then, given (9), we can conclude that you'd better give him the double dose. If you're unalterably going to do such a miserable thing, then you prudentially ought to do it in the way that's best for you. If we revise the example so as to make it fit the pattern of FDHI*6, then we can derive the statement of absolute prudential obligation.

Some who have reflected upon hypothetical imperatives have given a somewhat different suggestion concerning factual detachment. P. S. Greenspan suggests[24] that factual detachment fails for hypothetical imperatives because it is always possible to give up the end mentioned in the "antecedent". 'Whenever the agent can still produce action in accordance with his end, ..., he can and may give up his end instead.'[25] So the suggestion seems to be that while simple factual detachment fails, a sort of unalterability detachment is valid. More specifically, the proposal seems to be that this is a valid principle:

FDHI*7: $(HI^*s, t, q/p \& Us, t, (s \text{ wants } p)) \rightarrow POs, t, q$

This says that if the hypothetical imperative is true, and you unalterably went the antecedent, then you prudentially ought to see to the consequent. (Greenspan apparently would deny that FDHI*7 has any application, since, in her view, "it is always possible to give up the end". I take this to mean that there are no unalterable wants.)

If we accept my proposed account of the meaning of hypothetical imperatives, we must conclude that the fixity of the ends has no bearing on the derivability of absolute prudential obligations. The inference still fails. A simple case should suffice to show why FDHI*7 is invalid. Suppose you want to smoke, and simply cannot give up your craving for cigarettes. In this case, smoking is an unalterable end for you. You want to smoke, and there is no accessible world in which you don't want to smoke. Suppose that in the best-for-you accessible world in which you smoke, you smoke filter cigarettes. Surely, it does not follow that it would be best for you to smoke filters. Rather (given the natural assumptions about the dangers of smoking) it would be best for you to refrain from smoking altogether — even though this would mean that you would have to go through life with an unsatisfied craving for cigarettes. As I see it, there are worse things than having an unsatisfied desire. It is plausible to suppose that lung cancer is one of them.

So far as I can tell, my treatment of hypothetical imperatives yields acceptable results with respect to factual detachment. A hypothetical imperative tells me that best-for-me way to go about doing a certain thing. If I am going to do that thing no matter what, then I absolutely (prudentially) ought to do it in the specified way. On the other hand, if I still can avoid doing that thing (perhaps in favor of something more in my self-interest) then it may fail to to be in my interest to do it in the specified way. This may be so, clearly enough, even if I want to do it, will do it, and unalterably want to do it.

Furthermore, my treatment of hypothetical imperatives gives us a clear account of the reason why no statement of absolute *moral* obligation may be derived from a hypothetical imperative by anything like factual detachment. The hypothetical imperative is a special case of conditional *prudential* obligation. The relevant ranking of the accessible possible worlds is strictly in terms of the value-for-s. Thus, no statement of moral obligation, dependent upon the intrinsic value ranking, may be derived.

5.4.1. *Other Formal Features of HI**

Among the other formal features of HI*, we should note that deontic detachment, in one version, is valid. More specifically, we have the following principle:

   DDHI*: $(HI^*s, t, q/p \& POs, t, p) \rightarrow POs, t, q$

No other form of deontic detachment is valid for the hypothetical imperative.

Augmentation is straightforwardly invalid for this sort of sentence. We have to reject:

   AugHI: $HI^*s, t, q/p \rightarrow HI^*s, t, q/p \& r$

For example, suppose that if you want a good business reputation, you ought to give correct change. It may not be the case that if you want a good business reputation, but also want to cheat your customers, that you still ought to give correct change. The best-for-you accessible world in which you get a good reputation may be one in which you give correct change, even though the best-for-you accessible world in which you both get a good reputation and cheat your customers is not one in which you give correct change.

We can understand overridability for hypothetical imperatives to mean that sentences of the following form are possible:

OverHI*: $p \& r \& HI^*s, t, q/p \& HI^*s, t, \sim q/p \& r$

Reflection will reveal, I believe, that it is possible for such sentences to be true, and so hypothetical imperatives are overridable, in my sense. This fact is closely related to the fact that factual detachment, in the relevant sense, is not valid for these sentences.

My proposal concerning hypothetical imperatives generates clear answers to the questions set by Hare. We have already seen that, on my view, the 'want' in a hypothetical imperative is purely idiomatic. It can always be deleted without change of meaning. (Of course, I am disregarding such 'wants' as the second one in 'if you want to stop wanting to smoke, you ought to see a hypnotist'.) It seems to me that Hare was right when he said that the 'want' in an ordinary hypothetical imperative does not mean the same as "be affected by a recognizable state of the feelings known as desire".[26]

The other question suggested by Hare is the question whether a hypothetical imperative such as:

(15)   If you want to see the largest grocer in Oxford, then you ought to see Grimbley Hughes

"says no more than"

(16)   Grimbley Hughes is the largest grocer in Oxford.

If (15) and (16) are synonymous, or if (15) can be derived from (16), then we seem to have a breach of the doctrine that "you can't validly derive an ought from an is". Admittedly, the ought here would only be a hypothetical imperative. It is not a moral ought. Nevertheless, this would be of some interest.

It is clear that (15) and (16) are not synonymous. We can easily imagine cases in which (15) would be a true hypothetical imperative, but (16) would be false. For example, suppose that Grimbley Hughes is not a grocer, but is an extremely knowledgeable and helpful tourist guide in Oxford. Suppose no other person is as well qualified as he to take you to the largest grocer in Oxford. Then, understood as a hypothetical imperative, (15) might be true. (16), obviously, would be false.

Even though (15) and (16) are not synonymous, they are closely related. (16), together with certain other obviously factual premises, entails (15) — that is, the premises entail (15) if (15) is understood to be a hypothetical imperative. So this sort of ought can be derived from a collection of "is-es". We can see this if we reflect on the analysis I have proposed. Suppose (16) is true, the suppose you can't alter its truth. Then every world accessible to you is one in which Grimbley Hughes is the largest grocer in Oxford. Suppose also that there is at least one world accessible to you in which you see the largest grocer in Oxford. Then it must be that the best-for-you accessible world in which you see the largest grocer in Oxford is one in which you see Grimbley Hughes. Given my analysis, this means that:

(15a)   HIy, t, you see Grimbley Hughes/you see the largest grocer in Oxford.

is true.

This suggests a general principle connecting hypothetical imperatives to statements about unalterability. If every accessible p-world is a q-world, then the best accessible p-world is a q-world. So we may propose:

(17)   (U$s, t, p \rightarrow q$ & Ks, t, p & q) $\rightarrow$ HI$s, t, q/p$

and

(18)   (U$s, t, p \rightarrow q$ & Ks, t, p & q & K$s, t, \sim q$) $\rightarrow$ HI*$s, t, q/p$

I can't say whether these principles run counter to Hume's dictum or not. In any case, the fact that they are valid shows that certain sort of ought statement can be derived from some purely factual statements.[27]

5.4.2. *Kant's Thesis*

The third area of puzzlement had to do with the thesis, suggested by Kant, that there's an interesting connection between the categorical/hypothetical distinction and the moral/nonmoral distinction. The thesis itself is open to a variety of possible interpretations, and so I can't be sure that what I have to say on this score will have any bearing on anything Kant meant to affirm.[28] However, I can formulate a reasonably clear interpretation of the thesis that "the moral ought is the categorical ought". On this interpretation, the thesis is taken as a syntactic criterion for statements of moral obligation. So understood, the thesis is pretty obviously false. In any case, let us consider the view.

Let us say that a sentence is "syntactically categorical" if and only if it is of the form MOs, t, p or of the form POs, t, p. Thus, statements of absolute obligation (whether prudential or moral) are taken to be the "categorical oughts". Next we can say that a sentence is "syntactically hypothetical" if and only if it is of one of these forms: MOs, t, q/p; POs, t, q/p; HI*s, t, q/p. Statements of conditioned absolute obligation are neither categorical nor hypothetical, but contain parts that are categorical. Finally, we can extend this terminology to ordinary language ought-statements by saying that an ought-sentence of ordinary language is of the same form(s) as its most appropriate translation into the terminology I have introduced. This means that, in the case of typical ordinary language sentences, there will be several forms, depending upon the various ways in which the sentence can be used. Its form on a given occasion will be determined by the form of its most fitting translation.

A version of the Kantian thesis can now be stated fairly succinctly:

KT: A statement is a moral ought statement if and only if it is a syntactically categorical ought statement.

It should be pretty obvious that, under the proposed interpretation, this view is false. We have seen that there are moral oughts that are hypothetical ('If you give A on the first day, then you morally ought to give A on the second day.') and we have seen that there are non-moral oughts that are categorical ('You prudentially ought to give correct change.').

We can develop a slightly more interesting version of the Kantian thesis by revising the concept of hypotheticalness. Let us say that an ordinary language ought-statement is "end-hypothetical" if and only if it has the following features: (i) it is hypothetical in form; (ii) its antecedent is about some want, wish, desire, or end of some agent; and (iii) its consequent is a statement to the effect that that agent ought to perform a certain act. Now we can state a revised version of the Kantian thesis:

KT′:   Every end-hypothetical ought-statement is non-moral.

This thesis is also false. We have seen that standard hypothetical imperatives are non-moral. It seems to me that they are also "end-hypothetical". Hence, they do not refute KT′. However, it seems to me that any ordinary sentence that can be used to express a hypothetical imperative can also be used to express conditioned absolute moral obligation, or conditional moral obligation. In some cases, no doubt, the moral interpretation will be extremely implausible. For example, consider 'if you want to kill him, you ought to use a double dose'. However, in other cases the moral interpretation is relatively natural. For example, suppose you overhear someone saying:

(19)   If you want to become educated, then you ought to go to college.

I would maintain that, unless you were given some information about the context of utterance, you wouldn't be able to tell whether (19) was being used as a hypothetical imperative or as a statement of conditional moral obligation. Using the natural abbreviations, we have (at least) two plausible readings. First, the hypothetical imperative:

(19a)   HI*y, t, c/e

and, next, the statement of conditional moral obligation:

(19b)   MOy, t, c/y wants e.

Since (19) can be used to express what's more perspicuously expressed by (19b), we have to say that the second version of the Kantian thesis is also false. Some end-hypothetical ought-statements of ordinary language are moral oughts.

My own view is that there is simply no syntactic criterion of morality. Statements of moral obligation come in all forms. Some are categorical, some are ordinary conditionals, and some are of the intermediate form I have called conditional moral obligation. Similarly, non-moral ought-statement come in all forms. So you just can't tell a moral ought by its shape. You have to figure out what it means.

5.4.3. *The Hypothetical Imperative*

The final set of questions introduced earlier had to do with the connection (if any) between these particular hypothetical imperatives and the more general principle known as "The Hypothetical Imperative" (or "THI"). This latter is sometimes formulated as the doctrine that "he who wills the end, wills the means". Is this true? Is it analytic? How does it relate to particular hypothetical imperatives such as 'if you want to cure him, you ought to use aspirin'?

In order to answer these questions, we must have a clearer statement of THI. Once again, Kant is the leading authority. In one place, he formulates the principle in this way: 'Who wills the end, wills also (necessarily, if he accords with reason) the sole means which are in his power.'[29] It is hard to discern any interesting connection between this version of the principle and the particular hypothetical imperatives we have already considered. For one thing, this principle is restricted to cases involving people who "accord with reason". Whatever this may mean, it is clear that ordinary hypothetical imperatives are not subject to any such restriction. Secondly, this version of THI is also restricted to cases in which there is a "sole means". As we have seen in many examples above, ordinary hypothetical imperatives may be true even in cases in which there are many different ways of achieving the relevant end. Finally, this version of THI contains no 'ought' or any equivalent term. It is not a normative doctrine at all. It is merely a factual claim, although a very general one. It belongs to psychology, not to ethics, and not to the theory of prudence. It purports to describe the volitional behavior of certain people in certain circumstances. In light of all this, I think we must conclude that it is doubtful that there is any interesting connection between this version of THI and particular hypothetical imperatives.

There is a tradition according to which THI may be understood to have application to imperfectly rational beings. For them, it issues a command, or states an obligation. Roughly, it tells them that they ought to act in the way rational beings invariably do act. More specifically, it tells them that they ought to adjust their means to their ends. This suggestion may point the way to a version of THI that will have some relevance to ordinary hypothetical imperatives.

In his paper, 'The Hypothetical Imperative,' Thomas Hill formulates and defends a version of THI that contains an 'ought' and is directed toward ordinary, imperfectly rational people.[30] A preliminary version of the principle is put this way:

> THI-1: If one has decided to pursue a certain end, and remains constant in this commitment to it, then one ought to will the necessary means within his power.[31]

Hill is not satisfied with THI-1. One problem he finds with it derives from the fact that people sometimes decide to pursue bad ends. In those cases, they should not will the means within their power. Hill apparently feels that these cases raise a problem for this version of The Hypothetical Imperative. However, he also maintains that a fuller version is immune to this difficulty. Hill points out that, in addition to taking the necessary means, 'there is another alternative. He can abandon the end. Insofar as this remains a possibility, what the Hypothetical Imperative prescribes, in effect, is "take the necessary means or else give up the end" '.[32]

It appears, then, that the general principle in question may be stated as follows:

> THI-2: If a person, *s*, wills an end, *p*, and some means, *q*, is necessary to *p* and within *s*'s power, then *s* ought either to will *q* or else give up *p*.

As Hill understands it, the 'ought' in THI-2 is non-moral. It has to do with what he calls 'rational self-interest'. Presumably, what a person ought (in this sense) to do is what is, of all his alternatives, most in his own rational self-interest. In other words, the obligatory (in this sense) is what's best for the agent. I think it will be appropriate to assume that the relevant concept to obligation is adequately captured by our concept of prudential obligation. Furthermore, in light of the use to which Hill puts THI, it is clear that it must be understood as involving some sort of conditioned absolute obligation. This must be so, since Hill wants it to figure in "practical arguments" whose conclusions are absolute prescriptions. In other words, some sort of factual detachment must be valid for the iffy ought in THI. As we have seen, factual detachment is valid only for contitioned absolute obligation.

In light of these considerations, it seems to me that the fairest rendering of Hill's version of THI into the notation I have proposed would have to begin with something relevantly like this:

THI-3: $(s)(t)(p)(q)(s$ wills p as an end & q is a necessary means to p & q is in s's power at $t \rightarrow$ POs, t, [s wills q or else s gives up p])

THI-3 is not restricted to cases involving perfectly rational agents. It purports to apply to everyone. It purports to tell us our prudential obligation under certain circumstances. Specifically, the relevant circumstances occur when we have some end, and some necessary means to that end is in our power. THI-3 then tells us that we have a sort of disjunctive prudential obligation. The obligation in question is the obligation to either will the means or else give up the end. It should be noted that although this obligation is disjunctive, nevertheless it is absolute.

In virtue of the fact that THI-3 is conditional in form, it has the power to help us derive absolute prudential ought statements from suitable factual premises. The premises need not be unalterable or obligatory. They need only be true. Thus, to use one of Hill's examples,[33] we can argue from the premises that (i) Jack Glatzer wants to become a concert violinist, and (ii) practicing is in his power and a necessary means to that end, and (iii) THI-3, to the conclusion that (iv) Jack Glatzer prudentially ought either to practice or give up his musical aspiration.

Hill strongly suggests that he takes something like THI-3 to be true. He says it is a 'principle which any fully rational person would adopt and which men ought always to follow.'[34] I take this to be a statement of endorsement, although I have to admit a certain uneasiness about the claim that we "ought" to follow THI-3. Surely, Hill does not mean that we morally ought to do the things enjoined by THI-3 (together with the relevant factual premises). Presumably, Hill's point is that we really do have the prudential obligations that THI-3 says we have. In other words, the principle is true.

I have my doubts about the truth of THI-3. My doubts are based on the fact that, whatever its exact nature may be, *willing* is evidently an activity of some sort, and so it may have some value in its own right, unrelated to the value of the object willed. Thus, it might be good for someone to will something as an end, even though it wouldn't be good for him to will the necessary means to that end. In this sort of case, it might turn out that he prudentially ought to will the end, though he prudentially ought not to will the means.

An outlandish example will suffice to establish the possibility of this sort of case. Suppose a malicious mind reader threatens to impose terrible hardships upon you unless you will some end while refraining from willing the necessary means to it which are in your power. Assuming that your volitions are in your power, and assuming that he really would carry out his insane threat, it appears that you prudentially ought to do as he demands. That is, you prudentially ought to will some end, but refrain from willing the necessary means which lie in your power. In this case, purely extrinsic considerations about the value-for-you of various volitional patterns impose an odd prudential require-ment upon you. In virtue of the mind reader's threats, you prudentially ought to will a certain end while refraining from willing the means to that end. However outlandish the example, it seems to me to be possible, and so it seems to me to establish that it might be in some-one's rational self-interest to will an end without willing the means. Thus, the example refutes THI-3.

Once we recognize the possibility of this sort of case, we can see that relevantly similar things happen quite frequently in the ordinary affairs of life. A more prosaic example should drive this home. Suppose a man, Brown, wishes he could become a full-time bird-watcher. Suppose further that he could become a full-time bird-watcher — this is a possible end for him. However, he could achieve this end only at considerable expense. He would have to quit his job, leave his friends and family, and endure other similar hardships. Thus, it might be seriously contrary to Brown's self-interest for him to take steps toward the fulfilment of his life's ambition.

Nevertheless, it might also be very good for Brown to continue to will that he become a bird-watcher. Perhaps willing in this way gives "meaning" and "purpose" to an otherwise empty and pointless life. It is possible that the having of this end, though it goes unfulfilled, gives Brown the strength he needs to carry on.

In this case, as I see it, there is a person who has an end (full-time bird-watching), and there is a means (quitting his job) which is in his power, and necessary to that end, but it simply is not the case that he has a prudential obligation to either give up his end or take the means. It is good for him to have the end, but bad for him to will to take the means to it. So I think that non-outlandish examples refute THI-3, too.

These reflections show, I think, that there is no necessary connection between rational self-interest and rational consistency in willing. We cannot assume that it is always in a person's self-interest to adjust his volitions into a maximally consistent and rational pattern. As I understand it, that's just what THI-3 insists. It tells us that we have a prudential obligation always to see to it that we either set out to achieve our ends, or else give them up. If 'prudential obligation' is understood in terms of maximizing self-interest, then this is false. Volitional rationality may be useful in most instances, but there's no guarantee that it will always be so.

The final question concerning THI had to do with the relation between it and particular hypothetical imperatives. Since THI, no matter how formulated, seems to be false, it surely can't serve to explain why people ought to adjust their volitions in some specified way. Nor can it serve to explain why purely rational beings would so adjust their volitions. As I see it, purely rational beings might not abide by THI. I have attempted to describe a case in which it would be quite rational for a person to maintain a certain end while steadfastly refusing to adopt the necessary means to it. That was the case of the man who wished to become a birdwatcher.

In my view, there is no interesting logical connection between THI and particular hypothetical imperatives. THI is not, in any standard sense of the term, a "generalization" from particular hypothetical imperatives. Nor are the particular hypothetical imperatives "instances" of THI.

I can describe one line of though that might seem to connect hypothetical imperatives to THI. As we have seen, there is a connection between hypothetical imperatives and statements about essential means. For example, suppose Sam won't be able to smoke unless he first buys a pack of cigarettes. Suppose he can buy them, and that, if he does, he will be able to smoke them. In this case, the hypothetical imperative:

(13)   If Sam wants to smoke, then he ought to buy a pack of cigarettes.

seems to be true.

In general, we can say that if q is a necessary means to p, and p is in our agent's power, then a hypothetical imperative connecting p and q will have to be true. In other words, the following general principle is valid:

(17) $(Us, t, p \rightarrow q \, \& \, Ks, t, p \, \& \, q) \rightarrow HIs, t, q/p$

If we take certain liberties with (17), may be inclined to paraphrase it in ordinary English in some such terminology as this:

(17a)   If you can't achieve p without seeing to q, then, if you want p, you ought to see to q.

But (17a) is subject to misinterpretation. Someone might take it to be of the form:

(17b)   You can't achieve p without seeing to q → (you want p → you ought to see to q)

Then, noting a familiar equivalence, we can rephrase (17b) as:

(17c)   (You can't achieve p without seeing to q & you want p) → you ought to see to q.

(17c) looks like some form of THI. Thus, it might seem that some trivial transformations will get us from (17) — a truth about hypothetical imperatives — to (17c) — a version of The Hypotheticsl Imperative.

Obviously, however, the inference is fallacious. The move from (17a) to (17b) is unjustified. In (17b), a hypothetical imperative is treated as if it were some sort of materially conditioned absolute obligation, rather than a form of conditional obligation.

I don't know whether Kant or anyone else has ever travelled down this particular garden path. My point is merely that someone might feel the temptation to try to connect particular hypothetical imperatives to The Hypothetical Imperative in the way I have outlined. My view is that this temptation, like so many others, must be resisted.

CHAPTER 6

DEFEASIBLE COMMITMENT AND PRIMA FACIE OBLIGATION

The iffy oughts of ordinary language are a logically heterogeneous group. As we have seen, a given sentence with 'if' and 'ought' may express any of several different sorts of proposition. As I see it, this fact is responsible for one of the most serious defects in the literature concerning iffy oughts. We frequently find cases in which one writer, focussing on one sort of iffy ought, proposes an analysis. He claims to have given an account of "conditional obligation". A critic, appealing to examples of another sort of iffy ought, claims thereby to have shown the analysis defective. Obviously, however, the criticism misfires, since the two writers are talking about different classes of sentences.

This sort of problem arises especially frequently in the case of what I call 'defeasible commitment'. In light of the historical prominence of such sentences, it is all the more important that we identify them properly, distinguish them from other sorts of iffy ought, and consider various proposed analyses of their logical structure. These are the topics of the present chapter.

6.1. STATEMENTS OF DEFEASIBLE COMMITMENT

Many of us would be prepared to accept, as general rules, such statements as these:

(1)   If someone makes a promise, he ought to keep it.
(2)   If someone has injured someone, he ought to apologize.
(3)   If someone has benefitted from the generosity of another, then he ought to show gratitude.

There are, of course, many others in the same family. Ross suggested that there would be several other main sorts. In addition to the ones indicated here, there are ones having to do with justice, non-maleficence, beneficence, and self-improvement.[1] Other philosophers undoubtedly would fill out the list in other ways.

In every case, however, the sentence would exemplify certain essential features. One of these is very important, but a bit hard to pin down. Roughly, it is that the antecedent of the sentence picks out a factor that may be taken as the "ground" or "basis" or "foundation" of the obligation picked out by the consequent. Thus, we may hold that promise-making is the "ground" or "basis" for the obligatoriness of promise-keeping. The same fact may be expressed (equally obscurely) by saying that one has an obligation to keep a promise "in virtue of" the fact that he has made that promise.

Another crucial feature of such statements as (1)—(3) is that they are ordinarily taken to express a sort of connection that is deeply defeasible. Every one of them admits of all sorts of exceptions. Consider (1), for example. Even though we may want to accept (1), we still recognize that many promises ought not to be kept. If you have promised to return a weapon you have borrowed, and you now find that its owner is deranged and bent on mayhem, you shouldn't return the weapon. If you have promised to meet a friend for lunch, but now you have come across an injured stranger who desperately needs your medical attention, you shouldn't go to lunch. The other examples are equally exception-ridden. We ought to apologize to those we have injured. However, if I injure someone in self-defense while he is trying to mug me, I don't have any obligation to apologize to him.

In light of the defeasibility of the connection expressed here, some would say that sentences such as (1)—(3) are simply false as they stand. They might insist that we put a 'generally' or an 'ordinarily' or a 'ceteris paribus' into each of the sentences somewhere in order to make them true. Perhaps a truly fastidious speaker of English would never use (1) to express the sort of proposition in question here. Perhaps he would use something more like:

(1a)   If someone makes a promise, then, other things being equal, he ought to keep it.

I am inclined to think, however, that there is an acceptable, standard use of (1) in which it is understood to mean the same as (1a). So long as people a communicate adequately with each other, I see no reason to demand the longer expression. In any case, let's say that sentences such as (1)—(3), when understood in this way, express statements of "defeasible commitment". When a sensitive speaker of English makes use of such a sentence, he is generally aware of the fact that there are exceptions to the general principle. Somehow, this is thought to be compatible with what's intended by a statement of defeasible commitment.

As my reference to Ross makes clear, these statements of defeasible commitment are intimately related to the concept of "prima facie obligation". The connection is clear. If promise-making is connected to promise-keeping in the way suggested by (1), and Smith has made a certain promise, then Smith has a prima facie obligation to keep that promise. In general, we can say that prima facie obligations arise whenever the antecedent of one of these statements is satisfied. "All-in obligation" is another matter. We do not want to say that every prima facie obligation is all-in. That would commit us to an unpalatable collection of conflicts of obligation. Ross would have said that only the "most stringent" of a set of conflicting prima facie obligations in all-in.[2]

6.2. SOME FORMAL FEATURES OF DEFEASIBLE COMMITMENT

It is important to recognize that statements such as (1)–(3), if understood in the way intended by Ross and many others, are not statements of conditioned or conditional obligation. More exactly, they are not statements of *what I have called* 'conditioned obligation' or 'conditional obligation'. Indeed, their logical features distinguish them from everything we have so far seen.

I think it is pretty obvious that (1), for example, is not a statement of conditioned absolute moral obligation. To see this, let's compare (1) with the following statements:

(1b) $(x)(t)(p)$ (at t, x promises to bring about p $\rightarrow$ MOx, t, x brings about p)

(1c) $(x)(t)(p)$ (at t, x promises to bring about p $\leadsto$ MOx, t, x brings about p)

(1d) $(x)(t)(p)$ (at t, x promises to bring about p $\Rightarrow$ MOx, t, x brings about p)

(1b) expresses what I have called 'materially conditioned absolute moral obligation' or MCAMO.[3] It says, in effect, that the statement that someone has made a promise "materially implies" that he absolutely ought to keep it. (1c) expresses the idea that this is a "subjunctive implication".[4] If a person *were to* make a promise, then he *would have* an absolute obligation to keep it. (1d), finally, suggests that making a promise *entails* (strictly implies) that there is an absolute obligation to keep that promise.[5]

We have already see that factual detachment is valid for every one of these things. Any one of (1b), (1c), and (1d), in conjunction with

(4)   Smith promised at Noon that he would meet me for lunch.

entails

(5)   MOSmith, Noon, Smith meets me for lunch.

Thus, none of these explicates (1). Factual detachment is not valid for the exception-ridden statements of defeasible commitment. It is valid for every form of conditioned absolute moral obligation. Therefore, defeasible commitment is not a form of conditioned absolute moral obligation.

Although it is easy to miss this point, such statements of defeasible commitment are also distinct from statements of conditional obligation — at least, they are distinct from statements of conditional obligation if 'conditional obligation' is understood in anything like the way I understand it. Some other philosophers use 'conditional obligation' in such a way that what I call 'defeasible commitment' *must* be a form of conditional obligation. When introducing what they call 'conditional obligation', they use statements of defeasible commitment as examples. This, unfortunately, may generate misunderstanding here.

I should attempt to make my point clear. 'Defeasible commitment' and 'conditional obligation' are technical terms of moral philosophy. They have been used in various ways in the literature. So far as I know, there is no such thing as "the correct use" for either of these expressions. As I use them, they pick out different sorts of sentence. Statements of defeasible commitment are, for me, statements such as (1), (2) and (3). Such statements seem to express the idea that a certain condition or act "defeasibly commits" a person to some sort of behavior. For example, promise-making defeasibly commits the promisor to promise-keeping. Defeasible commitment is not a "doing-the-best-we-can" concept. On the other hand, statements of conditional obligation are statements that convey the idea (roughly) that in order to do the best you can consistent with some condition, you will have to see to some specified state of affairs. Thus, conditional obligation, for me, is a doing-the-best-we-can concept.

One important difference between defeasible commitment and conditional obligation concerns "unalterability detachment".[6] We have seen that while ordinary factual detachment for conditional obligation:

*FD/CMO: $MOs, t, q/p \& p \rightarrow MOs, t, q$

is not valid, unalterability detachment is valid for conditional obligation. That is, we have this principle:

UD/CMO: $MOs, t, q/p \& Us, t, p \rightarrow MOs, t, q$

Roughly, we can understand this principle to say that if the best accessible p-worlds are all q-worlds, and all accessible worlds are p-worlds, then the best accessible worlds are all q-worlds. It should be obvious that UD/CMO is valid.

The analogue of unalterability detachment is not valid for defeasible commitment. Even if Smith has already made his promise, and can't "undo it", or retract it, or make it "inoperative", we still cannot conclude that he absolutely ought to keep it. For if the promise was one that never should have been made in the first place, or if something more important has come up in the meantime, this obligation may fail to be forthcoming. For example, if Smith has already promised to commit murder and mayhem, then this fact is currently unalterable for Smith. Yet it would be absurd to conclude that Smith has an absolute moral obligation to commit murder and mayhem. In any case, we have to reject the principle that if a certain state of affairs, p, is unalterable for a person, s, at a time, t, and p defeasibly commits s to q, then s has an absolute moral obligation, as of t, to see to the occurrence of q. So statements of defeasible commitment, such as (1)—(3) above, cannot be understood as any sort of conditional obligation.

Another approach of these statements might involve a reconsideration of the scope of the obligation operator. Loosely, we might characterize this approach by saying that, according to it, a statement such as (1) really means something like this: everyone ought to see to it that, if he makes a promise, then he keeps it. More strictly, this approach would have us put some sort of conditional within the scope of the obligation operator. This would yield three main possibilities for (1):

(1e) $(x)(t)(p)(MOx, t, [x$ promises at t to bring about $p \rightarrow x$ brings about $p])$

(1f) $(x)(t)(p)(MOx, t, [x$ promises at t to bring about $p \rightsquigarrow x$ brings about $p])$

(1g) $(x)(t)(p)(MOx, t, [x$ promises at t to bring about $p \Rightarrow x$ brings about $p])$

The first of these can be eliminated without much ado. It should be clear that (1e) is entailed by something that does not entail (1). That would be the obligatoriness of the negation of the antecedent. Schematically, $\text{MO}x, t, \sim p \rightarrow \text{MO}x, t, p \rightarrow q$ is valid. But from the proposition that we shouldn't promise, it does not follow that if we do promise, we should keep our promise.

It should also be clear that (1g) won't serve here, either. For $\text{MO}x, t, p \Rightarrow q$ entails that there are some possible worlds in which $p \Rightarrow q$ is true. This, in turn, implies that $p \rightarrow q$ is true at all possible worlds. In the example in question, the corresponding implication fails. So (1g) is much too strong.

It may then appear that the most promising way of dealing with this would be the way represented by (1f). In general, we could propose that statements of defeasible commitment are to be understood as subjunctive conditionals within the scope of the obligation operator, MO. If we do treat these sentences in this way, several important logical features will be preserved. Notice first that factual detachment is (as it should be) invalid for the construction in (1f). There is no way to prove the validity of this:

*FD5: $(\text{MO}x, t, p \rightsquigarrow q \,\&\, p) \rightarrow \text{MO}x, t, q$

Loosely, this says that if $p \rightsquigarrow q$ is true at the best accessible worlds, and p is true here in the real world, then q is true at the best accessible worlds. There's no reason to suppose that this would have to be true. So far, so good.

Augmentation is also invalid. We reject:

*Aug5: $\text{MO}x, t, p \rightsquigarrow q \rightarrow \text{MO}x, t, p \,\&\, r \rightsquigarrow q$

This is another respect in which the present formulation seems to be adequate to defeasible commitment. Another has to do with overridability. This construction is overridable, as it should be. That is, sentences of this form are possible:

*Over5: $p \,\&\, r \,\&\, \text{MO}x, t, p \rightsquigarrow q \,\&\, \text{MO}x, t, p \,\&\, r \rightsquigarrow \sim q$

Nevertheless, the subjunctive conditional approach does not serve adequately to capture the logic of defeasible commitment. Once again, the problem has to do with factual detachment, and arises in the case of the unalterable antecedent. Reflection will reveal that the following principle is valid:

FD5: $(\text{MO}x, t, p \rightsquigarrow q) \,\&\, \text{U}x, t, p \rightarrow \text{MO}x, t, q$

If p occurs in all still possible worlds, and $p \rightsquigarrow q$ is true at the best of these, then q is true at the best of these, too. The impact of this should be clear. If we allow (1f) to express defeasible commitment, then we will be stuck with the unacceptable conclusion that once a promise has been made, and can't be "undone", it becomes absolutely obligatory that it be kept. The whole point of defeasible commitment is to avoid this.[7]

6.3. DEFEASIBLE COMMITMENT AND CHISHOLMIAN REQUIREMENT

At the beginning of 'The Ethics of Requirement',[8] Professor Chisholm makes a remarkable assertion. 'By taking "*p requires q*" as our single ethical primitive and making use of the concept of an *act*, we can define all the fundamental concepts of eithics.'[9] Among the concepts under consideration are 'obligatory,' '*prima facie duty*,' 'commitment,' 'defeasible,' and 'overrides.' In light of the examples cited, it should be clear that Chisholm meant to be dealing with the same family of concepts we're considering here.

By way of introducing us to the unanalyzed concept of requirement, Chisholm provides some examples. 'Promise-making requires — or calls for — promise-keeping. Being virtuous, according to Kant, requires being rewarded, . . .'[10] But requirement is not restricted to ethics. Examples can be found in aesthetics, too. 'One color in the lower left calls for a complementary color in the upper right.'[11] Chisholm goes on to mention some claims made by gestalt psychologists concerning some perceptual requirements — a certain curve allegedly requires a certain sort of completion. He also suggests that there are cases of epistemic requirement.[12] Perhaps he would say that there are some propositions, p and q, such that having p as evidence requires having q as a belief. For example, it may seem to be fitting, or epistemically required, to believe that the butler did it, given that you see the knife in his hand, you know about the will, etc.

Requirement is overridable. It may be that p requires q, but the conjunction of p and r does not require q. This happens in a case such as this familiar one: I promised to meet you for lunch. That requires that I meet you. I have met an injured person on the highway. He desperately needs my medical attention. That requires that I miss my luncheon appointment. The conjunction of my promising and my meeting the injured person fails to require that I meet you for lunch. So the requirement for lunch that was created by the promise has been overridden by the meeting with the injured person on the highway.

Chisholm makes use of a concept of "bringing about" or "seeing to the occurrence of". He uses Ap to mean 's brings about p' or 's sees to the occurrence of p'. Furthermore, he uses $p \, R \, q$ to mean 'p requires q'.

With this as background, Chisholm can introduce some defined terms. Oq, or 'it ought to be that q', is defined as follows:

(6)   "Oq" for: $(Ep) \, (p \& p \, R \, q \& \sim (Es) \, (s \& \sim (p \& s \, R \, q)))$

So a state of affairs ought to be if and only if there is a non-overridden requirement for it.[13]

The ought-to-do is allegedly definable in terms of this concept of the ought-to-be:

(7)   "S ought to bring it about that p" for: OAp [14]

So you ought to do something just in case in ought to be that you do it. And it ought to be that you do it just in case something requires that you do it, and nothing overrides that requirement. In Chapter 8, I will discuss the idea that the ought-to-do can be defined in this way by appeal to the ought-to-be, and I will explain why I think it fails.[15]

Chisholm says that he can give an account of Ross's concept of *prima facie* duty: 'We may say that a man has a *prima facie* duty to perform a certain act a, if there is a requirement that he perform a, and that he has a *duty proper* to perform a if he ought to perform a.[16] In other words, Chisholm's proposal is that there is a prima facie duty to see to the occurrence of p if and only if there is some true q, such that q requires Ap. There is an all-in duty to see to the occurrence of p if and only if there is some true q, such that q requires Ap, and no true s, such that $q \& s$ fails to require Ap.

If we apply Chisholm's proposals to the issues under consideration here, I think we come to the view that statement of defeasible commitment, such as (1)—(3) above, are to be understood straightforwardly as statements of requirement. Thus, (1) is supposed to be equivalent to:

(1h) $(x) \, (p) \, (x$'s promising to bring about p requires x's bringing about p)

The other examples would be treated is a relevantly similar manner. Each would be taken to be a statement to the effect that one sort of action requires another.

If understood in this way, statements of defeasible commitment would apparently be immune to factual detachment, they would be overridable, and they would be non-augmentable. I see no reason to suppose that they would be subject to deontic detachment, although this is not entirely clear. Thus, Chisholm's approach may seem to be right on target.

Furthermore, the account proposed here seems to capture all the prima facie duties. Any action for which there is a requirement is said to be a prima facie duty. Apparently, everything Ross would want to call a prima facie duty is an action for which there is some requirement, in Chisholm's sense. However, the fit here is not quite perfect. There are requirements for many actions that Ross would not consider to be prima facie duties. Suppose, for example, that we see a cat on the first roof, and a cat on the second roof, and a cat on the third roof. It would seem, then, that there is then a requirement that we believe that there is a cat on the fourth roof, too. This would be based on the more general epistemic requirement to believe that the unexamined roofs must be relevantly like the examined ones. If this is right, Chisholm's proposal yields the result that we have a prima facie obligation to believe that there is a cat on the unexamined roof. To my knowledge, Ross never suggested that we have a prima facie obligation to believe what our inductive evidence supports.

Similar points could be made concerning all the other non-moral sorts of requirement. For example, an artist who has drawn a certain curve would have a prima facie obligation to complete it in the most fitting way. A musician who has played certain notes would have a prima facie obligation to follow them up in the most fitting, or appropriate way. All these examples show, I think, that Chisholm's requirement-based concept of prima facie obligation is broader than the one introduced by Ross.

It seems to me, however, that problems with Chisholm's approach run even deeper than this. When I reflect on what comes to mind when I think of fittingness, or requirement, I find that it is a relation that has not only ethical, epistemic and aesthetic manifestations. It also has logical, or semantic, ones. So, for example, I find that being a mother requires being female — what could be more fitting, or appropriate,

than for a mother to be female? Similarly, I find that being red requires
being colored; that being spherical requires being extended; and so on.
In general, it seems to me that the following principle must be true:

(8) $(p)(q)(p \Rightarrow q \rightarrow p \,\mathrm{R}\, q)$

In other words, if a state of affairs, p, entails a state of affairs, q, then p
requires q.

This principle has serious impact on what Chisholm wants to say.
Notice, first, that any requirement based upon entailment must override
any conflicting requirement not based upon entailment. If p requires q
because p entails q, and r requires $\sim q$ for some other reason (e.g.,
ethical), then $p \& r$ requires q. This follows from the fact that if p
entails q, then $p \& r$ entails q, too. By (8), it follows that $p \& r$ requires
q. So, in a sense, we can say that entailment-based requirements
override all other sorts of requirement, and are the most stringent.

Second, we should note that entailment-based requirements support
a kind of factual detachment. If p requires q because p entails q, and p
occurs, then q absolutely ought to occur. This follows from Chisholm's
definition of the ought-to-be, together with the fact that something that
occurs (p itself) requires q in a non-overridable way.

In light of this, we can see that everything that occurs absolutely
ought to occur. The proof is straightforward. Suppose p is a state of
affairs that occurs. Since every state of affairs entails itself, p entails p.
In light of (8), it follows that p requires p. Since p entails p, this
"self-requirement" must be of the most stringent, non-overridable sort.
Hence, something that occurs (p itself) non-overridably requires p.
Given Chisholm's definition ((6) above) it follows that p ought to be.
Thus we have:

(9)   (p) (p occurs $\rightarrow$ Op)

The converse of (9) can be proven as well. Suppose $\sim p \& Op$ were
true. Then, since $\sim p$ would be true, $O \sim p$ would be true, too. (One
application of (9)). In this case, $Op \& O \sim p$ would be true. But
Chisholm (quite plausibly) tells us that this is impossible.[17] Hence, $\sim p$
$\& Op$ can't be true. This is equivalent to saying that $Op \rightarrow p$ must be
true. Hence we have the converse of (9). Conjoining this with (9) yields
the notorious:

(10) (p) (p occurs $\leftrightarrow$ Op)

It has been suggested that Chisholm could overcome these objections merely by ruling out all entailment-based requirements. In other words, he could simply legislate that when p entails q, p does not require q.[18] However, it seems to me that this stipulation will not entirely avoid difficulty, since further objection can be made concerning inductive connections. Suppose there is a cat on the first roof, and a cat on the second roof, and a cat on each other roof right up to the last one. It seems to me, then, that it would be fitting, or appropriate, for there to be a cat on the last roof, too. The harmony, symmetry, and uniformity of the vista would be broken if the last roof were catless. Hence, I'm inclined to think that when p provides good enough inductive evidence for q, p requires q.

If my inclination is correct, we can see that there will be a whole bunch of rather implausible prima facie obligations. Consider a man who has regularly broken his promises in the past. Each day he promises to meet us for lunch, and each day he fails to show up. His past behavior is good enough inductive evidence for the conclusion that he will break his promise again today. In this case, Chisholm's proposal yields the result that he has a prima facie obligation to break his promise. This seems to me to be wrong.

Furthermore, if these induction-based requirement are non-overridable, we will be able again to establish the truth of the unacceptable principle (10).

Chisholm could simply deny that entailment and inductive support are forms of requirement. He could say that requirement obtains only in the more plausible ethical and asesthetic cases. I find it hard to see how such a claim could be justified. Requirement, as I see it, is a relation that holds between states of affairs regardless of their subject matter, and regardless of their deductive and inductive connections. Every case in which q would be fitting, or appropriate, given p, is a case in which p requires q. Fittingness, or appropriateness, as I understand them, occur in the ethical and aesthetic cases, but also in the epistemic, deductive, and inductive cases, too. Thus, I am inclined to believe that we cannot properly understand the strictly moral concept of prima facie duty in the way suggested by Chisholm.

6.4. DEFEASIBLE COMMITMENT AND PROBABILISTIC REQUIREMENT

In his paper, Chisholm remarked upon the formal analogy between his own concept of requirement and the concept of confirmation, or epistemic probability.[19] Some of his comments and examples suggest another possible way of dealing with these troublesome statements of defeasible commitment. The approach would have us understand:

(1)   If someone makes a promise, he ought to keep it

as

(1i)   Given that someone has made a promise, it is probable that he absolutely ought to keep it.

Thus, statements of defeasible commitment would be understood to be statements of conditional probability, where the consequent is a statement of absolute moral obligation. Let us investigate this idea.

Consider this truism:

(10)   If you lie down with dogs, you'll wake up with fleas.

If we use (10) to express a truth, we don't use it to mean that absolutely everyone who lies down with dogs wakes up with fleas. For we recognize that there are plenty of exceptions. Those who lie down with flealess dogs may arise flealess. Equally, flea-protected individuals who lie down with dogs (flea-ridden or not) may arise flealess. What (10) means is that if you lie down with dogs, you'll *probably* wake up with fleas. This is a statement of conditional probability. The logic of such statements is somewhat puzzling, primarily because of the quantifiers.

Suppose we use $\Pr(q/p) = n$ to mean that the probability of q, given p, is equal to n. N can be anything between 0 and 1. Let us also agree that there is some number, k, between 0 and 1, such that when $\Pr(q/p) \geqslant k$, then we say that q is "probable", or "probably true", given p. Now, to see the trouble about the quantifiers in (10), let's consider some fancier statements. We can use Fx and Dx to mean, respectively, 'x wakes up with fleas' and 'x lies down with dogs.'

(10a) $(x)(\Pr(Fx/Dx) \geqslant k)$
(10b) $(Ex)(\Pr(Fx/Dx) \geqslant k)$
(10c) $\Pr((x)(Fx)/(x)(Dx)) \geqslant k$
(10d) $\Pr((Ex)(Fx)/(Ex)(Dx)) \geqslant k$

None of these is a suitable paraphrase of (10). (10a) is wrong. It says that everyone, x, is such that if x lies down with dogs, then x will probably wake up with fleas. But there are undoubtedly some few individuals who are protected against fleas. For these individuals, the probability of waking up with fleas, given that they lie down with dogs, is not very high at all. So not everyone is such that if he lies down with dogs, he will probably wake up with fleas.

(10b) say that there is someone such that if he lies down with dogs, he will probably wake up with fleas. Clearly, however, this is too weak. It could be true even if (10) were false. All we'd need is some already flea-ridden person. It's almost certain that if he were to lie down with dogs (or chickens, for that matter) he'd wake up with fleas.

(10c) says that it is probable that if everyone lies down with dogs, then everyone will wake up with fleas. This is unacceptable, since it is unlikely that absolutely everyone would wake up with fleas, even if everyone were to lie down with dogs. Surely, at least a few flea-protected individuals would remain flea free. Finally, (10d) is also wrong. It says that it is probable that if someone were to lie down with dogs, then someone would wake up with fleas. This is much too weak. Even if no one lies down with dogs, it is probable that someone will wake up with fleas. (10d) could be true even if (10) were false.

Clearly, what we need here is a statement to the effect that an "arbitrarily selected individual" who lies down with dogs will probably wake up with fleas. But who is this "arbitrarily selected individual"?

Let us use SFx and SDx to mean, respectively, that x arbitrarily selects an individual who wakes up with fleas, and x arbitrarily selects an individual who lies down with dogs. So SFx does not mean, or even imply, Fx. Rather, SFx means that x arbitrarily selects someone, y, such that Fy. Similarly for SDx and Dx. Now, for (10), we can propose:

$$(10e) \quad (x)(\Pr(SFx/SDx) \geqslant k)$$

This just means that given that someone, x, has arbitrarily selected an individual who lies down with dogs, x has probably arbitrarily selected an individual who will wake up with fleas. Since we require arbitrary selection, this seems to me to be true, and adequate to (10). It also seems to me to be ontologically benign, since it does not commit us to the existence of any "arbitrary individuals".

Now let us return to the statements of defeasible commitment. On the present proposal, a statement such as (1) is to be understood as a statement of quantified conditional probability. Following the pattern of (10e), let us use SKx and SPx to mean, respectively, x arbitrarily selects an individual who absolutely ought to keep his promise, and x arbitrarily selects an individual who makes a promise. Now we can try:

(1j) $(x)(\mathrm{Pr}(\mathrm{SK}x/\mathrm{SP}x) \geqslant k)$

In other words, everyone is such that if he arbitrarily selects someone who has made a promise, then he has probably arbitrarily selected someone who absolutely ought to keep his promise. As I see it, the picture is this. Gather together a huge number of promise-makers. Now let a blindfolded person randomly select someone from the group. Chances are the selected promise-maker is someone who has an absolute obligation to keep a promise. In other words, the fact that someone has made a promise makes it probable that he has an absolute obligation to keep that promise.

The interesting relation between promise-making and promise keeping holds, of course, in many other cases as well. This is a relation between properties in which the having of one of the properties makes probable the obligatoriness of the having of the other. We can call this relation "probabilistic requirement", and we can define it as follows:

PR: P1 probabilistically requires P2 = df. $(x)(\mathrm{Pr}(x$ arbitrarily selects an individual who absolutely ought to have P2$/x$ arbitrarily selects an individual who has P1$) \geqslant k)$

We can put this into simpler English by saying that property P1 probabilistically requires property P2 just in case anyone having P1 probably ought to have P2. If you have a large collection of people with P1, and you pick someone randomly from the group, you've probably picked someone who ought to have P2. Some examples of this sort of requirement might be these: being a parent probabilistically requires seeing to the welfare of your children; injuring someone probabilistically requires apologizing to him; being benefitted by someone probabilistically requires showing gratitude.

From the logical point of view, this concept of requirement is very weak indeed. Virtually none of the standard deontic principles turns out to be valid for it. For example, let's consider a form of factual detachment. The idea would be this: if one property probabilistically requires another, and someone in fact has the former property, then he absolutely ought to have the other. More strictly:

*FD/PR: P1 probabilistically requires P2 & x has P1 $\rightarrow$ MO$s, t, s$ has P2

This is clearly invalid, as is the non-deontic analogue. if you lie down with dogs, you'll probably wake up with fleas. But there are some people who in fact do lie down with dogs, and who do not wake up with fleas. Some of these are people who selected flealess dogs for bed-partners. Others dusted themselves liberally with flea powder before lying down. Similarly, if you make a promise, you probably ought to keep it. But there are some people who have in fact made promises and who have no obligation to keep those promises. For example, consider the man who promised to murder the Pope. In this respect, then, probabilistic requirement may seem to capture what's meant by statements of defeasible commitment.

However, there are other respects in which probabilistic requirement seems wide of the mark. For one thing, probabilistic requirement occurs far too frequently to account for any traditional concept of prima facie duty. There are pairs of properties that are pretty clearly related by probabilistic requirement, but which just as clearly do not fit the standard pattern noted by Ross and others. For example, if you arbitrarily select someone who has been indicted a grand jury, you've probably selected someone who absolutely ought to be punished for a crime. Yet we wouldn't think that being indicted gives rise to a prima facie duty to be punished. Surely, there is no hint of "commitment" or Chisholmian requirement here.

The central question, however, is the question whether we should understand statements of defeasible commitment, such as (1)—(3), as statements of probabilistic requirement. In other words, are the following sentences equivalent in meaning?

(1)   If someone makes a promise, then he ought to keep it.
(1h)   Promise-making probabilistically requires promise-keeping.

My answer to this question is a bit complicated. I believe that sentences relevantly like (1) are sometimes used to mean what's meant by corresponding sentences relevantly like (1h). Surely, we sometimes use iffy oughts of this form merely to express the idea that the obligation mentioned in the consequent is much more likely, given the factors mentioned in the antecedent. Probabilistic requirement is a fact of ordinary language.

However, I also think that probabilistic requirement does not not provide an analysis for sentences such as (1), when such sentences are used in the Rossian, prima facie duty way.

If we reflect on (1h) for a moment, we'll recognize that it only says that promise-making makes probable the obligatoriness of promise-keeping. It does not say that promise-making is the "ground" or "basis" or "foundation" of the obligatoriness of promise-keeping. It does not say that promise-making "commits" one to promise-keeping, nor does it suggest that it is "in virtue of" having made a promise that one incurs the obligation to keep that promise. The connection alleged by (1h) not intrinsically moral. It is merely conditional probability. Given the standard frequency interpretation of such statements, it says only that a large percentage of those who have made promises have an obligation to keep their promises. So, if it should turn out that a large percentage of persons with long, pointy noses have lied, then having such a nose would probabilistically require apologizing for your lie. However, it would be the lying that gives rise to the need for the apology, not the long pointy nose. Rossians would view as absurd the suggestion that Pinocchio had a duty to apologize for his lies in virtue of the fact that he had such a long nose.

My conclusion, then, is this. In its interesting use, (1) is supposed to express some sort of intrinsically moral connection between promise-making and promise-keeping. It suggests (allegedly) that promise-making is the defeasible "ground" or "basis" for the obligatoriness of promise-keeping. When used in this way, (1) does not means the same as (1h). Statements of probabilistic requirement simply do not express any such connection. They do not indicate any sort of moral "commitment" or "foundation" or "ground". Thus, probabilistic requirement is real enough, but provides no analysis of statements of defeasible commitment.

6.5. THE TRUTH ABOUT DEFEASIBLE COMMITMENT AND PRIMA FACIE DUTY

My current, somewhat pessimistic view about defeasible commitment is that these sentences demand a historical, psychological explanation, rather than a formal analysis. Let me attempt to sketch the explanation I have in mind.

As children, most of us undergo some sort of moral training. Sometimes this is fairly rigorous, and sometimes it is extremely casual, and even lax. In any case, we are introduced to a variety of maxims and principles. 'Never tell a lie', 'always keep your promises', 'return what you have borrowed', etc. are typical examples. To small children, with limited experience, these may seem fairly plausible. Furthermore, we learn these maxims from respected (and often intimidating) adults, and so we are naturally inclined to accept them.

I suspect that this may be a bit artificial, but it is not unreasonable to suppose that child who accepts

(1)   If someone make a promise, then he ought to keep it

understands it in such a way that

(1c) $(x)(t)$ (at t, x promises to bring about $p \rightsquigarrow x$ morally ought to bring about p)

would be an adequate, if somewhat too tidied-up rendition of his thought. That is, he thinks of (1) as meaning that if anyone were to make a promise, then he would have an absolute obligation to keep that promise. In general, I think we first take these as statements of subjunctively (or perhaps strictly) conditioned absolute moral obligation.

As we get a bit older, we begin to realize that, however useful it may be to believe these things, none of them is actually true. Numerous exceptions are noted. At first, we may try to accommodate these exceptions by expanding the antecedents of the rules. But soon enough we find that we can't keep track of all the provisoes. So we're in a bind. Childhood training has made us unwilling to reject these things outright. Experience has taught us that, taken on the model of (1c) or (1d), they are all false. Out of desperation, we seek a compromise. We need a way to maintain our commitment to the sentences, while acknowledging that they are subject to exceptions. In this sad situation, we hear some phrase such as 'other things being equal' or 'inasmuch as', or 'ceteris paribus'. Although we don't know exactly what these things mean, they seem to resolve the perplexity. All we have to do is put one of them into each of the rules. In this way, we can keep the rules, but take the sting out of the exceptions. So, instead of saying the troubling (1), we advance to saying

(1i)   If someone makes a promise, then, other things being equal, he ought to keep it.

In my view, however, these added phrases don't have any clear meaning. The revised verions of the rules are not accurate expressions of some new thought — rather, they are forms of language that record the inner conflict between respect for our parents and respect for what we have seen for ourselves.

My conclusion, then, has a number of elements. In the first place, the sentences associated with defeasible commitment, such as (1)—(3), are used meaningfully. Such sentences can be used to express a variety of interestingly different sorts of proposition. In some uses, they express conditioned absolute obligation. In others, they express conditional obligation. In yet others, they may be used to express the sort of connection Chisholm has dubbed "requirement". Finally, they can be used to express probabilistic requirement. In their most puzzling use, however, in which they do not express any of the things we have attempted to explain here, they don't express any proposition at all. Rather, they represent the attempt to maintain allegiance to grand and impressive moral principles, such as (1c) which, unfortunately, are all known to be false.

The upshot is that prima facie obligation begins to look like a moral mirage. To say that a person has a prima facie obligation to do something, it would appear, is just to say that there is one of these degenerate moral principles that requires it. Since the moral principles have been modified by the addition of such dubious phrases as 'other things being equal', it is no longer clear that they have any meaning. Hence, it is no longer clear that statements of prima facie obligation have any clear meaning.

With this I conclude my discussion of iffy oughts. While I suspect that there are sorts of iffy ought that I have not discussed here, I hope I have said enough to establish my main point. The iffy oughts of ordinary English are an extremely heterogeneous group. Many of them can be analyzed by appeal to suitable concepts of possibility and value. These are the doing-the-best-we-can iffy oughts. They include all the forms of conditioned absolute obligation, conditional moral obligation, conditional prudential obligation, hypothetical imperatives, etc. Others, such as requirement and defeasible commitment, are birds of a different feather.

PART THREE

EXTENSIONS

CHAPTER 7

INDIVIDUAL OBLIGATION AND GROUP WELFARE

Many moral thinkers have accepted the notion that there is an important connection between moral obligation and group welfare. More specifically, they have thought that the welfare of a social group would more-or-less automatically be maximized if all the members of that group were to do their moral obligations.[1] We can say that any doctrine to this effect is a version of the "principle of moral harmony" (PMH).

Some moral philosophers have argued in favor of utilitarianism, claiming that is alone of moral theories is consistent with PMH.[2] It apparently has seemed obvious to them that if each member of a group does the best he can — as utilitarianism requires — then the group will be doing its best, and so will be best off. Other moral philosophers have argued against traditional act utilitarianism, saying that it must be false, since it conflicts with this very same principle.[3] They have claimed that even when everyone in a group does his best, it is still possible that the group will fail to achieve its best possible outcome.

So we have a bunch of questions: does the utilitarian concept of obligation verify PMH? If not, then are there other, more plausible concepts of obligation that do verify PMH? In any case, if the utilitarian concept fails to verify PMH, does that show that utilitarianism is false?

In this chapter, I attempt to answer these questions. In Section 1, I discuss some preliminary difficulties that must be dealt with before we can attempt to formulate a version of PMH. Then, in Section 2, after developing a suitable first version of PMH, I show that my own neo-utilitarian concept of moral obligation fails to verify PMH. Then, in Section 3, I develop a concept of obligation ("social obligation") that may naturally be thought to verify a version of PMH. I go on to show that even this strange concept of obligation in fact fails to verify PMH. Then, in Sections 4 and 5, I consider two concepts of obligation that do verify the principle. One of these concepts ("civic obligation") is my own creation. The other ("cooperative obligation") is based on the work of Donald Regan. My aim is to drive home the fact that only some rather peculiar concepts of obligation verify PMH. Thus, the fact that MO fails to verify PMH ought not to be taken as a mark against MO. No plausible concept of obligation verifies PMH.

147

Let's begin, then, by considering some preliminary difficulties that arise when we set out to formulate PMH.

7.1. SOME PRELIMINARY DIFFICULTIES FOR PMH

PMH is the view that when individuals perform their moral obligations, their group enjoys a maximum of welfare. For this doctrine to stand any chance of being true, there must be a pretty tight fit between the way group welfare is measured, and the way individual obligation is determined. To see this, consider what happens when we measure group welfare in one way, and determine individual obligation in another. Suppose, for example, that the welfare of a group is determined strictly hedonistically. That is, to find out how well off a group is, all you must do is add up the amounts of pleasure enjoyed by the members, add up the amounts of pain suffered by the members, and subtract the latter number from the former.

On the other hand, suppose that individual obligation is determined by appeal to something like Ross's deontological theory. Many different act types are prima facie obligatory. Among these are promise-keeping debt-paying, gratitude-showing, justice-doing, etc. In any given case, an individual's moral obligation is to do the act which is the most stringent of the prima facie obligations open to him.

If all the members of some social group were to do their moral obligations, thus determined, then many promises would be kept, many debts would be paid, much gratitude would be shown, and justice would be widely done. However, it is questionable whether the group would be maximally happy. Perhaps all this debt-paying and gratitude-showing would make people depressed. If many of the debts, both monetary and gratitudinal, were owed to foreigners, perhaps the group would become despondent and poorer as a result of paying them off.

It seems pretty clear, then, that if we want PMH to turn out true, we are going to have to assume that individual obligations are determined in some other way. Specifically, we are going to have to assume that individual obligations are determined by appeal to the notion that obligatory acts maximize beneficial outcomes. Then there's chance that, when everyone does his duty, thus determined, the group will be best off.

Clearly, however, this assumption will not suffice to establish PMH. To see this, suppose that individual obligation is determined by appeal to the maximization of some benefit, but the benefits are assessed according to some pluralistic axiology. Suppose that several different things are intrinsically good. These may include pleasure, knowledge, freedom, beauty, and justice. Suppose several corresponding things are intrinsically bad. Suppose that what a person morally ought to do is that act which, of the alternatives available to him, would produce the greatest balance of intrinsic good over intrinsic evil. Suppose, however, that we continue to determine group welfare strictly hedonistically, as we did before. If we determine group welfare and individual obligations in these divergent ways, there will be no reason to suppose that our obligations will harmonize in the manner suggested by PMH. It may seem plausible to maintain that if everyone does what he morally ought to do, then intrinsic value will be maximized. However, since the maximization of intrinsic value (pluralistically assessed) does not guarantee the maximization of group welfare (hedonistically assessed), it would not be reasonable to say that if we all do what we morally ought to do, our group will have to enjoy a maximum of welfare.

In light of this, we can see that PMH stands a reasonable chance of being true only if we assess group welfare by appeal to the same criterion that's used to determine individual obligation. Thus, if we determine individual obligation by appeal to the maximization of intrinsic value, and we accept a pluralistic axiology, then we must use the same pluralistic axiology when we assess group welfare.

7.2. MORAL OBLIGATION AND PMH

In Chapter 2, I presented an analysis of a concept of obligation that I find especially attractive. According to that analysis, a person morally ought, as of some time, to bring about a state of affairs just in case there is a world then accessible to him in which it occurs, and no intrinsically better world then accessible to him in which it fails to occur. Roughly, the idea is that a person ought to do a thing if it occurs in the instrinsically best worlds accessible to him. The intrinsic value of a world is said to be the sum of the intrinsic values of the basic intrinsic value states that occur there. According to the view I sketched in 2.2.6, basic intrinsic value states come in a variety of main sorts — some record the fact that someone is enjoying some pleasure, others have to do with justice, (perhaps) freedom, (perhaps) beauty, and (perhaps) knowledge. These are the intrinsic goods. Others have to do with pain,

injustice, (perhaps) bondage, (perhaps) ugliness and (perhaps) ignorance. These are the intrinsic evils. I apologize for the sketchiness of my
axiological intuitions. For present purposes, however, the details of the
axiology don't matter. What matters is that what a person ought to do is
determined by the intrinsic value of the accessible possible worlds. I
call this concept of obligation 'MO'.

In order to determine whether MO verifies PMH, we have to
construct a suitable measure of group welfare. As we have seen above,
unless we assess group welfare in the same way we determine individual
obligation, there isn't much chance that PMH will be verified. In light of
this, it seems to me that we must say that group welfare is strictly a
matter of the extent to which the group enjoys the things that are of
intrinsic value — whatever they may be.

If pleasure is the only intrinsic good, and pain is the only intrinsic
evil, then group welfare is a relatively determinate matter. Take the
extent to which the members of the group enjoy pleasure and subtract
the extent to which the members of the group suffer pain. The result is
the group's "intrinsic welfare".

If knowledge, beauty, freedom, justice, or other complex states of
affairs also have instrinsic value, then things become far more difficult.
In this case, we will have to imagine some way of assessing the extent to
which the group enjoys justice (or suffers injustice). Furthermore, to
make the calculation significant, we will have to assume that the
measurements of justice, pleasure, knowledge, beauty and freedom are
suitably commensurate. This strikes me as being at best a very difficult
business. Let's assume, for purpose of argument, that it can be done.
More specifically, let's assume that if k is a social group, w is a possible
world, and k exists in w, then there is a number that represents k's
"intrinsic welfare" in w. This is the extent to which k shares in the
things that have intrinsic value — whatever they may be.

The crucial thing here, and the thing I am trying to assure, is that
the factors that contribute toward the intrinsic welfare of a social group
are exactly the same as the factors that are maximized by the performance of individual acts of moral obligation. The individual must
always maximize intrinsic value. The group is best off if it gets the
largest possible share of intrinsic value. The question before us now is
this: if we determine individual obligation in this (MO) way, and we
assess group welfare in this (intrinsic welfare) way, then is PMH true? If
every member of a social group does every one of his MO-obligations

during some period of time, will the social group enjoy the greatest intrinsic welfare that was possible for it during that period of time?

It seems perfectly obvious to me that this version of PMH is false. Consider a simple example. Suppose the citizens of the United States constitute a social group. Suppose a horrible famine is raging in Africa, and that enormous quantities of food, medicine, and money are needed to stave off very great evils. Then it may be that each citizen of the United States has a moral obligation (as determined by MO) to give a substantial portion of his wealth as a charitable contribution for the suffering Africans. In order to make actual the best of the accessible worlds, we may have to give a lot of food, medicine, and money to the Africans. We may even have to "give until it hurts". That is, we may have to give so much that our own opportunity for the enjoyment of the things of intrinsic value is slightly decreased. If this sort of thing can happen (and it seems clear that it can) then there can be cases in which, by doing our moral obligations, we make our own social group somewhat worse off. Thus, MO fails to verify PMH.

More obvious counterexamples to this version of PMH can easily be developed. Suppose some international superpower threatens to enslave the free nations of Western Europe. If the threatened enslavement occurs, then the world-wide level of freedom would diminish. Then we may have an obligation, as determined by MO, to go to war to defend freedom. Nevertheless, our own welfare might not be threatened by the malicious international superpower. We might be much worse off for doing the acts that are obligatory.

The general point should be clear: intersocietal altruism is sometimes morally obligatory. There are cases in which we have a moral obligation, as determined by MO, to behave in ways that will significantly increase the intrinsic welfare of some other social group, at cost to the intrinsic welfare of our own group. In such cases there is no other way to maximize the intrinsic value of the world as a whole. Thus, even if we assess group welfare by appeal to intrinsic value, and we determine individual obligation by appeal to the same measure, there is no assurance that the performance of obligatory acts by the members of a group will increase *that group's* share of intrinsic value. Thus we have the answer to our first question. My own neo-utilitarian concept of obligation fails to verify PMH.

In light of the fact that MO fails to verify PMH, some moral philosophers may be prepared to reject MO. In my view, however, any such conclusion would be premature. Perhaps PMH is the source of the trouble. Perhaps no plausible concept of obligation will be found to verify PMH. In this case, the fact that MO also fails to verify PMH should not be taken as a mark against MO. Let us then consider the question whether there is some other reasonably attractive concept of obligation that yields PMH. If there is, then we may wish to adopt that concept of obligation rather than MO. If there is not, then we needn't be troubled by the fact that MO fails to verify PMH.

7.3. SOCIAL OBLIGATION AND PMH

MO doesn't verify PMH. The reason is fairly obvious. Our MO-obligations are determined by consideration of the total intrinsic values of the accessible possible worlds. What we ought to do is what we do in the accessible worlds with the greatest overall intrinsic value. However, the intrinsic welfare of our own social group may not be at a maximum in the worlds with the greatest overall intrinsic value. It may happen that in the best accessible worlds, our group gets a smaller share of the goods than we get here in the real world. Though the pie is bigger, our slice may be smaller.

7.3.1. *Social Obligation*

A trivial revision of MO will generate a new concept of obligation that may seem to verify PMH. We can construct this concept (which we'll call "social obligation" or "SO") in such a way as to assure that when a person does his social obligations, he *must* maximize the welfare of his social group. Then it may turn out that social obligations harmonize. In other words, when all the members of a social group perform all of their social obligations during some time, then the welfare of the group will be maximized.

Let's suppose again that, for every social group and possible world, if the social group exists at the world, then there is a certain share of intrinsic value that the group enjoys (or suffers) at the world. Let this be the intrinsic welfare of the group at the world.

Suppose some individual is exclusively concerned about the intrinsic welfare of some group of which he is a member. Perhaps the group is a certain nation, and this individual is a fanatical patriot. In this case, we may represent this person's normative view by saying that he wants to maximize the intrinsic welfare of his nation. He wants to realize the possible world, of all those accessible to him, in which his nation enjoys the greatest intrinsic welfare. Such a person tries to act in accord with the demands of what I call 'social obligation'. He always strives to do what he does in the best-for-his-nation accessible world.

We cannot introduce social obligation by saying that a person's social obligation is to do what he does in the accessible worlds in which the social group to which he belongs enjoys a maximum of intrinsic welfare. The problem is that, for most individuals, there is no such thing as "*the* social group to which he belongs". Each person belongs to many social groups. Thus, it will be better to relativize the concept of social obligation. Let's suppose that a person may have different social obligations relative to different social groups. In each case, the person's social obligation is to maximize the intrinsic welfare of the group. Thus our fundamental concept here will be this: as of a time, t, a person, s, has a social obligation, relative to some social group, k, to see to a certain state of affairs, p. We can abbreviate this as: $SO s, t, k, p$.

Now we can introduce the official account of social obligation:

SO: $SO s, t, k, p$ is true at a world, w iff $(Ew')(As, t, w', w \& p$ is true at $w' \& \sim(Ew'')(As, t, w'', w \& \sim p$ is true at $w'' \&$ the intrinsic welfare of k in $w'' \geq$ the intrinsic welfare of k in $w))$

Loosely, then, the idea is that s has a social obligation, relative to a group, k, to see to p just in case p occurs in the best-for-k worlds accessible to s. If s does the very best he can for k, p will occur. It should be clear that this new concept of social obligation is formally quite like the old concept of moral obligation. There are just two differences. In the first place, this concept of obligation is relativized to social groups. In the second place, accessible worlds are evaluated by appeal to a different concept of value. Instead of total intrinsic value, we here consider the intrinsic welfare of the relevant group. Clearly, this is another "doing the best we can" concept of obligation.

7.3.2. *The Disharmony of Social Obligations*

We can now formulate a new version of the Principle of Moral Harmony. According to this version of the principle, social obligations harmonize. When all the members of a group perform their social obligations relative to some group, the intrinsic welfare of that group is maximized. More exactly, the idea is this: If k is a social group, and t is a period of time, and every member of k brings about every state of affairs that is socially obligatory for him relative to k during t, then the intrinsic welfare of k will be maximized — no other pattern of behavior available to the members of k would have resulted in k's enjoying a greater intrinsic welfare. I will abbreviate this doctrine by saying that "social obligations harmonize".

Although the concept of social obligation has been created here with an eye toward verifying the principle of moral harmony, social obligations do not harmonize. The current version of the principle is also false. To see this, consider a relatively straightforward voting example: Suppose a certain small nation, G, is about to elect a new president. Suppose Smith and Jones are the only candidates, and each citizen must cast exactly one vote. Suppose G would be best off if Smith were to get all the votes. G would be next-best off if Jones were to get all the votes. G would be worst off if some votes were cast for Smith, and some for Jones. Suppose each voter is able to vote for either candidate, but in fact is going to vote for the less-good candidate, Jones. Suppose, finally, that it's too late for anyone to influence anyone else's vote.

Consider the issue from the perspective of some voter, v1. V1 has his choice of either voting for Jones or voting for Smith. If he votes for Jones, he will contribute to the production of the second-best possible outcome — a unanimous victory for the second-best candidate. On the other hand, if he votes for Smith, he will be nothing more than a "spoiler". He will be ruining Jones' chance for a unanimous victory, but he won't thereby get a better outcome. He'll guarantee a worse outcome by assuring a split vote. Since v1 has no other choice (he can't make the other voters vote for Smith) it seems that v1's social obligation relative to G is to vote for Jones.

Similiar considerations will show that each other voter also has a social obligation, relative to G, to vote for the second-best candidate. In each case, the voter has the choice of voting for Smith or voting for Jones. However, in each case, if the voter were to vote for Smith, he would cast the only vote for Smith. By stipulation, no voter can influence any other voter's vote, and in fact each voter is going to vote for Jones.

In this case, if every member of G does his social obligation relative to G on election day, Jones will win in a landslide. While this outcome is good, it is not the best outcome available to G. Each voter is able to vote for the better candidate, Smith. Nothing prevents them from voting for Smith unanimously. Thus, G could have elected Smith and could have secured a better outcome. Social obligations do not harmonize.

This example is an instance of a sort that has been widely used in the literature. Another instance[4] involves an oppressed society. Each member is able to secure a weapon and come to the capital city. If all were to do this simultaneously, the tyrant would be overthrown in a successful revolution and the nation would be best off. However, no individual is able to coordinate the plot. Each is such that if he were to revolt, he would revolt alone and unsuccessfully. Thus, each has a social obligation, relative to this oppressed society, to avoid revolution. If everyone does his or her social obligation, the society fails to achieve the best outcome available to the society as a whole. Yet another example[5] involves a group of ice-skaters. Each can save a child who has fallen through the ice. Each is such that the group would be best off if he were to try to do it. Thus, each has a social obligation to try to save the child. However, these social obligations do not harmonize. If all were to try to save the child, too many would skate on thin ice, and many would needlessly get cold and wet. Another example[6] involves a pair of button-pushers, Whiff and Poof. Each has his choice of either pushing or not pushing his button. If both push, the world is best off. If neither pushes, the world is not so well off. If one pushes and the other doesn't, the world is worst off. Suppose Whiff is not going to push. Then Poof shouldn't push. Suppose he doesn't. Then Whiff shouldn't push either. In this case, when each refrains from pushing, each does what's best under the circumstances, but the group does not achieve the best possible outcome.[7]

The essentials of the voting case may be illustrated by a very simple matrix (Fig. 7.1.).

		v1	
		vote for Smith	vote for Jones
v1	vote for Smith	+10	−5
	vote for Jones	−5	+5

Fig. 7.1.

In this example, we assume that G is a social group consisting of just two members, v1 and v2. Each member has his choice of voting for

Smith or voting for Jones. The numbers in the cells indicate the intrinsic welfare for G that would be secured by each combination of votes. Thus, the '+10' in the upper left cell indicates that if both votes are cast for Smith, G enjoys 10 units of intrinsic welfare. Suppose v2 is in fact going to vote for Jones, and v1 cannot influence v2's vote. Then v1 seems to have just two choices: either he can vote for the better candidate (Smith) and thereby assure a worst-case outcome (-5 intrinsic welfare for G) or he can vote for the less good candidate (Jones) and thereby secure a better outcome (+5 intrinsic welfare for G). Clearly, v1's social obligation, relative to G, is to vote for Jones.

Smilar considerations show that v2's social obligation, relative to G, is to vote for Jones. If both members of G vote for Jones, G ends up in the lower right cell with just +5 units of intrinsic welfare. Since each voter could have voted for Smith, G could have ended up in the upper left box with +10 units of intrinsic welfare. Thus, even though each does his social obligation relative to G, G does not thereby secure the best-for-G possible outcome. The social obligation version of PMH is false.

7.4. CIVIC OBLIGATION AND PMH

In order to develop a concept of obligation that in fact will verify a version of PMH, it will be necessary to devote some attention to a number of matters concerning the powers of groups, and the obligations of groups.

7.4.1. *Group Accessibility*

According to preanalytic common sense, social groups can do things. For example, the group consisting of all the voters in the United States can elect a certain person to the office of President. More prosaically, a group consisting of a bunch of football players can run a certain play. A group consisting of a bunch of actors and actresses can act out a certain drama. If a group of football players runs a certain play, they do it in virtue of the fact that the center passes the ball to the quarterback, and the quarterback carries the ball, running from one spot to another, and the linemen block, etc. Thus, the group's act is in some sense "reducible" to the acts of the members. Nevertheless, when the members behave in the specified way, it is correct to say that the team has executed a certain play. No *individual* executes the play. The *team* does it.[8]

According to common sense, groups do things. Furthermore, according to common sense, groups have options. In many case, various alternative group actions are somehow available to the group. Consider an election. Suppose Smith and Jones are running. Suppose every voter is free to vote as he or she pleases. Each can vote for Smith, and each can vote for Jones. Clearly, then, the group can elect Smith and the group can elect Jones. Assuming standard voting practices, the group cannot elect *both*, but it can elect either candidate. Similar considerations apply to a football team. They can execute a certain pass play in a certain situation, and they can also execute a certain running play. Other plays may be conceivable, but beyond the collective power of the team. They can't execute these.

In 2.1.1—4, I introduced and explained a concept that I called 'accessibility'. Using that concept, we can say that, at some time, some possible world is accessible to some person from some world. Roughly, the idea is that a world is accessible to a person at a time if and only if he can still see to it at that time that that world is actual, or occurs. Since there are groups, and they can do various things, we can say that worlds are accessible to groups, too. So, for example, if a certain social group is holding an election, and two candidates are running, and the group can elect either, then we should say that a world in which the first candidate is elected is accessible to the group, and a world in which the second candidate is elected is also accessible to the group. If the group has standard voting procedures, no world in which both candidates are elected is accessible to the group.

Let us use GAk, t, w', w to abbreviate 'world w' is accessible to social group k at time t from world w', and let us refer to this concept of accessibility as 'group accessibility'. The concept of group accessibility has the same logic as the old concept of individual accessibility. It is transitive, reflexive, and symmetric (in slightly extended senses of these expressions. For an explanation, see 2.1.2). Anything that is accessible at a time to a group was accessible to that group at all previous times. As time goes by, less and less is accessible.

Making use of this undefined concept of accessibility, we can define a concept of the "group can do":

GK: GKk, t, p is true in $w =$ df. $(Ew')(GAk, t, w', w$ & p is true at $w')$

In other words, a group can still see to the occurrence of a state of affairs provided that there is a world still accessible to the group in which that state of affairs occurs.

We can also define a concept of unalterability applicable to groups:

GU: GUk, t, p is true in w = df. (w') (GAk, t, w', $w \rightarrow p$ is true in w')

Aside from the fact that these concepts are defined only for the case in which the "agent" is a social group, they are just like the corresponding concepts of individual possibility and unalterability, which were explained in 2.1.3.

The relations between individual and group accessibility may be somewhat surprising. One attractive but false principle is this:

*A1: GAk, t, w', $w \rightarrow$ (s) (s in K $\rightarrow$ As, t, w', w)

This says that the worlds that are group accessible to a group are individually accessible to each member of that group. *A1 is false. A group of voters might have it in its power to elect a certain candidate. However, if the group is not going to elect that candidate, and a certain member can't influence the votes of his fellow citizens, then that member does not have it in his power to elect that candidate. So a world is which that candidate is elected is accessible to the group, but not to that member.

Obviously, if *A1 is false, then the corresponding "can do" principle is also false. From GKk, t, p we may not infer that for any s in k, Ks, t, p. From the fact that group (collectively) can see to the election of a certain candidate, it does not follow that each member (individually) can see to the election of that candidate.

Furthermore, from the fact that we can do it, it does not follow that any of us can do it. We must also reject this principle:

*A2: GAk, t, w', $w \rightarrow$ (Es) (s in k & As, t, w', w)

The same example should explain what's wrong with *A2, too. Suppose that the group can elect a certain candidate, but in fact won't. No member can influence the vote of any other and no single member can, by changing his own vote or by doing anything else, insure the election of the candidate in question. Then a world in which that candidate is elected is accessible to the group, but not to any member.

In light of this, we also have to reject·the claim that GK k, t, p entails (Es) (s in k & Ks, t, p).

Some people find it hard too see how *A2 can be false. ('How can a group see to the occurrence of a state of affairs,' you might ask, 'if no member can see to its occurrence?' As I see it, the question is little more than an invitation to comment on the fallacy of division. One might just as well ask how a group can weigh over a ton, when no member weighs anywhere near a ton.

Perhaps another example will help to clarify the point. Suppose some people have been driving in a car. It runs out of gas at the bottom of a hill. There's a gas station at the top. If every member of the group pushes, they will be able to push the car to the top of the hill, but if any one of them tries to do it alone, he will fail. Each member of the group can push, but in fact none of them is going to. There's nothing any one of them can do that will make the others join in a cooperative effort. Thus, it appears that the group is able to push the car to the top, but no member of the group is able to push the car to the top.

As I see it, this shows that there might be a world accessible to a certain group at a certain time, but inaccessible to each member of that group. So *A2 is false.

It might appear, then, that there is no interesting connection between individual and group accessibility. In fact, however, there are some true principles relating these notions. One of them is this:

A3:   As, t, w', w → (k) (s in k → GAk, t, w', w)

In other words, if a certain world is accessible to a certain individual, then that world is group accessible to every group of which the individual is a member. If I can see to the election of a certain candidate, then the electorate (of which I am a member) can see to that candidate's election.

It's not too hard to see why A3 is true. Suppose I am a voter and a member of the electorate. Suppose I have it in my power to see to the election of a certain candidate. It's not that I have lots of influence over other voters. Rather, it's just that enough others are going to vote for this candidate so that I will be able to assure his election merely by casting my own vote for him. Thus, there is some pattern of behavior open to me such that, if I follow it out, this candidate will be elected. Now consider the complex pattern of behavior that the electorate as a whole follows in some accessible world in which I do see to the election of the candidate. That pattern consists (loosely) of my voting for him, and their doing all the things they all would be doing if I were to see to his election. Clearly, that complex pattern of behavior must be possible for the group — after all, it's just the pattern of behavior they would follow if I were to vote for the candidate of my choice, and I can vote for him.

If we make one not-too-implausible assumption, we can identify another interesting connection between individual and group accessibility. The assumption is that each person constitutes a minimal social group all by himself. Then, for any person, s, $\{s\}$ is a social group. The interesting connection is captured by this principle:

A4: $A s, t, w', w \leftrightarrow GA\{s\}, t, w', w$

This just says that a world is accessible to an individual if and only if it is group accessible to the minimal social group of which that individual is the sole member. It does not seem to me that A4 sheds a whole lot of light on either concept of accessibility, nor is it entirely clear to me that each individual does constitute a social group. So my commitment to A4 is tenuous.

We must not suppose that the conjunction of the things individually possible for some individuals must be collectively possible for the group consisting of just those individuals. That is, we have to be careful to reject this:

*A5: $Ks, t, p \& Ks', t, q \rightarrow GK\{s, s'\}, t, p \& q$

Suppose we are the only voters and neither of us is going to vote for Smith, although each of us could. Then I can cast the sole vote for Smith, and you can cast the sole vote for Smith. However, we as a pair cannot bring about the state of affairs in which I cast the sole vote for Smith and you also cast the sole vote for Smith. So *A5 is false.

7.4.2. *Group Moral Obligation*

If we assume that there are social groups, and that they can do various things, then we face the question what these groups *should* do. My answer, as might be expected, is that social groups should do the best they can. So if we are talking about moral obligation, my view is that what a group morally ought to do is just what it does in the intrinsically best worlds accessible to it. More strictly, I want to maintain this thesis about group moral obligation:

GMO: GMOk, t, p is true at w iff $(\text{E}w')\,(\text{GA}k, t, w', w$ & p is true at w' & $\sim(\text{E}w'')\,(\text{GA}k, t, w'', w$ & $\sim p$ is true at w'' & $\text{IV}(w'') \geqslant \text{IV}(w'))$

A group has a group moral obligation to see to a state of affairs if there is some world accessible to the group in which that state of affairs occurs such that there is no intrinsically as good world in which it fails to occur.

Aside from the fact that this concept applies only to groups, and MO applies only to individuals, the two concepts are virtually indistinguishable. The logical features of GMO are just like those of MO. I shall not burden the reader with a detailed account of the deontic principles true of GMO. The application of GMO should be clear enough. Suppose the citizens of the United States are about to elect a new President. Suppose they can elect Smith, and the world as a whole would be best off it they were to do so. Then the electorate has a group moral obligation to elect Smith.

GMO thus constitutes another concept of obligation that is explicated by appeal to a concept of possibility and a concept of value. The value concept here is the same as the one used in MO — intrinsic value. The concept of possibility is new. It is group accessibility.

So far as I can tell, there just isn't any interesting connection between what an individual morally ought to do and what his various social groups morally ought to do. It should be clear, for example, that this principle is false:

*GMO/MO: GMOk, t, $p \rightarrow (s)\,(s$ in $k \rightarrow \text{MO}s, t, p)$

In the best world accessible to the group, a certain candidate may be elected. So the group ought to elect him. Yet it may also be true that the group is not going to elect him, and a certain member, s, cannot influence his fellow citizens. There is nothing s can do to get them to vote for the best candidate. In other words, no world in which that candidate is elected is accessible to s. Hence, it is not the case that s morally ought to see to the election of that candidate.

A weaker principle is also false:

*GMO/MO':   GMOk, t, $p \rightarrow (\text{E}\,s)\,(s$ in k & $\text{MO}s, t, p)$

Suppose again that the group ought to elect a certain candidate, but isn't going to do so. Suppose no memeber can influence the vote of his fellow citizens. Then the group has a group moral obligation to see to the election of the best candidate, but no member has an individual moral obligation to do so.

Principles in the other direction seems to fail, too. Consider the case in which every member of a certain group ought to do a certain thing. It might appear, then, that the group as a whole ought to do it. Strangely, this result does not follow. More precisely, what I want to reject is this:

$$*MO/GMO: \quad (s)(s \text{ in } k \rightarrow MO\,s, t, p) \rightarrow GMO\,k, t, p$$

To see why *MO/GMO is false, consider this example. Suppose a little social group, k, is composed of just two members, v1 and v2. Suppose they are going to vote for President, and their best choice would be to cast two votes for Smith. Suppose in fact each is going to vote for Jones, and neither can influence the other's vote. Suppose a split vote would be very bad, while two votes for Jones would not be so bad. Then each should vote for Jones, but the group should cast two votes for Smith. Hence, if we let p be 'a vote for Jones is cast', we have a counterexample to *MO/GMO.

If A4 (a few pages back) is true, then there is one very tight, but pretty trivial connection between these two concepts of obligation. It is this:

$$MO/GMO': \quad MO\,s, t, p \leftrightarrow GMO\{s\}, t, p.$$

7.4.3. *Group Prudential Obligation*

GMO is another "doing the best we can" concept of obligation. In this case, the value concept is intrinsic value, but the concept of possibility is the somewhat novel concept of group accessibility.

There is a tradition according to which political entities have no duty to look out for the welfare of the world as a whole or for the welfare of other political entities. According to this tradition, each such politicial entity has a sort of prudential obligation to enhance its own welfare.[9] On the international scene, the law of the jungle prevails. Each society has a fundamental obligation to maximize its own welfare. Let us consider one way of formulating a version of this view.

I suggest about that we can assume that if a social group exists at a possible world, then that group enjoys or suffers a certain share of that world's intrinsic goods and evils. Although it would undoubtedly be very difficult to measure such a thing, let us assume that there is a measure of this "share of intrinsic value". We can call this the group's "intrinsic welfare" at that world.

By substituting intrinsic welfare for total intrinsic value in GMO, we get a concept of group prudential obligation. The fundamental principle is this:

GPO: GPOk, t, p is true at w iff (Ew') $(GAk$, t, w', w & p is true at w' & $\sim(Ew'')$ $(GAk$, t, w'', w & $\sim p$ is true at w'' & the intrinsic welfare of k at w'' is as great as the instrinsic welfare of k at $w'))$

The idea behind GPO is that each group has a duty to maximize its own intrinsic welfare. The group prudentially ought to see to the things that occur in the best-for-it accessible worlds.

7.4.4. Civic Obligation

With the concept of group prudential obligation at hand, we may now proceed to the development of a concept of individual obligation that will indeed verify PMH. I call this "civic obligation". It may appear at first that there is little difference between civic obligation and social obligation, but, as I will show shortly, these concepts are in fact utterly unlike one another. Consideration of an example will serve to introduce civic obligation. Suppose a football team is in the midst of a crucial game. In order to win, and thereby maximize the team's intrinsic welfare, it will be necessary for the team to run a certain play. The pass receivers will have to run downfield in certain patterns, the linemen will have to block their opponents in certain ways, and the quarterback will have to wait until the proper moment, and then pass the ball to a certain receiver. If each does his part properly, the play will succeed and the team will win the game. Any other play will fail. Thus the team has a group prudential obligation to run just this play.

In this sort of case, it seems fairly natural to say that the linemen ought to block, the pass receivers ought to run their patterns, and the quarterback ought to throw the pass. After all, the team has a group prudential obligation to run the play, and the team can run the play only if the players perform their parts. Thus, relative to the team, each player seems to have some sort of obligation to do his part.

The sort of obligation in question here is what I call 'civic obligation'. Each player in the example has a civic obligation, relative to the team, to do his part in the collective action that is the team's group prudential obligation. More generally, we can say that if s is a member of some social group, k, and k has a group prudential obligation to see to some state of affairs, p, and k cannot see to p unless s sees to q, then s has a civic obligation, relative to k, to see to q. The official account of this notion is this:

> CVO: CVOs, t, k, p is true at w iff (i) k is a social group in w, and (ii) s is a member of k, (iii) GPOk, t, q is true in w, and (iv) necessarily, if q occurs, then s sees to p.

A simple voting example may serve to make the idea behind CVO clearer. Suppose there is a little group consisting of just two voters, v1 and v2. Suppose this group would be best off if both members voted for Smith. Then the group has a group prudential obligation to see to it that v1 votes for Smith and v2 votes for Smith. Clearly, the group cannot see to this compound state of affairs unless v1 sees to it that v1 votes for Smith. Thus, v1 has a civic obligation, relative to this little group, to vote for Smith.

A version of PMH is verified by this latest concept of obligation. In this form, the principle says that civic obligations harmonize. More exactly, the principle says that if every member of a social group sees to all of his civic obligations relative to the group during some period of time, then the intrinsic welfare of the group will be maximized. There is no other pattern of behavior available to the members of the group during that time which would have a more salutary influence on the group's intrinsic welfare.

A possible objection to this version of PMH should pershaps be mentioned.[10] Consider a group of ten voters, v1—v10. Suppose the group has a group prudential obligation to cast exactly nine votes for Smith. Suppose further that it doesn't matter which nine vote for Smith, and which one votes against him. The only thing that matters is that exactly nine vote for Smith. In this case, it seems, the group has a group prudential obligation to cast nine votes for Smith, but it is not the case that there is some subgroup of nine members each of whom has a civic obligation to vote for Smith. Each voter can truly claim that the group will be able to do its group prudential obligation without his assistance. Thus, no member of the group has a civic obligation to vote for Smith. Doesn't this show that even civic obligations may fail to harmonize?

I think that the example does not refute the current version of PMH. It is correct to conclude in this example that no member of the group has a civic obligation to vote for Smith. Each voter is such that the group can achieve its best outcome without his vote. However, this does not show that PMH is false. We must notice that each member of the group has a civic obligation to see to it that exactly nine votes are cast for Smith. You can see that each member has this duty by reflecting on CVO. The group has a group prudential obligation to see to it that nine votes are cast for Smith. Necessarily, if nine votes are cast for Smith, then nine votes are cast for Smith. So each member has a civic obligation, relative to the group, to see to it that this happens. Precisely how they do it does not matter. What matters is that each member must see to it that some group of nine votes for Smith. If every member of the group fulfils this civic obligation, then some nine-membered subset of the group will vote for Smith, and the group will be best off. Thus, the objection fails. Civic obligations do harmonize.

This does constitute a sort of vindication for PMH. We have found a sort of obligation that harmonizes. But questions remain: How serious are these obligations? Ought we to be concerned about our civic obligations? Is civic obligation a most important sort of obligation?

It seems to me that civic obligation is a very strange sort of obligation. One respect in which it differs from every other sort of obligation we have so far discussed is this: the Kantian dictum ("ought implies can") fails for civic obligation. We must reject this principle:

*OK/CVO: CVO$s, k, t, p \to$ Ks, t, p

To see that *OK/CVO is false, consider the football example again. Suppose I am the player who would receive the pass if our team ran the play most in its self interest. The team has a group prudential obligation to run the play, and to see to it that I catch the pass. But suppose the quarterback calls a different play — one in which no pass in thrown. Suppose further that the other players are determined to run the play as called. Nothing I can do will get them to run the more beneficial pass play. In this case, no pass is thrown. No world is accessible to me in which I receive the pass. Hence, I cannot see to my civic obligation relative to my team.

A second odd feature of CVO has to do with conflicts of obligation. We saw above in Chapter 2 that MO-obligations cannot conflict. This "no conflicts" principle can be formulated in several ways, but perhaps the most typical is:

NC/MO: MO$s, t, p$ & MO$s, t, q \rightarrow$ Ks, t, p & q

Given the proposed analysis of MO, it is clear that NC/MO will have to be true. If p is true at all the best accessible worlds, and q is also true at all the best accessible worlds, then p & q is true at some accessible worlds.

The corresponding CVO-version of the "no conflicts" principle is obviously false:

*NC/CVO: CVOs, t, k, p & CVO$s, t, k, q \rightarrow$ Ks, t, p & q

As we have just seen, there's no guarantee that *any* civic obligation will be possible, and so there's no hope that conjunctions of civic obligations will always be possible. We have to find another way of expressing the "no conflicts" principle.

Perhaps we can capture the fundamental idea here by saying that it will never be the case that someone has logically incompatible civic obligations. The revised principle would be:

NC/CVO: CVOs, t, k, p & CVO$s, k, t, q \rightarrow \Diamond (p$ & $q)$

If, in order for k to do its group prudential obligation, you must see to p, and furthermore, in order for k to do its group prudential obligation, you must also see to q, then p and q must be logically consistent. So long as we hold t and k constant, this principle is true.

Nevertheless, it seems to me that CVO runs into trouble with respect to conflicts of obligation. The problem is that each person is simultaneously a member of very many different social groups. For example, you might be a member of the faculty union at a school, but also a member of the school board, and also a member of the PTA. Relative to one of these groups, it might be your civic obligation to go on strike. Relative to another group, it might be your civic obligation to accept the proposed contract. Thus, we can have cases in which there are two groups, k1 and k2, such that some individual, s, is a member of both, and CVO$s, t, $k1$, p$ and CVO$s, t, $k2$, \sim p$.

I am not here suggesting that there is some formal difficulty concerning CVO. Rather, the problem is a moral one. Suppose someone maintains that my most important obligations are my civic obligations. What I really ought to do, according to this person, is what I civically ought to do. This advocate of CVO now faces a most serious problem: he has to tell me *which* of my incompatible civic obligations are the ones I ought to carry out. In other words, he has to tell me which, of the many social groups to which I belong, is the one that carries the moral weight. Which of these groups is the one such that I ought to carry out my social obligations relative to it?

Perhaps the most serious problem for CVO concerns what happens in cases of partial compliance. Reconsideration of the possibility of "spoilers" in a voting example should make the problem clear. Suppose a group, k, consisting of ten voters is about to vote in a very important election. Smith and Jones are the only candidates. Suppose k would be best off if every voter voted for Smith. Suppose k would be slightly less well off if all voted for Jones. Suppose k would suffer eternal torment if there were a split vote. In this case, $v1$ has a civic obligation, relative to k, to vote for Smith. That's what $v1$ does in the best-for-k worlds accessible to k. However, it may also turn out that every other member of k is going to vote for Jones, and nothing $v1$ can do will alter their votes. In this case, if $v1$ carries out his civic obligation relative to k, k will get the worst of all possible outcomes.

Clearly, in cases of partial compliance, doing your civic obligation relative to a group may be detrimental to the intrinsic welfare of the group. Since partial compliance seems to be a near-universal fact of life, one wonders why anyone would think that we ought to carry out our civic obligations.

Let me now make clear my conclusions concerning CVO. This concept of obligation does verify a version of the Principle of Moral Harmony. However, it is a very strange concept of obligation. It conflicts with the thesis that 'ought' implies 'can'. It faces certain difficulties concerning conflicts of obligation. It directs us to do counter-productive things in cases of partial compliance. Thus, as I see it, the fact that CVO verifies PMH does not show PMH to be a *more* plausible moral doctrine. Rather, it casts some doubt on the accept-ability of PMH. If the only sort of obligation that verifies PMH is this weird thing, then so much the worse for PMH.

7.5. THE 'OUGHT' OF COOPERATIVE UTILITARIANISM

In a most impressive recent book, Donald Regan developed and defended a novel concept of obligation.[11] In certain respects, this concept of obligation is a clear improvement over CVO. Central among these is that while it does verify a version of the principle of moral harmony, it does not run into difficulty in cases of partial compliance. It deserves attention here.

I noted above that, when your compatriots are not doing their parts the best group action, it may make no sense for you to do your part in it. Why run out for a pass when the quarterback is not going to throw it? Why vote for Smith when your vote will only ruin the chances for a moderately beneficial Jones landslide? These examples point out a serious deficiency in CVO. CVO requires me, relative to each group, to do my part in the best group action open to the group — regardless of the behavior of others.

7.5.1. *Cooperative Utilitarianism*

It might seem that it would make much more sense to be more sensitive to what the others are going to do. Far better results could be assured if, instead of following CVO, the agent would determine what his group-mates are going to do, and then choose for himself the best available act, given the behavior of the others. Consider the football example again. Assume that even though a pass would be most advantageous for the team, the rest of the team is going to execute a certain running play. In this case, I will only be a spoiler if I go out for the pass. Better results will be achieved if I do my part in the running play. Admittedly, if I do this, the group will not be able to achieve its best possible outcome. However, that outcome seems unattainable anyway. Nothing I can do would assure it.

In a slightly different example, suppose I'm not the only one willing to do his best for the team. A few other players are also willing to coordinate their behavior in order to achieve the team's best outcome. Unfortunately, not all other team members are prepared to be cooperative. Some are set on executing a less-than-ideal running play. What should the cooperators do? Clearly, they would be wasting their energy if they cooperatively participated in the team's best choice, the pass play. The problem, once again, is that since some players will not cooperate, this play will surely fail. A better idea would be for the cooperators to recognize each other as potential cooperators; for them to identify the noncooperators; for them to identify the behavior of the noncooperators; for them to identify the best course of action for the cooperators, given the anticipated behavior of the noncooperators; and then to do their parts in this best course.

This little football scenario displays, with only some trivial differences, the fundamental idea behind Regan's theory of co-operative utilitarianism. He summarizes the view as follows:

> According to the theory I call 'co-operative utilitarianism' (hereafter 'CU') what each agent ought to do is to co-operate, with whoever else is co-operating, in the production of the best consequences possible given the behavior of non-co-operators.[12]

In another place, Regan presents a much more detailed account of his theory. He distinguishes five main steps that an agent must follow if he is to be in accord with CU. The steps are:

> ... *first*, he should be willing to take part in a joint attempt to produce the best consequences possible by co-ordinating his behavior with the behavior of other agents who are also willing. That is, he should hold himself ready to do his part in the best pattern of behavior for the group of co-operators, whoever precisely the other members of that group turn out to be. *Second*, he should consider the other agents involved in the co-ordination problem he is making a decision about and determine which of those other agents are available to be co-operated with ... *Third*, he should assertain how other agents who are *not* ... available to be co-operated with are behaving or are disposed to behave. *Fourth*, the should identify the best pattern of behaviour for the group of co-operators. *Fifth*, he should do his part in the best pattern of behaviour just identified.[13]

Let's slightly modify and abbreviate Regan's proposal. Let's say that a person "follows the procedure" relative to a group, k, if and only if he (i) first holds himself ready to cooperate with other members of k, then (ii) identifies other cooperators in k, then (iii) identifies the impending behavior of non-cooperators in k, then (iv) identifies the best group act for cooperators, given the expected behavior of non-cooperators, and then finally, after going back through steps (iii) and (iv) to be sure that no one has changed his plan of action, (v) does his part in that group act.

Now we can introduce a new concept of obligation, based on this procedure.

CUO: S cooperatively ought, as of t, relative to k, to see to p (CUOs, t, k, p) iff necessarily, if s follows the procedure relative to k at t, then s sees to p.

Regan draws an important, if somewhat obsure distinction between "act-oriented" and "procedural" theories.[14] Virtually all traditional normative theories are act-oriented. Such theories purport to give necessary and sufficient conditions for an act's being morally right, or obligatory. They do not specify the procedure one must use to choose the act. MO seems to be an act-oriented theory since it tells us to do what we do in the intrinsically best accessible worlds. It does not tell us how to discover which worlds are accessible, nor does it tell us how to figure out how much each is worth.

Regan's theory is different. Its whole point is to specify the procedure that must be followed in every case of moral choice. He is not claiming that our moral duty is to perform the act that would be selected if the specified procedure were followed. Rather, he is claiming that our moral duty is to follow the procedure.

By appeal to an ingenious argument,[15] Regan shows (in effect) that the act-oriented variant of his own view does not verify the principle of moral harmony. To see this, consider a typical voting case. Suppose two votes for Smith would be best, two votes for Jones would be intermediate, and a split vote would be worst. Suppose there are two voters, v1 and v2. Suppose each voter is going to vote for the second-best candidate, Jones. In this example, each voter is such that if he were to vote for Smith, he would cast the sole vote for Smith, and thereby produce a tie — the worst possible outcome.

Now consider the act that v1 would perform if he were to follow Regan's procedure. He would discover (to his dismay) that v2 is not cooperating and is going to vote for Jones. He would then recognize that his own best choice, under the circumstances, is to vote for Jones. After all, a vote for the better candidate, Smith, would only produce a split vote. Then he would vote for Jones. Similiar considerations apply to v2. Thus, if each voter votes as he would have voted if he had followed the procedure, each voter votes for Jones, and the group ends up with the second-best outcome. This shows that the act-oriented variant of Regan's view does not verify PMH.

On the other hand, suppose each voter in fact adheres to Regan's view, and actually follows the specified procedure. In this case, v1 first holds himself ready to cooperate. Then he scouts around to see who else is willing to cooperate. He discovers that v2 is one such. Each then recognizes that the best group act for $\{v1, v2\}$ is the one they perform when they cast two votes for Smith. Each then does his part, and Smith wins in a landslide. The group gets the best possible outcome. So the 'ought' of Regan's cooperative utilitarianism, in virtue of this procedural feature, verifies a version of the principle of moral harmony. If every member of a group acts in accordance with the specified procedure, the group will secure the best possible outcome.[16]

It should be clear that Regan's view does not run into trouble in cases of partial compliance. To see this, suppose the group is a football team. Suppose the team's best choice would be a certain pass play. Suppose five team-members are unwilling to participate in that play. The remaining six members are more open-minded. They are Reganians. Each of them then holds himself ready to cooperate. Each recognizes each other as a potential cooperator. Each also recognizes the non-cooperators, and identifies the impending behavior of the non-cooperators. In light of this, each then locates the best course of behavior for the Reganians and (after ascertaining that the others are going to do their parts) does his part in the most beneficial pattern of behavior for the cooperators, given the behavior of the non-cooperators. Perhaps this will be a running play. In this case, nobody pointlessly does his part in the play that would have been best if all had co-operated. Rather, each does his part in the play that in fact will be best, given that some are intent on being uncooperative. Thus, in cases of partial compliance, those who abide by CUO collectively do the best they can, given the unfortunate behavior of those who don't. In this respect, CUO seems superior to CVO.

7.5.2. Problems for CUO

Regan's proposal has been subjected to the most penetrating sort of criticism. In a review[7] Blake Barley pointed out that Regan's theory violates the Kantian dictum about 'ought' and 'can'. According to Regan, there is a certain procedure that each person ought to follow, in every situation of moral choice. Clearly, however, it is possible for there to be a person capable of moral choice, but incapable of following Regan's procedure. A good, if farfetched example would be the example of a person incapable, as a result of the implantation of electrodes in the brain, of entertaining some of the beliefs one must entertain in order to follow Regan's procedure.

Even ordinary people will have trouble following CUO. If you are a member of a very large group, and you are not acquainted with all the other members, then you may not be able to form all the beliefs you must form in order to follow the procedure. For example, if you have no knowledge whatsoever of Smith, it may be impossible for you to believe that Smith is a cooperator. But CUO requires that, for every cooperator, x, you believe that x is a cooperator.[18]

Another problem for Regan's view[19] concerns cases in which following the procedure would independently lead to terrible consequences. Regan's "mad telepath" case illustrates the point.[20] Suppose a mad telepath can read your mind, and is bent on blowing up Macy's if you follow the Reganian procedure. Utilitarian intuitions suggest that, in this strange case, it would be best not to follow the procedure. Although Regan discusses the case at some length[21] it is hard to see just how he proposes to answer the objection.

Some readers will not be impressed by examples involving mad telepaths. Such readers are invited to consider the general point of the objection. CUO requires that a certain procedure be followed in absolutely every case. Surely there can be ordinary cases in which following the procedure will be counterproductive. For example, consider any case in which time is of the essence, and following the procedure will take too much time.[22] The mad telepath example is farfetched, but the general point behind it is not.

It seems to me that Regan's theory is open to yet another sort of objection. This objection also involves the Kantian dictum. Suppose a certain group has two subgroups. One subgroup consists of Reganian cooperators. The second subgroup consists of "disruptors". These are people who steadfastly adhere to a procedural theory much like Regan's. However, instead of going through the procedure and then cooperatively performing their best group act, given the behavior of non-cooperators, the disruptors go through the procedure and then attempt to perform their *worst* possible group act, given the behavior of the others.

Now let us consider what happens when the members of such a mixed group find themselves in some situation of moral choice. Each cooperator will hold himself ready to cooperate, and then will identify all the other cooperators. Next, the cooperators are supposed to recognize the non-cooperators, and identify their impending behavior. But here's the rub. In the present case, the non-cooperators are all disruptors. They have been going through a procedure of their own. At this point, each disruptor has identified the other disruptors, as well as the cooperators. However, the disruptors will steadfastly refuse to settle on any plan of action until they have identified the impending behavior of the cooperators. Thus, the disruptors have not settled on any plan of action, and so it will be impossible for the cooperators to identify that plan, and make their own plans accordingly.

If the cooperators form a tentative plan, (or "current best plan"), the disruptors will identify it and formulate a "current worst plan" of their own. The CWP will be selected in such a way as to make the CBP backfire. If the cooperators revise their CBP in light of the disruptors' tentative CWP, the disruptors will have to do likewise. Clearly, then, in a case such as this, each subgroup will continue looping back through the procedure, and neither will ever be able to reach the final stage. This shows yet another sort of case in which CUO violates the Kantian dictum. When disruptors are present, it will be impossible to do all the things required by the Reganian procedure.[23]

I think that these considerations establish that CUO is a very strange and implausible concept of obligation. Perhaps some will think that no more needs to be said about it. Nevertheless, I want to consider Regan's view from another perspective. Specifically, I want to focus more narrowly on the question whether there are cases in which satisfaction of CUO would yield better results than satisfaction of a more familiar view. This seems to be the central claim that can be made on behalf of cooperative utilitarianism. If (as I believe) it cannot be sustained, then we will be justified in sticking with the more traditional sort of view illustrated by MO, even though MO doesn't verify PMH.

7.5.3. *MO and CUO*

My own view is that individual moral obligations are specified by MO. Individuals morally ought to do the best they can. According to cooperative utilitarianism, each individual morally ought to follow the Reganian procedure in every situation of moral choice. Regan has suggested that cooperative utilitarianism has one central advantage over any view such as mine. The alleged advantage he calls "adaptability". To say that a normative theory is adaptable is to say that in any case in which a subgroup of a group satisfies the theory, the subgroup will produce, by their satisfaction of the theory, the best results possible given the behavior of the non-satisfiers.[24]

Let us attempt to recast the issue in terms of MO and CUO. MO is not adaptable. There are cases in which every member of a group satisfies MO, but the group fails to achieve the best possible results. CUO does not have this defect. In every case in which every member of a group satisfies CUO, the group achieves the best results possible. Thus, it would be natural to conclude that there are cases in which the results of satisfying CUO would be better than the results of satisfying MO. Are there any such cases?

Let's consider a case of the sort Regan used in this context.[25] Suppose there is a little group, k, consisting of two voters, v1 and v2. Suppose the best outcome would be achieved if both voted for Smith; the second best outcome would be achieved if both voted for Jones; and the worst outcome would be achieved if one voted for Smith and one for Jones. Suppose that each voter is able to vote for either candidate, but in fact is going to vote for the less good candidate, Jones.

It appears that when both proceed to vote for Jones, both satisfy MO. The appearance is backed by the following reasoning. Since v2 is going to vote for Jones, v1 has two choices. Either he votes alone for Smith, and thereby produces the worst outcome, or he joins v2 in voting for Jones, and thereby helps to produce the second best possible outcome. MO seems to imply that v1 ought to vote for Jones. Similar considerations apply to v2. Hence (it might seem) in this case both voters satisfy MO by voting for Jones, and the group ends up with a less-than-ideal result.[26]

It might appear that better results would be achieved if both voters were to satisfy CUO in this case. For if both satisfy CUO, each will identify the other as a potential cooperator; each will recognize that two votes for Smith will be best; and each will go on to vote for Smith. The group will end up with the best possible outcome. Thus, it appears that joint satisfaction of CUO in this case produces better results than joint satisfaction of MO.

It seems to me, however, that the argument does not succeed. The central problem turns on the question whether, in the case described, both voters have in fact satisfied MO. It is not clear to me that they have. In order to clarify the point, let me draw a distinction. We can say that voter is "intransigent for" a candidate if he is going to vote for that candidate, and will vote for that candidate no matter what anyone else does. Although an intransigent voter is able to vote for another candidate, no one else can get him to do so. In terms of accessibility, we can put this point by saying that there are worlds accessible to the voter in which he votes for another candidate, but there are no worlds accessible to anyone else in which he (the intransigent voter) votes for another candidate. On the other hand, we can say that a voter is "open-minded" if he is prepared to change his voting plans if it should turn out that a change would be for the best.

In the description of the example, I stated that both voters were going to vote for Jones, but I failed to mention whether they were intransigently for Jones, or open-minded and planning to vote for Jones. Let's consider the main possibilities.

Case One. Assume that both voters are intransigently for Jones. Look at the example from the perspective of v1. No matter what v1 does, v2 will vote for Jones. Thus, v1 has two main choices. In some accessible worlds, he votes for the better candidate, Smith. However, in all such worlds, he casts the sole vote for Smith, and worst results are produced. On the other hand, in some other accessible worlds, he joins v2, and votes for the lesser candidate, Jones. In these worlds, better results are secured. Similar considerations apply to v2. Each voter is such that in the best worlds accessible to him, he votes for Jones. Hence, when both voters are intransigent for Jones, MO indeed does approve of their votes.

What does CUO say about this case? In order to satisfy CUO, each voter must be prepared to cooperate. Since, as the case has been described, each voter is intransigently for Jones, we can see that neither satisfies CUO in this case. Each violates the first step of the Reganian procedure. Thus, it is impossible to assess the results of joint satisfaction of CUO in Case One. CUO cannot be satisfied in Case One. Let us consider a case in which CUO can be satisfied.

Case Two. Assume that both voters are open-mindedly for Jones. Now they can satisfy CUO. Consider the case from the perspective of v1. He first holds himself ready to engage in cooperation. He then notices that v2 is similarly prepared to cooperate, and that two votes for Smith would be their best choice. After looping back to be sure that everyone is on board, v1 votes for Smith. Smiliar considerations apply to v2. Best results are achieved.

Now let's see what happens when both voters satisfy MO in Case Two. Again consider the case from the perspective of v1. In some accessible worlds, v1 votes for Jones. In those, v2 adjusts his vote accordingly, and fairly good results are achieved by the group. In other worlds accessible to v1, he votes for Smith. Since v2 is open-minded, v2 also votes for Smith in these worlds and the group achieves best results. Similar considerations apply to v2. Hence, if both voters satisfy MO in Case Two, both voters vote for Smith, and best results are achieved.

Clearly, then the results of satisfying CUO in Case Two are no better than the results of satisfying MO in Case Two.

Case Three. Assume now that v2 is intransigent for Jones, and v1 is open-minded. Consider the case from the perspection of v1. In some accessible worlds, v1 votes for Smith. In these, worst results are achieved. In other accessible worlds, he joins v2 and votes for Jones. In these, better results are achieved. Since v2 is intransigently for Jones, there is no world accessible to v1 in which two votes are cast for Smith. Hence, v1 satisfies MO by voting for Jones. Second best results are achieved.

Clearly, v2 does not satisfy CUO in Case Two. What happens when v1 satisfies CUO? He scouts around and discovers that v2 is intransigent for Jones. He settles on a best plan according to which both vote for Jones. Finally, v1 votes for Jones, and second best results are achieved. Therefore, in Case Three, only v1 can satisfy either theory, and if he does satisfy either theory, second best results will be achieved.

This line of reasoning is rather complicated, and so it may be useful to summarize the conclusions. There are three main cases to consider:

Case One. Each voter is intransigent for Jones. Each voter satisfies MO by voting for Jones. Second best result are achieved. Neither voter satisfies CUO in this case as specified.

Case Two. Both voter are open-minded. If both satisfy MO, both vote for Smith, and best results are achieved. If both satisfy CUO, both vote for Smith, and best results are achieved.

Case Three. V1 is open-minded; v2 is intransigent for Jones. If v1 satisfies MO, he votes for Jones, and second-best results are achieved. If v1 satisfies CUO, he votes for Jones, and second-best results are achieved. In the case as specified, v2 does not satisfy either MO or CUO.

There are other cases that could be considered here. However, there is none in which CUO might be thought to yield better results than MO. Thus, my conclusion is that the alleged superiority of CUO is a mirage. It is created by comparing the results of satisfaction of MO in cases relevantly like Case One with the results of satisfaction of CUO in cases relevantly like Case Two. If we keep the cases constant, we will find that there is none in which satisfaction of CUO yields superior results.

There is only one further point that needs to be made concerning this example. It has to do with Case One. In Case One, each voter is intransigently for Jones, and each voter satisfies MO. Nevertheless, best results are not achieved. In the same case, when both voters vote for Jones, they violate CUO. It might seem that there is a certain advantage for CUO here. Since best results have not been achieved, it seems plausible to maintain that somebody must have done something wrong. Since both voters satisfied MO, we cannot locate any wrongdoing by appeal to MO. On the other hand, since they have violated CUO, we may be able to locate the wrongdoing in the case by appeal to CUO.

However, it is not clear to me that either voter does anything wrong in Case One. Consider v1. Admittedly, he was intransigently for the less-good candidate, Jones. However, since v2 was equally intransigent, no better results would have been achieved if v2 had been open-minded. Thus, under the circumstances, there is nothing wrong with v1's attitude. Similar considerations apply to v2.

As I see it, the error here was not committed by either voter. The error was committed by the group.[27] No world in which Smith wins in a landslide was accessible to either voter in Case One. Thus, neither voter is to be blamed for the less-than-ideal outcome. However, a world in which Smith wins in a landslide was accessible to the group − and the group failed to realize that world. Hence, in voting for Jones the group violated its group obligation. As I see it, this explains the sense that someone (or something) has violated some obligation in Case One.

Let me now draw some conclusions concerning MO and CUO. While CUO seems to verify a version of the principle of moral harmony, it is a very strange concept of obligation. It violates the Kantian dictum in several different ways. It requires us to follow to certain procedure even when following the procedure has horrible results. Finally, it seems that there is no case in which joint satisfaction of CUO by the members of a group would yield better results than would joint satisfaction of MO by the members of that same group.

Admittedly, there are cases (such as Case One above) in which joint satisfaction of MO will not guarantee best possible outcomes. Thus, MO conflicts with a version of PMH. CUO does not have these disappointing results in this case. However, CUO does not have *better* results in this case, either. Since CUO cannot be satisfied by either group member in this case, CUO has no results in Case Three.

7.6. MO AND GROUP WELFARE

At the beginning of this chapter, I raised several questions about utilitarianism and group welfare. The first of these was the question whether utilitarianism verifies PMH. In Section 1, I explained why my own neo-utilitarian concept of obligation, MO, fails to verify PMH. There are cases in which all the members of a group satisfy MO, but the group nevertheless fails to achieve its best possible outcome. Some may take this to be a defect in MO.

The second question was the question whether any plausible concept of obligation verifies PMH. In Section 3, I developed the concept of social obligation — a concept that might easily be taken to yield PMH. However, I went on to show that this concept also fails to verify PMH. In Section 4, I discussed some issues concerning the powers and obligations of groups, and then I introduced the concept of civic obligation. Civic obligation yields a version of PMH. However, civic obligation is a very odd sort of obligation. It violates the Kantian dictum. It runs into trouble with respect to conflicts of obligation. It generates absurd results in cases of partial compliance.

In Section 5, I discussed another concept of obligation that verifies PMH. This is Regan's CUO. I attempted to show that CUO is at least as strange as CVO. Furthermore, contrary to appearances, there is no case in which satisfaction of CUO yields better results than satisfaction of MO.

The third question was the question whether failure to verify PMH is a bad thing. By describing two sorts of obligation that verify PMH, I have suggested my view. Only some pretty odd concepts of obligation verify PMH. The fact that MO does not verify PMH does not reveal any defect in MO.

CHAPTER 8

WHAT OUGHT TO BE

Sometimes, instead of saying that a certain person ought to do a certain thing, we may say that a certain state of affairs ought to be, or ought to occur. For example, someone who is annoyed by loud motorcycles might say that there ought to be a law against such things. Someone who thinks government is getting corrupt might say that there should be more honesty in government. Someone who feels that the present distribution of wealth is unjust might say that there ought to be a more equal distribution of wealth in the world. Each of these could very well be a statement of the ought-to-be.

These statements differ from the more familiar statements of the ought-to-do. When someone says that the legislature ought to prohibit loud motorcycles, he makes use of the ought-to-do. His statement affirms some sort of connection between a certain agent (in this case, the legislature) and a certain state of affairs (in this case, the prohibition of loud motorcycles). The statement as a whole seems to affirm that the agent ought to see to the occurrence of the state of affairs.

Statements of the ought-to-be are, at least superficially, different in structure. Each such statement says of some state of affairs, that it ought to occur. It does not say that someone (or something) ought to see to its occurrence. Thus, the difference between the ought-to-be and the ought-to-do appears, roughly, to be a structural difference. The ought-to-do involves a relation between an agent and a state of affairs. The ought-to-be involves a property of a state of affairs.

In this chapter, I investigate the ought-to-be. In Section 1, I consider some attempts to explain the ought-to-be by appeal to the ought-to-do. I try to show that each such attempt fails. In Section 2, I give my own account. In Section 3, I explore the relations between the ought-to-be and the ought-to-do. I go on to consider the general principle that it ought to be that we do what we ought to do.

8.1. SOME PROPOSALS CONCERNING THE OUGHT-TO-BE

There is a persistent inclination to suppose that the difference between

179

the ought-to-be and the ought-to-do is nothing more than a trivial, stylistic difference. We might think, for example, that we tend to speak in the ought-to-do mode when we have some particular agent and some particular act in mind, and we tend to speak in the ought-to-be mode when we have no particular agent in mind, or when we have some state of affairs that is not an action in mind. Nevertheless, we might suppose, statements of the two sorts are, strictly speaking, directly intertranslatable.

It is important to recognize at the outset that this inclination, however natural, is not obviously correct. Statements of the ought-to-be cannot be understood directly as mere stylistic variants of more familiar statements of the ought-to-do. To see this, consider the following fairly typical example:

(1)   There ought to be a peaceful way of ending the arms race.

It should be clear that (1) is not simply a disguised statement of absolute moral or prudential obligation. Such statements are always person- or group-relative. They say, with respect to some person or group, that he or she or it ought to see to the occurrence of the state of affairs in question. But in the case of (1), there is apparently no person or group to which we can relativize.

Obviously, it would be wrong to understand (1) as a statement of absolute moral obligation directed at me now. That is, we cannot take (1) to mean that, as of now, I morally ought to see to it that there is a peaceful way of ending the arms race. For, even if there is some way of realizing this important goal, it is not something I can do. In my jargon, we can say that although there are plenty of possible worlds in which there is an amicable end to the arms race, no such world appears to be accessible to me from here. So I can't be obliged (morally or prudentially) to actualize one of them.

Even if we introduce quantifiers here, we cannot account for (1). Suppose, for example, that we let p abbreviate 'there is a peaceful way of ending the arms race', and we let n name now. Suppose we allow quantification into our absolute moral obligation operator, MO. Then we might take (1) to mean to same as:

(2) $(Es)(MOs, n, p)$

(2) says that there is someone, s, such that as of now, s ought to see to it that there is a peaceful way of ending the arms race. Who could this

be? Surely not you or me! Probably not even the President or the Secretary of State. Perhaps there is nothing any of us can do that would assure the occurrence of *p*. Maybe a lot depends on luck, such as the accidental coming-to-power of several individuals who happen to be well suited to mutual negotiation. So it appears that while (1) is true, (2) may be false.

It might naturally be thought that the 'ought' in a statement such as (1) serves to express group moral obligation, where the group is humanity as a whole.[1] That is, we might think that what ought to be is the same as what would be if humanity as a whole did the best it could.

This proposal might seem plausible in connection with examples such as (1), but there are other examples that make it seem somewhat less plausible. It seems to me that there are some states of affairs that ought to be, but which not even the joint efforts of the whole human race could secure. For example, consider the state of affairs of there being a more equitable distribution of natural resources in the world. It seems to me that this would be a good thing, and that it ought to happen. But nothing we can do will make it happen. Therefore, we have no group moral obligation to see to it. Similarly, there ought to be a cure for various horrible diseases, but maybe no one and no group is currently able to effect a cure. There ought to be fewer destructive tornadoes, hurricanes, and earthquakes. Surely, however, no person or group of persons has a duty to see to these things.

These reflections show, I believe, that the ought-to-be is not simply a stylistic variant of the ought-to-do. At least I hope I have said enough convince the reader that if there is some connection between the ought-to-be and the ought-to-do, it isn't connection that is immediately obvious. It needs to be discovered.

8.1.1. *Deontically Perfect Worlds and the Ought-to-be*

One proposed analysis of the ought-to-be is based on the concept of the "deontically perfect world". A world, *w'*, is deontically perfect relative to a world, *w*, provided that at least the following conditions are satisfied: (i) whatever is obligatory in *w* is actually done in *w'*; (ii) whatever is obligatory in *w'* is done in *w'*; and (iii) whatever is obligatory in *w* is also obligatory in *w'*. We can also assume that if something is obligatory in *w*, then there is at least one deontically perfect world, w', relative to w, in which that thing is obligatory and is done.[2]

Now we can say that what ought to be at a world is just what occurs at every deontically perfect world relative to it. In other words:

OB1:   OBp is true at w iff (w') $(w'$ is denotically perfect relative to $w \rightarrow p$ is true at $w')$

This approach is seriously flawed. The main problem seems to be that the concept of the deontically perfect world is of doubtful value. We have already seen that one person's obligations may shift from time to time.[3] As of now, the doctor ought to give A tomorrow. By tomorrow, maybe he'll have an obligation to avoid A tomorrow. Thus, there is no world in which the doctor fulfills all the obligations he ever has.

Equally, and perhaps more importantly, one person's obligations at a time may conflict with another person's obligations as of that same time. We have already considered a number of cases that illustrate this point.[4] Suppose it would be best if exactly one of us were to cast a vote for Smith. Suppose that in fact neither of us is going to vote for him, and neither of us can influence the other's vote. Then I ought to cast the sole vote for Smith, and you ought to cast the sole vote for Smith. While there are worlds in which we both vote for Smith, there are no worlds in which we jointly fulfill the specified obligations. That is, there is no world in which I cast the sole vote for Smith and you also cast the sole vote for Smith. Since these things are, ex hypothesi, obligatory here in the real world, we conclude that no world is deontically perfect relative to the real world.

A second problem with this approach is its circularity. Deontic perfection is defined in terms of obligation. That is, a deontically perfect world is one in which all *obligations* are fulfilled. In order to determine whether a world is deontically perfect relative to a given world, we have to know what's obligatory in the given world, among other things. This may be no defect for some projects, but if we hope to give a non-circular explication of some concept of obligation, it clearly would be a problem.

8.1.2. *"Best Worlds" and the Ought-to-be*

These difficulties are avoided by a second sort of approach. Instead of explaining the ought-to-be by appeal to the concept of obligation, we may attempt to explain it by appeal to the concept of intrinsic value. On one version of this view, we assume that for each possible world, there is a set of worlds evaluable from there. These worlds are alike in that they are subject to the same standards of evaluation, or can be ranked on the same scale of value. Otherwise, they may be as different as possible. We also assume that, of these evaluable worlds, each has some intrinsic value — positive, negative, or zero. We call a world a "best" relative to a given world if and only if it is evaluable from there, and no better world is also evaluable from there. Now we can say that what ought to be is what happens in all the bests. In other words:

OB2: $\text{OB}p$ is true at w iff $(w')(w'$ is a best relative to $w \rightarrow p$ is true at $w')$

On any plausible value system, however, OB2 yields the unfortunate result that everything ought to be. This is a consequence of the fact that, on such systems, there is no upper limit on the values worlds may have. For every world, no matter how good it may be, there is sure to be a better one. To see this, assume that some form of simple hedonism is true. It seems to be the case that, for any world, no matter how much pleasure is enjoyed there, there is sure to be another world in which more pleasure is enjoyed. We merely need to imagine that there are more people in the second world, or that there is more time for the people to enjoy the pleasures of that world. There is just no reason to assume that there has to be an upper limit to the amount of pleasure that can be enjoyed at a world. Thus, it appears that this axiological view implies that no world is a best relative to any world, and so (according to OB2) everything ought to be.

8.1.3. *Another Approach*

David Lewis has suggested that we will get an adequate semantics for certain systems of denotic logic if we let $\text{O}p$ be true at a world if and only if p is true "throughout a sphere around that world".[5] His idea, adapted to the present purpose, would have us define the ought-to-be in some fashion such as this:

OB3: $\text{OB}p$ is true at w iff $(\text{E}w')(w'$ is evaluable from w & p is true at w' & $\sim(\text{E}w'')(w''$ is evaluable from w & $\sim p$ is true at w'' & $\text{IV}w'' \geqslant \text{IV}w'))$

So even if there is no "best" relative to w, OBp may be true at w. All that's required is that, as the worlds evaluable from w get better and better, a point is reached at which p starts being true, and p is, "from there on up", never false again.

This proposal has been criticized by Alan McMichael.[6] He suggests that, on many standard theories of intrinsic value, OB3 yields unacceptable results. Take simple hedonism for example. Consider the statement, (1), that there ought to be a peaceful way of ending the arms race. This may seem to be true. We can represent it as OBp. Yet, if every evaluable possible world is to be counted, it would seem that for any world, no matter how good, if p is true at it, there is a better one in which p is false. The falsehood of p at a world does not seem to put any limit on the amount of pleasure that might be enjoyed there. As before, all we need to do is imagine a world with more people, or more time for them to have fun. Thus, OBp seems to come out false at the real world according to OB3. Most other typical examples would be treated similarly. So while OB3 may serve to define some interesting notion, it apparently does not define any recognizable concept of the ought-to-be.[7]

8.2. AN ANALYSIS OF THE OUGHT-TO-BE

I believe that at least some of the time when we say that something ought to be the case, what we mean is, roughly, that it would be the case if things turned as well as they still might. According to this view, we have to consider all the possible worlds that are still physically possible, and see what happens in the best of them. If p occurs in one of them, and $\sim p$ doesn't occur in any as good or better, then p ought to be. This way of understanding the ought-to-be makes it yet another concept of obligation explicable by appeal to a concept of possibility and a concept of value. The value concept here is intrinsic goodness again. The concept of possibility, however, is one I have not yet discussed. Thus, while it won't be necessary for me to say anything further about the concept of value, I will have to explain the concept of possibility.

When I say that a possible world is "still possible", I think I mean something like what some philosophers mean when they say that such a world is "physically possible". But this is a somewhat tangled topic.[8] We can use [P] and $\langle P \rangle$ as sentence operators to indicate physical necessity and possibility respectively. These are sometimes understood as follows: $\langle P \rangle p$ is true at a world, w, just in case p is true at some world with the same laws of nature as w. $[P]p$ is true at w iff p is true at every world with the same laws of nature as w.[9]

In my view, however, this account won't suffice. The problem, as I see it, is that what's physically possible at one time may fail to be so later. For example, consider some acorn. Suppose it is still viable. We may want to say that it is possible for it to grow into a mighty oak. Yet if a squirrel finds it, and nibbles on it, and it begins to rot and it dies, then we will no longer want to say that it is possible for it to grow into a mighty oak. But now consider the statement:

(3) $\langle P \rangle$This acorn grows into a mighty oak.

Since there undoubtedly are plenty of possible worlds governed by our laws of nature in which the acorn grows into a mighty oak, it appears that (3) is simply true on the standard account. Furthermore, nothing we or the squirrel can do to the acorn can make it stop being the case that there are worlds governed by our laws of nature in which the acorn grows into a mighty oak. Thus, even after the acorn has been nibbled and has died, (3) will still be true. We'll still have to say that the acorn can grow into a mighty oak. That seems wrong.

These facts about physical possibility and necessity, it seems to me, show that we have to introduce a time relativization into our operators. We can do this in a number of different ways. I want to use $\langle P \rangle t$, p and $[P]t$, p to express the ideas, respectively, of p's being physically possible as of t, and p's being physically necessary as of t. So, where t is some time at which the acorn is still viable, we can affirm:

(4) $\langle P \rangle t$, this acorn grows into a mighty oak.

If t' is a later time, when the acorn has begun to rot, then we will be able to say:

(4′) $\sim \langle P \rangle t'$, this acorn grows into a mighty oak.

If we do choose to proceed in this way, then, obviously enough, we can't understand physical possibility simply as truth in some world with the same laws of nature. For on that approach, what's physically possible at any time would be eternally so. Thus it appears that we must make use of the notion of a world's being "still possible" from a world *at a time*. In order to secure uniformity with what has gone before, let us introduce the notion of "world accessibility", and let us use WAw', w, t to express this idea. WAw', w, t is taken to mean, roughly, that, as of t, w' has not yet been physically ruled out by what has happened in w. So if the combination of the history of world w up to t, together with the laws of nature of w, leaves open the possibility that things might turn out as they do in w', then WAw', w, t is true.

Now I can introduce my physical necessity and possibility operators as follows:

PP: $\langle P \rangle t$, p is true at w iff (Ew') (WAw', w, t & p is true at w')

PN: $[P] t$, p is true at w iff (w') (WAw', w, $t \rightarrow p$ is true at w') & (Ew') (WAw', w, t & p is true at w')

So the idea here is that what's physically possible (necessary) at a world at a time is just what occurs in some (every) still world-accessible world from there then.[10]

This account of the physical modalities is not of much interest until some further details concerning world accessibility are given. Since world accessibility is, in a number of respects, relevantly like regular accessibility, it won't be necessary to say very much. The following points seem to me to be fairly important.

i. From the formal point of view, world accessibility is much like regular accessibility. This relation is, in suitably extended senses, transitive, reflexive, and symmetric.[11]

ii. As time goes by, the set of world-accessible worlds from any given world is pared down. Less and less is still possible at every passing moment. If a world lapses into some "end state", then the only world accessible from it from then on will be itself. In this case, everything that occurs in that world will, from then on, be physically necessary. The only physical possibilities will be the truths.

iii. Any world that is accessible in the regular way to a person in a world is world-accessible to the world. In other words:

A/WA: $(s) (t) (w) (w')$ (As, t, w', $w \rightarrow$ WAw', w, t)

is true. The same principle holds true for groups. If some world is accessible to group in w at a time, then that world is then world accessible to w. To deny these principles would be to say that some individual or group can see to the occurrence of some state of affairs that is physically impossible. As I understand it, this amounts to the belief in miracles.

The converses of these principles, however, seem to me to be false.

From the fact that some possible world is accessible to the world at a time, it does not follow that that world is accessible to any individual or group. Suppose, for example, that a certain subatomic particle is about to undergo a certain change. It might gain property p1, but then again it might not. Suppose that in fact it gains p1. Nothing any individual or group could have done would have assured that the particle would not gain p1. Then there was a world accessible to the world in which the particle failed to gain p1, but there was no such world accessible to any individual or group. In other words, we have to reject:

*WA/A: $(t)(w)(w')(\text{WA}w', w, t \rightarrow (Es)(s \text{ in } w \ \& \ As, t, w', w)$

as well as the corresponding principle concerning group accessibility.

iv. Any world that is world-accessible from a world must be very like that world in certain important respects. One of these respects is reflected in the traditional way of explaining the physical modalities. It is this: every still world-accessible world must have the same laws of nature as a given world. So, for example, if $E = mc2$ is a law of nature at this world, then it is also a law of nature at every world-accessible world. To deny this principle would be equivalent to maintaining that that it is still physically possible for the laws of nature to change, or to have been different. That seems to me to be wrong. It seems to me that it is physically necessary that the laws of nature are true.

On the other hand, it does not seem to me that it is *metaphysically* necessary that the laws of nature be true. As I see it, there are some possible worlds in which our laws of nature are not true. My point in the previous paragraph is just that no such world is world-accessible to our world.

Another respect in which every world-accessible world is like the actual world is this: every logical or metaphysical principle that is true at the actual world is also true at every world that is world-accessible from here. To deny this would be to maintain that it is physically possible that some such logical or metaphysical principle be false.

v. There is a temptation to maintain that worlds that are still accessible from a given world must be even more like that world than I have so far allowed. Specifically, there is the temptation to say that all such worlds are "past-wise indiscernible" from the given world.[12] In my view, this temptation must be resisted. One problem is that it is very hard to formulate the idea precisely. Clearly, we cannot simply say that if WAw', w, t is true, then, for any time, t', if t' is earlier than t, then whatever is true in w' at t' is also true in w at t'. The problem here is that many of the things that are true at a world at a time are "future infected". That is, they are true at that time in virtue of the fact that certain other things are going to be true in the future. To see the impact of this, imagine a case in which a certain subatomic particle still might swerve to the left and still might swerve to the right. Then there are world accessible worlds in which it swerves to the left, and others in which it swerves to the right. Suppose, furthermore, that thousands of years ago Democritus and Leucippus were discussing this particle, and Democritus predicted that it would swerve to the right and Leucippus predicted that it would swerve to the left. It follows that there are now world-accessible worlds in which when Democritus made his prediction thousands of years ago, he predicted the path of the particle correctly, and others in which when Democritus made his prediction thousands of years ago, he predicted the path of the particle incorrectly. So we can see that, just as there are now future-wise discernible world-accessible worlds, so there are past-wise discernible worlds. Admittedly, these differences in the pasts ride piggy-back on some more "solid" differences in the futures of the worlds. Nevertheless, the worlds seem to differ in at least some trivial ways in their pasts.

Another reason to reject the idea that world-accessible worlds are past-wise indiscernible is that, in some contexts, we talk as if, in spite of causal determinism, various possibilities for the future are still open. For example, we might say that even though causal determinism is true, it is possible that a peaceful way of ending the arms race will be found, and then again it is also possible that no such way of ending the arms race will be found. Clearly, if we have a plurality of future-wise discernible worlds still accessible, and causal determinism is true, then we must have an equal plurality of past-wise discernible worlds still accessible. I prefer to let the metaphysical scheme leave this sort of possibility open.[13]

Making use of this concept of world-accessibility, we can now explain the present proposal concerning the ought-to-be. What ought to be, in this sense, at a world at a time, is what happens in the best still accessible worlds from there then. More strictly, what I want to consider is this:

OB: OBt, p is true at w iff $(Ew')(WAw', w, t$ & p is true at w'
        & $\sim(Ew'')(WAw', w, t$ & $\sim p$ is true at w'' & $IVw'' \geqslant$
        $IVw'))$

So when we say that there ought to be a peaceful way of ending the arms race (p), what we may mean is that some p-world is still possible from here such that no $\sim p$-world that is still possible from here would be as good as or better than it. More simply, if things turned out as well as they still might, there would be a peaceful end to the arms race.

Associated with this notion of the absolute ought-to-be, there is the expected array of notions of conditioned and conditional ought-to-be. I shall not burden the reader with an account of all of these. It will suffice to say that they are relevantly like the notions introduced in Chapter 4 for the ought-to-do. They are materially-, subjunctively- and strictly-conditioned absolute ought-to-be, as well as conditional ought-to-be.

From the logical point of view, this concept of the ought-to-be, in its absolute and conditional forms, is like the concept of the ought-to-do. The only significant differences are induced by the lack of person-relativization and the substitution of world-accessibility for regular accessibility. So a version of the Kantian "ought implies can" principle is true. That is:

OK/OB: $OBt, p \rightarrow \langle P \rangle t, p$

Furthermore, there is a version of the principle that tells us that what unalterably is going to be the case, ought to be the case. That is:

U/OB: $[P]t, p \rightarrow OBt, p$

The various factual, unalterability, and deontic detachment rules, as well as the augmentation and overridability doctrines run parallel to those for conditioned, conditional, and absolute individual moral obligation.

Also related to this concept of the ought-to-be are the expected concepts of the "permitted-to-be" and the "forbidden-to-be". The former, expressible in English by such phrases as 'it would be OK, alright, acceptable, if p were to occur', may be defined as follows:

RB: RBt, p is true at w iff $\sim OBt, \sim p$ is true at w

The latter, "it shouldn't be that p", is introduced in this way:

FB: FBt, p is true at w iff $OBt, \sim p$ is true at w.

These also may appear in a wide variety of conditioned and conditional forms.

OB introduces a concept of the ought-to-be that is, in certain important respects, more successful than the one introduced in OB3. We have already seen that some plausible-looking statements of the ought-to-be come out false on OB3. The statement about the arms race, for example, came out false because no matter how good a p-world we select, there is sure to be an even better $\sim p$-world. However, on OB this problem does not arise. Consider p again. Focus on worlds that are still accessible from here. While there may be an infinite supply of such worlds, there is no reason to suppose that for every accessible p-world, there is sure to be an even better $\sim p$-world still accessible. Somewhere along the line, as we consider better and better worlds that are still accessible, we'll reach a point at which p starts being true, and is never false again. There are undoubtedly better and better $\sim p$-worlds "out there", but, from the perspective of the person who affirms (1), these are no longer accessible. They are irrelevant on OB.

Reflection of the ways in which people actually speak leads me to believe that OB introduces a concept that is somewhat too rigid to account for all the uses of 'it ought to be the case that . . .' in ordinary English. In fact, I believe that we speak as if there are many grades of the ought-to-be, each tied to a corresponding grade of possibility. An example may help to clarify this view.

Imagine a discussion of the arms race. Suppose one speaker suggests that high-level negotiation is the answer:

(5)   There ought to be a meeting at the summit.

Another speaker might express a somewhat bolder approach:

(6)   There ought to be a gradual, progressive build-down of the weapons stockpiles of the nuclear powers.

Still another speaker might make a statement that makes the preceding ones look timid:

(7)   It ought to be that all nuclear weapons are promptly deactivated, and plans developed for their rapid dismantlement.

It seems to me that statements (5)–(7) could be used in such a way as to express truths. This fact suggests that, as our conception of what's still possible expands, our notion of what ought to be may change, too. If we take a narrow view concerning what's still possible, we may find that a not-too-impressive state of affairs is about the best of the lot. We may then think that that is what ought to be. (5) above represents this sort of thinking. However, if we take a more generous view about possibility, then more alternatives present themselves. The best of these may be something that we formerly took to be impossible, and which is better than the best of the earlier possibilities. (6) represents such a move. As we move toward more and more generous conceptions of possibility, we find ourselves confronted with better and better worlds, and so we also find that richer concepts of the ought-to-be arise.

In light of this, I think we should recognize that world-accessibility comes in various "degrees". Each such degree corresponds to a concept of the ought-to-be. Thus, we have to introduce a schema that provides for all of these concepts. We can use WAi, w', w, t to mean that w' is accessible, in degree i, from w at t. Then we can say:

OBi: OB$i, t, p$ is true at w iff $(Ew') (WAi, w', w, t \& p$ is true at $w' \& \sim(Ew'') (WAi, w'', w, t \& \sim p$ is true at $w'' \& IVw'' \geqslant IVw'))$

Sometimes, it must be admitted, we make use of a concept of the ought-to-be that is even more generous than the most generous of the concepts covered by my schema OBi. We may say, for example:

(8)   I know it's totally impossible, but still it ought to be the case that all weapons of war are immediately transformed into plowshares, and other agricultural implements.

This sort of remark, as I see it, serves to express a sort of wishful thinking — a fond daydream. It has nothing to do with what's possible, or what would be best. It can be represented by the truth-valueless exclamation, 'Ah, if only there were no more weapons of war!' For this sort of remark, emotivism should suffice. Such statements are immune to the sort of treatment I am proposing.

Although I can't say that is the most widely used, I think that the concept introduced in OB is relatively clear and interesting. It represents something that we might have in mind when we say that some state of affairs ought to occur. Furthermore, each of the degree-relativized concepts of the ought-to-be is formally like that one. So it provides a sort of model for the behavior of the concepts introduced by OBi. Let us consider it as our representative of the various ought-to-be's.

8.3. CONNECTIONS BETWEEN THE OUGHT-TO-BE AND THE OUGHT-TO-DO

There is a persistent inclination to suspect that there must be a connection between what ought to be and what we ought to do. A loose version of this view seems to stand behind certain utopian thought. When a visionary writer describes some utopia, he seems to be describing how, according to him, things ought to be. But there is generally some practical message, too. Perhaps the writer means to suggest that we should observe the behavior of the citizens of utopia in order to gain some insight into the ways in which we should behave. If this is right, then the visionary presupposes that what we ought to do is somehow revealed by consideration of how things ought to be. Of course, this is all very vague. In 'The Ethics of Requirement', Professor Chisholm presented a clear account of his conception of the connection between the ought-to-be and the ought-to-do.[14] According to the view he there proposed, to say that someone ought to do something is to say that it ought to be that he does it. A variety of other claims about connections between the ought-to-be and the ought-to-do might be maintained. Let us investigate such claims, making use of the concepts introduced in MO and OB.

The boldest thesis concerning the ought-to-be and the ought-to-do is one that, to my knowledge, no one has ever affirmed. It is the thesis that something ought to be if and only if someone ought to do it. Translated into my terminology, this is:

*OB/MO: $(t)\,(p)\,(\mathrm{OB}t, p \leftrightarrow (\mathrm{E}s)\,(\mathrm{MO}s, t, p))$

If we understand the ought-to-be and the ought-to-do in anything like the ways I have proposed, we will have to reject *OB/MO. Indeed, we will have to reject it "in both directions". The problems arise because what's accessible to the world as a whole may be markedly different from what's accessible to some person in it. This means that the best that's still possible for the world as a whole may be better than the best that's still possible for the person. Thus, what's obligatory for the world may be different from what's obligatory for the person. Let's consider a case to see how this works.

Suppose that civil strife is going to break out in a foreign country, and it will be best for me to give to a relief found for innocent victims. The citizens of the country can still avoid the strife, but are not going to do it. I can't do anything to stop it. From my perspective, it is unalterable. In this case, I have an absolute moral obligation to contribute to the relief fund. However, it is still possible for these people to avoid the civil strife altogether. Since what's possible for them must be possible for the world, it follows that there is a world-accessible world in which they settle their differences amicably, no relief fund is set up, and I don't contribute to one. It is reasonable to assume that some such world is better than any accessible world in which the civil strife occurs, and innocent victims require assistance from the likes of me. It appears, then, that it ought to be the case that the strife does not occur, and I don't contribute to the relief fund.

Thus we have a case in which there is someone (me) who morally ought to do something (give to the relief fund) but this is not something that ought to be. This refutes *OB/MO from right to left.

It is not clear that this same example can be used to refute *OB/MO in the other direction. The problem is that it might be insisted that if it is still possible for the strife to be avoided, then someone (or perhaps some group) in the foreign nation has an obligation to see to it that the strife is avoided. In order to refute *OB/MO from left to right, we need to find a case in which the thing that ought to be is something very good that is not accessible to anyone (or to any group), but which nevertheless still might happen.

Let's suppose that the old adage about the weather is true. That is, let's suppose that everyone talks about the weather, but nobody can do anything about it. Let's suppose, further, that tomorrow's weather is not fully determined. It's still possible for there to be severe thunderstorms, and it's still possible for them to blow over. Suppose it would be best for them to blow over. Suppose, finally, that they are not going to blow over. In fact, severe thunderstorms are going to do a fair amount of damage to some newly-planted crops. Now consider this state of affairs:

(9)   There are no severe thunderstorms tomorrow

Since this state of affairs is so good, and still might occur, it might be something that ought to be. Let's suppose it is. However, since it is not going to occur, and no one can do anything about the weather, no world in which (9) is true is accessible to anyone (or any group) in this world. Hence, it is not the case that there is anyone (or any group) with a moral obligation to see to the occurrence of (9). Thus, *OB/MO is refuted from left to right.

Reflection on these examples should suffice to show that, if understood in our way, Professor Chisholm's thesis must be rejected. Recall that he said that the ought-to-do can be defined directly by appeal to the ought-to-be, together with the concept of "bringing about". Using Ap for 's brings about p', and Op for 'it ought to be the case that p', he said that 's ought to bring it about that p' can be understood to mean the same as 'OAp'.[15] The examples just cited show that this thesis is false, if the concepts of obligation are relevantly like the ones I have introduced. In the civil strife case, I maintained that I ought to give to the relief fund, but that it is not the case that it ought to be that I give to the relief fund. In an expanded version of the thunderstorm case, we can maintain that it ought to be that we work in our fields during tomorrow's fine weather, but it is not the case that that work is something that we ought to do (because no world in which the weather is fine is accessible to us).

It should be pointed out that Professor Chisholm did not understand the ought-to-be and the ought-to-do in my neo-utilitarian way. His concepts of obligation are based on the notion of "requirement". Hence, it is not clear that the examples I have introduced would have much impact upon his thesis, if that thesis is understood in the way he intended.[16]

We might want to propose a weakened version of half of *OB/MO. That would be the thesis that if something ought to be, and someone can make it happen, then he ought to. More precisely, what I have in mind is this:

*OB/MO': $(s)\,(t)\,(p)\,(OBt, p \,\&\, Ks, t, p \rightarrow MOs, t, p)$

Not surprisingly, *OB/MO' is false. Among the things I can bring about are some I would bring about if things turned out in the best way possible. Some of these would be pretty pointless if in fact things don't turn out in the best way possible. Recall the thunderstorm example from a few paragraphs back. In that example, a certain state of affairs (the storm blowing over) was said to be something that ought to be, but which no one had a moral obligation to bring about. Of course, none of us can bring about or prevent such things as thunderstorms, and so the example has no direct bearing on *OB/MO'.

However, the example does provide the elements of a counter-example to *OB/MO'. Suppose a certain person is the weatherman at the local TV station. He is called upon to forecast tomorrow's weather.

It would be best if the storm were to blow over, and it would also be best if he were to forecast that the storm is going to blow over. This follows from the fact that in the best still possible worlds, that's what happens. However, since the storm in fact is not going to blow over, and nothing he can do will make it blow over, it would be wrong for him to forecast that it will. Hence, if we let s be the weatherman, t be now, and p be 's forecasts that the storm will blow over', we have a counterexample to an instantiation of *OB/MO'. I see no way to modify this principle so as to make it true, while still retaining its fundamental flavor.

In spite of all this, it may still appear that there simply must be some connection between the ought-to-be and the ought-to-do. Perhaps it is not the case that we ought to do all and only those things that ought to be. Nevertheless, it still might seem that it ought to be that we do what we ought to do. Let us consider this somewhat ambiguous doctrine.

On one interpretation, the doctrine in question would have it that things that in fact ought to be done, ought to occur. In other words:

*MO/OB: $(t)\,(p)\,(((Es)\,(MOs, t, p) \rightarrow OBt, p)$

This says that if somebody ought to do p, then p ought to be. We have already considered and rejected something relevantly like *MO/OB. That was the right-to-left half of *OB/MO. The counterexample involved giving to a relief fund for victims of civil strife in a foreign land. I shall not repeat the example here.

There is a far more plausible way of understanding the doctrine that it ought to be that people do what they ought to do. On this reading, the ought-to-do operator is entirely within the scope of the ought-to-be operator. The idea is the utopian notion that, if things were as they really ought to be, then people would be doing all the things that they would, under those ideal circumstances, ought to be doing. More exactly, it is this:

MO/OB': $(t)\,(OBt, ((s)\,(MOs, t, p) \rightarrow s$ sees to $p))$

In order to see whether MO/OB' is true, we would have to inspect the best worlds still world-accessible from here. We would then have to identify the moral obligations of the inhabitants of those best worlds. If MO/OB' is true, we would then find that those inhabitants uniformly discharge all of their moral obligations.

In order to make discussion of MO/OB′ more straightforward, let us assume that for each world, w, and time, t, there is a world, $w′$, such that $w′$ is the unique best world accessible to w at t. Let's suppose that u (for 'Utopia') is the unique best world accessible from our world now, and let's ask whether in u people do the things they there ought to do. To suppose that someone fails is to suppose that someone in u has a moral obligation to bring about some state of affairs, but doesn't do it. Let's suppose that s is such a person, and p is such a state of affairs. Then we have:

(10)   MOs, t, p is true at u & $\sim p$ is true at u

So we can see that u is a $\sim p$-world, and that there is a somewhat better p-world (call it $u′$) accessible to s at t from u. If $u′$ is accessible to s from u, then $u′$ must be accessible to u itself. Thus we can see that $u′$ is better than u and world-accessible from u. Since world-accessibility is transitive, it follows that $u′$ is also world-accessible from the real world, and better than u. This contradicts our original assumption that u is the unique best world still world-accessible from here. Thus, (10) can't be true. If there is a unique best world world-accessible from here, then the people in it do the things that they there morally ought to do.

So it turns out that there is a connection between the ought-to-be and the ought-to-do. It's not that there is a connection between what ought to be relative to the real world and what we (here in the real world) ought to do. The differences between world-accessibility and regular accessibility rule that out. Rather, it's that it ought to be (given our assumption) that people do the things that would be their moral obligations if things were as they ought to be. If there is a best world out there, then the people in it fulfil the obligations they there have.

Some may see in this a hint of Hintikka's deontically perfect worlds, or Kant's Kingdom of Ends. I gladly acknowledge that there are hints of such things in what I have said. Yet I must insist on some important differences. We must not lose sight of the fact that in the wonderful worlds where things are as they ought to be, the moral obligations that people have (and invariably fulfil) may be quite different from the moral obligations that we have (and often violate) here in the less-than-perfect real world. Thus, it seems to me that this link between the ought-to-be and the ought-to-do is not of any crucial significance to normative ethics.

CHAPTER 9

CONFLICTS OF OBLIGATION

In the preceding chapters of this book, I have introduced a variety of concepts of absolute (nonconditional) obligation. Among these are individual moral obligation, individual prudential obligation, social obligation, and civic obligation. I have also introduced and discussed some forms of "collective" obligation — group moral and prudential obligation, for example. There is also the concept of the ought-to-be. Each of these is a "doing-the-best-we-can" concept of obligation, defined by appeal to some concept of possibility and some concept of value. In addition to all of these, there are also some concepts of obligation that have not been discussed here. Among these are various society- and code-relative forms of obligation, such as legal obligation and etiquettical obligation. Such concepts as these are not doing-the-best-we-can concepts of obligation. They would require a rather different sort of analysis.

One of the main themes that I have been concerned to stress here is that, since there are so many concepts of obligation, it is inevitable that there will be conflicts among them. It is of course obvious that prudential and moral obligation may conflict. The best world accessible to me may fail to be the one in which I fare best. Equally, my real moral obligation may conflict with the obligations imposed upon me by the socially accepted moral code of my most important social group. The best world accessible to me may be one in which I tell a lie, or break a promise, even though my most important social group deems such things to be wrong.

I have attempted to establish (in Chapter 7, Section 3.2) that individual moral obligation may conflict with what I have called social obligation. Doing the best I can may be incompatible with doing the best I can for some group of which I am a member. Going beyond these relatively obvious cases, I have attempted to show that an individual's real moral obligation may conflict with the real moral obligation of some group of which he is a member. I tried to show this by considering some voting examples in Chapter 7, Section 4.2.

Furthermore, I have tried to establish that what a person morally ought to do may be incompatible with what ought to be. What ought to be depends upon what's still possible "for the world". What a person ought to do depends upon what's still possible for that person. Since the relevant accessibility relations are different, the obligations based upon them may be different, too. This issue was discussed in Chapter 8, Section 3.

Even if we focus exclusively upon absolute moral obligation, we will find plenty of opportunities for conflict. I pointed out (in Chapter 2, Section 3.2) that a given person's moral obligations, as of one time, may conflict with that same person's moral obligations as of some other time. As of Sunday, the doctor ought to give medicine A on Tuesday. As of Monday night, when he has already given the wrong medicine once, he has an incompatible obligation. Now he ought to avoid giving medicine A on Tuesday.

I also pointed out (in Chapter 2, Section 3.2) that one person's moral obligations at a time may conflict with another person's moral obligations as of that same time. Such conflict may occur, for example, in the following sort of case: suppose our town needs a surveyor of fences, and two residents are well-suited for the job. Only one can serve. Suppose that in fact neither is going to volunteer, though each could. In this case (given some innocent assumptions) it turns out that each has a moral obligation to serve as surveyor of fences, even though it would be impossible for both to serve. Reflection on the accessible worlds shows how this can happen. The first qualified person has accessible to him a good world in which he is surveyor of fences, and his neighbor is not. He does not have accessible to him as good a world in which his neighbor is surveyor of fences and he himself is not. This is the impact of the assumption that the first person cannot make the second one volunteer for the job. So the first person morally ought to serve. Corresponding reflections establish that the second person is in a relevantly similar situation. In the best worlds accessible to him, he serves as surveyor of fences, and his neighbor does not.

Letting Fx abbreviate 'x serves as the sole surveyor of fences in our town' and letting a, b, and n name our two residents and now, we have:

(1) $MOa, n, Fa \ \& \ MOb, n, Fb \ \& \ \sim\langle P\rangle n, Fa \ \& \ Fb$

It might seem, in light of all this, that I would be sympathetic to the view, recently defended by Bas van Fraassen, Ruth Marcus, and Bernard Williams (among others) that an individual's real moral obligations as of a time may conflict among themselves.[1] However, I am not sympathetic to that view. I think it is false.

9.1. MORAL DILEMMAS

Before I turn to a consideration of the arguments that lead some to think that there are genuine moral conflicts, I think I must clarify the issue. As I see it, the conflicts-of-obligation thesis is the thesis that it is possible for there to be an individual and time, such that, relative to that time, the individual has two absolute moral obligations that cannot be jointly fulfilled. As a working formulation of the thesis, subject to later revision, I propose:

(2) $\langle\,\rangle$ (Es) (Et) (Ep) (Eq) (MOs, t, p & MOs, t, q & ~Ks, t, p & q)

Given my account of the meaning of MO, (2) must be false. This can be seen easily enough. Suppose MOs, t, p and MOs, t, q are both true. Consider the possible worlds accessible to s at t, ranked in terms of intrinsic value. At some point in the ranking, we find a pretty good p-world than which there is no better ~p-world. All the worlds as good as or better than that one are also p-worlds. Similarly, at some point in the ranking, we find a q-world than which there is no better ~q-world. All the worlds as good as or better than that one must also be q-worlds. Hence, the upper reaches of the ranking must consist entirely of p & q-worlds. This generates the so-called "agglomeration principle":

AG: MOs, t, p & MOs, t, q $\rightarrow$ MOs, t, p & q

Since Ks, t, p just means that p is true at some accessible world, and MOs, t, p entails that p is true at the best of the worlds accessible to s at t, we can see that the Kantian "ought implies can" principle is true:

MO/K: MOs, t, p $\rightarrow$ Ks, t, p

Putting together these two principles yields the desired result:

(3)   MOs, t, p & MOs, t, q $\rightarrow$ Ks, t, p & q

Thus it can be seen that (2) cannot be true. If a person ought to see to p and ought to see to q, then he can see to p & q. Moral conflicts are impossible, given my account of moral obligation.

But, of course, the question is not whether this is the way it turns out on my view. The question is whether this is the way it is in fact. If there are in fact moral conflicts, then my view must be wrong. So we must consider the reasons that have been given in favor of thinking that there are moral conflicts.

9.1.1. *Five Arguments for Moral Conflicts*

Although there are many variations, it seems to me that there are five main arguments for moral conflicts. The first of these is a straight-forward appeal to moral intuition. We are asked to consider a case that allegedly illustrates conflict in a compelling way. Virtually everyone who writes on this topic comments on a case described by Sartre.[2] A young man in wartime France has a "deeply afflicted mother". Various misfortunes have made her wholly dependent upon him. He now has to choose between (a) staying with her, and thereby "helping her live", and (b) going off to England to join the Free French Forces. There are apparently good moral reasons on each side. He seems to have some sort of patriotic obligation to join the Free French Forces — but this would require leaving his mother. Clearly, since his mother depends upon him, he has some sort of filial obligation to remain with her — but then he must fail to join his comrades in the effort to free his country.

Defenders of moral conflicts have appealed to Aeschylus, Shakespeare, and Ibsen for examples. In every case the argument seems to be the same: 'Consider the example. Don't you just *see* that Agamemnon (or Nora, or Isabella) was in a real moral dilemma?'

This appeal to intuition strikes me as being inconclusive. Surely, the cases might be (a) no more than particularly wrenching cases of conflicting prima facie obligations. Equally, they might be (b) no more than cases in which a part of the evidence supports one obligation, and another part of the evidence supports an incompatible obligation, and, taken as a whole, the evidence is insufficient to determine which obligation is genuine. Finally, these cases might be (c) no more than cases illustrating conflicts of obligations of different sorts (civic and moral, for example, in Sartre's case). While I certainly do not mean to denigrate the literary talents of Aeschylus, Shakespeare, and Ibsen, I think we have to agree that their examples prove very little about moral dilemmas. Let us turn to a second sort of argument.

Marcus briefly suggests a different line of argument.

There is always the analogue of Buridan's ass. . . . The lives of identical twins are in jeopardy, and, through force of circumstances, I am in a position to save only one. Make the situation as symmetrical as you please. . . . [H]owever strong our wills and complete our knowledge, we might be faced with a moral choice in which there are no moral grounds for doing x over y.[3]

The argument might be developed in this way: imagine a case in which the life of one child is in jeopardy, and I alone am in a position to save him with relative ease. For example, suppose I am lounging at poolside when a child falls into the pool right before my eyes. Suppose the child can't swim, but I can. I could easily grab him, and haul him out. Suppose no one else is there to save the child. Clearly, in this sort of case, I have an obligation to save the child. Now convert the child into identical twins, and stipulate that I am able to save only one. Since I had an obligation to save one when there was one, and now we have two just like that one, it appears that I have an obligation to save each. But I can't. So there are moral dilemmas.

This "Buridanical" argument seems to me to fail. There is an obvious and important difference between the case in which one child is drowning and the case in which twins are drowning. When one child is drowning, failure to save him would be wrong. If I don't save that child, then, no matter what I do, I do something wrong. Nothing else I can do would be as good. However, when twins are drowning, I face a different bunch of alternatives. I can fail to save twin A, and still do something just as good — I can save twin B. When twins are drowning, I can fail to save one of them but still do something that's not wrong. As I see it, one's duty in this sort of symmetrical case is to save one or the other of the twins. Failure to save any twin at all would be wrong. The choice of the first twin would be right, and the choice of the second twin would be right. Neither choice is obligatory.

Marcus mentions that in symmetrical cases there are no moral grounds for choosing one course of action over the equally good other. I think this is right. If I choose to save twin A instead of twin B, my choice is not based upon moral reasons. I have moral reasons to make some choice or other since, if I don't make a choice, both twins will drown. But when I do choose one of the twins, my reason for choosing him cannot be moral. This follows from the fact that the twins are morally indiscernible. In this sort of case, it seems to me, one must impose some difference upon the twins. That is, one must see to it that one twin has some property that serves to distinguish him from the other. Flipping a coin, or saying 'eeny, meeny, miney, moe' will do the trick.

In the passage just quoted, Marcus suggests a third line of argument for moral dilemmas. She mentions the case in which I have made 'two promises in all good faith and reason that they will not conflict, but then they do, as a result of circumstances that were unpredictable and beyond my control'.[4] I can think of two different ways in which the argument might be developed. In the first way, it would be a version of the Buridanical argument just discussed. (This seems to be Marcus's argument in the passage quoted.) In the second way, the argument is based on the notion that promises ought to be kept. If I have promised to do something, then I ought to do it. Thus, if I have promised to do each of two incompatible things, then I ought to do each of them — but can't.

The general maxim about promises ("if I have promised to do something, then I ought to do it") seems to me to be an iffy ought of extraordinary ambiguity. Taken as a statement of conditioned absolute moral obligation, it will generate the desired conclusion. However, so understood, the principle is clearly unacceptable. Some promises ought not to be fulfilled. Taken as a statement of defeasible commitment, the principle is obscure, but far more plausible. However, if understood in this way, it will not generate the desired conclusion. Factual detachment is not valid for defeasible commitment. Thus, there is no sound way of establishing the existence of two incompatible absolute obligations in the two-promise case. The mere fact that I have made some promises is insufficient to generate the conclusion that I have any absolute moral obligations. Surely, it does not establish that I have two incompatible absolute moral obligations.

A number of writers on the topic of moral dilemmas have focussed attention on certain facts about the moral emotions. Specifically, they have claimed that feelings of guilt, remorse, and regret about the rejected obligation serve to show that dilemmas are real. In Sartre's case, for example, it might be alleged that no matter which course of action he chooses, the young man will feel regret about failing to choose the other. If he joins the Free French, he will regret having left his mother. If he stays with his mother, he will regret having failed to fight for his country. In either case, it has been alleged, the regret is genuine and appropriate. This is thought to show that whichever course of action he chooses, he thereby rejects a course of action that was also morally obligatory. He feels regret (or guilt) because he knows that he has failed to do something he should have done. ' . . . [I]t is inadequate to insist that feelings of guilt about the rejected alternative are mistaken and that assumptions of guilt is inappropriate. Nor is it puritanical zeal which insists on the reality of dilemmas and the appropriateness of the attendant feelings. For dilemmas, when they occur, are data of a kind.'[5]

Even in a quite simple case involving promises, it is alleged that this same phenomenon appears. Williams puts it this way:

> A man may, for instance, feel regret because he has broken a promise in the course of acting (as he sincerely supposes) for the best; and his regret at having broken the promise must surely arise *via* a moral thought. . . . A tendency to feel regrets, particularly creative regrets, at having broken a promise even in the course of acting for the best might well be considered a reassuring sign that an agent took his promises seriously.[6]

I am inclined to believe that these philosophers are right about the guilt and wrong about what it shows. I agree that it would be appropriate for the young man in Sartre's story to feel genuine guilt no matter which of the two alternatives he selects. For in either case, he will be directly responsible for the occurrence of a bad state of affairs — and one that matters to him, too. If he abandons his mother, he will surely make her very sad. That seems to be a bad thing, and one that would be directly caused by the young man's choice. If he is a decent young man, he will care deeply about his mother's sorrow. Equally, he'd be right to feel guilty about failing to come to the aid of his country in a time of dire need. That would also be a bad thing to do, and one about which decent people care.

However, there is a big difference between feeling guilt because you have caused something bad to happen, and feeling guilt because you have failed to do something you morally ought to have done. In my view, the guilt in the cases under consideration is to be explained in the former way, but not in the latter. Surely, it is clear that when one chooses the lesser of two great evils, one nevertheless chooses an evil. That should be sufficient to account for the emotional reaction.

Furthermore, it seems to me that we should distinguish between two different comments that might be made about such feelings of guilt. On the one hand, someone might say (as Williams seems to do) that it is morally fitting, or 'reassuring', for a promise-breaker to feel some regret, even when he recognizes that his promise-breaking was for the best. This fact is to be explained, I think, by pointing out that decent people are normally brought up to believe that (typical) promises ought to be kept. As children, we are taught to feel guilty about broken promises. Such childhood training stays with us. As Professor Hare has emphasized, it is a good thing, in general, that we feel as we do when we break promises. If we don't feel some compunction about promise-breaking, the whole institution of promising would be in danger of extinction. But from the fact that it is fitting or reassuring and in general a good thing that we feel guilty about a broken promise, it surely does not follow that we ought to have kept that promise.

On the other hand, advocates of dilemmas could get some mileage out of the claim that such feelings of guilt or regret are not merely morally fitting, but are also somehow "true". We might say that "true" guilt is guilt concerning a genuine moral lapse. If we could show that the guilt felt about the broken promise is in this way true guilt, we could reach the desired conclusion. I see no way to establish this point. Perhaps some who are moved by the argument from guilt are moved by it because they have failed to see the difference between guilt that is morally fitting, and guilt that is, in this way, true.

The fifth line of argument in favor of moral dilemmas strikes me as being in some ways paradoxical. To my knowledge, only a few philosophers have suggested this sort of argument. In each case, the philosopher in question apparently sees himself as an *opponent* of moral dilemmas. Nevertheless, in the midst the argument, each of these philosophers suggests that there is at least one type of case in which dilemmas arise. Such cases are ones in which an agent gets himself into a moral dilemma by doing something he should not have done.

Terrance McConnell strongly suggests this fifth line of argument. After stating that he intends to argue against moral dilemmas, McConnell goes on to make his target more explicit. He says:

> ... I am not necessarily ruling out the possibility that an agent can, by doing something forbidden, put himself in a situation where no matter what he does he will be doing something wrong. For example, one can [m]ake two promises that he knows conflict. Thus no matter what the agent does, he will break one of the promises. The situation arose, however, because the agent did something wrong. One might call situations like this dilemmatic; but if this were the only kind of dilemma that one could encounter, we would not be tempted to say that moral dilemmas show that our reasoning about ethical matters is incoherent.[7]

In his recent paper on dilemmas, Alan Donagan makes virtually the same point. He mentions a case (due to Donald Davidson) in which someone has made incompatible promises to Lavinia and Lolita. He then considers the cogency of the claim that the promisor would be justified in breaking one of the promises. He apparently finds the claim deficient:

> Has not the promisee reason to complain: "You should have thought of that when you gave me your word, which I accepted in good faith on the conditions on which you gave it; but it does not follow, because you did wrong to give it, that you do not also do wrong in breaking it"? This seems unanswerable; and if it is, those who wrongly give their word may entangle themselves in genuine conflicts of duties.[8]

Donagan goes on to maintain that the "no conflicts" thesis is ambiguous. On a strong reading, it is (roughly) the thesis that there are absolutely no cases of moral conflict. On a weak reading, it is (again, roughly) the thesis that, aside from cases arising from past wrong, there are no moral conflicts. Donagan suggests that the relevant distinction can be found in the writings of Aquinas, who distinguished between "perplexity *simpliciter*" and "perplexity *secundum quid*". The main point, however, is that Donagan apparently accepts the notion that one can entangle himself in a moral dilemma by doing something wrong.

Donagan's position here strikes me as being somewhat odd. On the one hand, he seems to be very favorably inclined toward both the agglomeration principle and the "ought implies can" principle. As he acknowledges, if these principles are true, then moral dilemmas are impossible. Yet, on the other hand, Donagan also seems to want to maintain that if a person does certain kinds of wrong, he can generate a dilemma. But this is impossible. Sinning can get you into some pretty uncomfortable spots, but it can't get you into a conceptually impossible spot.[9]

Suppose I have made incompatible promises to Lavinia and Lolita — for example, suppose I promised each that I would dine with her alone today at noon. Since these acts of promising generate expectations some of which are bound to be frustrated, it appears that I shouldn't have made both promises. Of course, in order to be sure about this, we'd have to know more about the accessible possible worlds. Nevertheless, it is reasonable to assume, in a case such as this, that prior to the time at which I made them, I should not have made both promises.

To simplify discussion, let us use the following abbreviations: f for me; t for a time before the promises were made; p1 for 'I promise to meet Lavinia for lunch today'; p2 for 'I promise to meet Lolita for lunch today'; k1 for 'I meet Lavinia for lunch today'; and k2 for 'I meet Lolita for lunch today'. As I said above, I accept the claim that I ought not to have made both promises:

(4) $MOf, t, \sim(p1 \,\&\, p2)$

Furthermore, it is reasonable to assume that I ought to keep at least one of the promises. In other words:

(5) $MOf, t, (k1 \lor k2)$

But it would be impossible to keep both:

(6) $\sim Kf, t, (k1 \,\&\, k2)$

Donagan points out that, if I settle on lunching with Lavinia, and therefore find myself unable to meet Lolita, Lolita will have grounds for complaint. She may say: 'You should have thought of that when you gave me your word'. Equally, if I dine with Lolita, and therefore fail to keep my promise to Lavinia, Lavinia will have equal grounds for making the same complaint.

All this seems to me to be true — but insufficient to establish what is, after all, the relevant point. What needs to be shown here is not merely that it was wrong to make the pair of promises, or that each promisee has reasonable grounds for complaint. Rather, what needs to be shown is that, having made the promises, I come to have a pair of incompatible obligations. In other words, what needs to be shown is:

(7) $MOf, t+1, k1 \,\&\, MOf, t+1, k2$

It does not seem to me that (7) is true. Something close to (7), however, probably would be true in a case such as the one described. Using a1 for 'I apologize to Lavinia' and a2 for 'I apologize to Lolita', we have:

(8) $MOf, \overset{.}{t}+1, (k1 \lor a1) \,\&\, MOf, t+1, (k2 \lor a2)$

But, of course, the obligations specified in (8) are jointly fulfillable. So I agree that, in this case, the promisor comes to "owe something" to each promisee. However, as I see it, the things owed are compatible. The promisor owes each promisee this: either to show up or to apologize. I see no reason to suppose that he owes more than this.

9.2. MO AND MORAL OBLIGATION

These reflections on the conflicts-of-obligation thesis give rise to a puzzle that may have been brewing for some time now. Marcus, van Fraassen, Williams and others believe in the possibility of real moral conflicts. Yet we have seen that the proposed definition, MO, entails that there can't be such conflicts — at least, this may seem to be what I have been claiming. We seem to be driven to the conclusion that either Marcus, van Fraassen, Williams and the rest are guilty of a relatively simple logical error, or else they don't understand the meaning of the thesis they have undertaken to discuss. Neither of these alternatives seems credible. How is this dilemma to be resolved?

In order to deal with this problem, it will be necessary to recall some facts about the concept introduced in the definition, MO, in Chapter 2. That definition was:

MO: MOs, t, p is true at w iff (Ew') $(As, t, w', w$ & p is true at w' & $\sim(Ew'')$ $(As, t, w'', w$ & $\sim p$ is true at w'' & $IV(w)'' \geqslant IV(w')))$

This is intended to be a "stipulative" definition. It tells us what MOs, t, p means. Roughly, the idea is that MOs, t, p is true of a person, s, a time, t, and a state of affairs, p, if and only if, as of t, there is a p-world accessible to s, such that there is no as good $\sim p$-world accessible to s.

Although it has not been stated explicitly, a certain utterly fundamental normative principle has been assumed here from the start. That principle is that we in fact morally ought to do all and only those things that fall under the concept MO. In other words, I mean to affirm the equivalence of the defined concept MO and the concept of real moral obligation. So the principle is:

(9) $(s)(t)(p)$ (s morally ought, as of t, to see to p if and only if MOs, t, p)

Some readers may be puzzled by my attitude toward (9). They may have expected that I would take (9) to be an empty tautology. If my definition, MO, had been intended as an "analysis" of the concept of moral obligation, then this expectation would perhaps be justified. But that definition was not intended to be an analysis of some concept we already have. It was intended to be a stipulative definition of a concept to which I wanted to draw attention.

If we compare (9) with the following principle, I think the difference between moral obligation and MO will emerge:

(10) $(s)\,(t)\,(p)$ (MOs, t, p if and only if MOs, t, p)

If we grant (as I think we must) that MOs, t, p has a meaning, then we should grant that (10) is an empty tautology. It tells us nothing of interest about morality. Even those who think that my approach is hopelessly wrongheaded, and that the concept MO is utterly irrelevant to ethics, will accept (10). On the other hand, (9) is intended to tell us how we ought to behave. It tells us that we morally ought to bring about all and only those states of affairs that fall under the concept MO. It tells us, roughly, that we morally ought to do the best we can. So even if (9) is a necessary truth, it is not an empty tautology. It is a fundamental moral doctrine.

Some philosophers, I fear, will claim to be unable to focus on the proposition expressed by (9). They may insist that they don't know what some of the terms in it mean. Others, however, will grasp all the relevant concepts, and will thus be able to appreciate the proposition expressed by (9). Of these, some will undoubtedly want to reject that proposition. They may hold that the utilitarian flavor of (9) makes it an unpalatable dish. Some will insist that our moral obligations are determined by another principle — perhaps something more Kantian, or Rawlsian, in flavor. These philosophers, no doubt, will not reject (10). The trivial truth of (10) is almost beyond debate.

Since some will disbelieve the proposition expressed by (9) while not disbelieving the one expressed by (10), these propositions are distinct. And since the propositions are distinct, we must conclude that the concept MO is distinct from the concept of moral obligation — for the propositions are alike in all respects save that one has the concept MO where the other has the concept of moral obligation.

This "open question" argument serves to emphasize the fact that my definition, MO, is not an analysis of the concept of moral obligation. It is a stipulative definition of what I take to be an utterly crucial, but perhaps not widely recognized normative concept.

Here, of course, is where we find the solution to the problem mentioned above. When Marcus, van Fraassen, Williams and the others affirm that it is possible for a person to have conflicting moral obligations, they can be understood to be affirming something relevantly like this:

(11)   ⟨⟩(Es)(Et)(Ep)(Eq)(s morally ought, as of t, to see to p
        & s morally ought, as of t, to see to q & ~Ks, t, p & q)

One who affirms (11) has not committed a logical error. It's not as if such a person simply failed to see that, given the appropriate definitions, (11) can be proven false. For the concept of moral obligation that appears in (11) has not been defined. Nor must we say that one who affirms (11) must fail to understand the meaning of the statement. For all I have said, Marcus and the others may have a fully satisfactory grasp on the meaning of the thing they assert.

However, I think that (11) is false. Since, in my view, (9) is a necessary truth, I believe that the logic of MO is exactly the same as the logic of the concept of moral obligation. As we have already seen, the MO-analogue of (11) is false. That is:

(2)   ⟨⟩(Es)(Et)(Ep)(Eq)(MOs, t, p & MOs, t, q & ~Ks, t,
        p & q)

is false. Thus, I think that the question whether there are conflicts of obligation, in the sense indicated by (11), turns on the question whether we ought to do the best we can. Since I think we morally ought to do the best we can, I think there are no such conflicts.

Two further points should be made here. The first of them is this: I do not take myself to have *proven*, or even to have attempted to prove, that (9) is true. As I see it, "questions of ultimate ends are not amenable to direct proof". Ever since Mill, utilitarians have been attracted by the tarbaby of proof. I have attempted to keep my hands off.

The second point I want to emphasize here is that I have not provided an analysis of the concept of moral obligation that appears in (11). I have not said what we mean when we say that someone morally ought to bring about a certain state of affairs. I find that I am unable to provide any such analysis. Some, finding themselves in this predicament, might conclude that the concept of moral obligation is a simple, unanalyzable concept. I am inclined to accept this conclusion, but I see no way to to establish it. At any rate, my open question argument is not intended to establish that the concept of moral obligation is simple and unanalyzable. It is only intended to establish that the concept of moral obligation is distinct from the concept MO.

9.3. WHY SHOULD I BE MORAL?

At least since the time of Plato, moral philosophers have struggled with the question 'Why be moral?' Some, reflecting on this question, see a triviality. They can't understand why anyone would be puzzled. Others, seeing the question in a different light, are moved to construct hopelessly implausible metaphysical schemes in order to make it seem that maybe, after all, we ought to be moral. Still others simply conclude that perhaps there just isn't any reason to be moral.

I am inclined to believe that these different philosophers have been focussing on different questions. In each case, the solution adopted may be appropriate to the question asked. However, since the questions have not been carefully distinguished, it appears that we have a plurality of incompatible answers to a single question. Furthermore, I fear that some philosophers, reflecting on such words as 'Why should I be moral?', have entertained a mish-mash of propositions from which no single question emerges clearly. It is no wonder that such reflections are often fruitless.

I think we are now in a good position to attempt to distinguish these questions. In previous chapters, I have introduced and explained a number of different concepts of obligation. By considering various combinations of them, we get various interpretations of the 'should' and the 'moral' in 'Why should I be moral?' Let's look at some of these.

Plato apparently thought it self-evident that each of us has good reason to do what's most in his own self-interest. I have explicated a concept of individual self-interest by appeal to a certain relativized value of possible worlds. A state of affairs maximizes someone's self-interest it and only if it occurs in some accessible world, and its negation does not occur in any accessible world in which that person fares as well. Such states of affairs are, in my jargon, prudentially obligatory for the person in question as of the time in question.[10] If we look at things in this way, we can understand the platonic view to have been that there is a certain sense of 'good reason' for which it is correct to say that one has good reason to see to the occurrence of a state of affairs if and only if it is prudentially obligatory for him.

If we ask why we should be moral, we may be asking why it is that each of us has good reason to do the things that are morally obligatory for him to do. 'What good reason do I have for doing what I morally ought to do?' If we understand good reasons in the suggested way, this, in turn, amounts to the question 'Why is it prudentially obligatory for me to do what's morally obligatory?' In the *Republic*, Plato suggests an answer to this question based on an alleged analogy between health and justice. Justice is to the soul as health is to the body. Each is a sort of harmony. Health is a harmony of the body, and justice is a harmony of the soul. Surely, one does not have to explain why it is in my self-interest to have a healthy body. The same allegedly holds for the having of a just soul. So the platonic answer seems to be that you ought to be moral because if you are moral you will have a harmonized soul.

In my view, this approach is unacceptable. The question presupposes that it is prudentially obligatory for me to do what's morally obligatory. The question then is, 'Why is this so?' In my view, however, the presupposition is clearly untenable. I see no reason to accept this principle:

(12) $(s)(t)(p)$ (POs, t, p iff s morally ought, as of t, to see to p)

I have already explained why I think (12) must be rejected.[11] The ordering of accessible possible worlds according to their intrinsic values surely differs from the ordering of accessible possible worlds according to how well I fare in them. Thus, for example, devoting my life to charity might be morally obligatory (because I do it in the intrinsically best accessible worlds) but not prudentially obligatory (because I don't do it in the best-for-me accessible worlds).

The upshot is that if we take the question to be 'Why is it prudentially obligatory for me to do what's morally obligatory?', then the correct answer is, 'It isn't.'

Another approach to the question is apparently based on the idea that the 'should' in 'Why should I be moral?' expresses moral obligation. In that case, the question as a whole may turn out to be equivalent to this one: 'Why is it morally obligatory for me to do what's morally obligatory?' This amounts to little more than a request for an explanation of the fact expressed by this uninteresting principle:

(13) $(s)(t)(p)$ (s morally ought, as of t, to see to p iff s morally ought, as of t, to see to p)

It's no wonder that some moral philosophers are not motivated to spend much time thinking about this puzzle. If you understand the puzzle in the way suggested by (13), you won't find it very puzzling.

There are several different ways in which we can modify (13) so as

to make it non-trivial. One of these involves the introduction of some
concept of social morality. We can put the question in this way: 'Why is
it morally obligatory for me to do what's required by the moral code of
my most crucial social group?' This version of the question also has a
presupposition. That is:

(14) $(s)\,(t)\,(p)\,(s$ morally ought, as of t, to see to p iff p is is re-
            quired of s at t by the moral code of s's most crucial social
            group)

I think (14) is false. As I see it, we have no real moral obligation to
abide by the rules of the codes of our various social groups. In typical
cases, it appears that a variety of historical and psychological factors
shape the development of a group's moral code. Some of these factors,
such as superstition, ignorance, xenophobia, vengefulness, etc., often
lead to the establishment of hopelessly defective rules. Other factors,
such as the requirement that the rules be easy to teach and easy to
apply, may lead to serious oversimplification. So there's little reason to
suppose that the rules in such codes are actually true.

In light of this, I think we must say that the thesis formulated in (14)
needs no explanation. It isn't true. So, once again, we have an inappropriate formulation of the question 'Why be moral?'

In order to formulate the question in a suitable way, I propose that
we investigate the idea that the 'should' in 'Why should I be moral?'
expresses neither prudential nor moral obligation. In my view, we can
make good sense of the question if we let that 'should' express what I
call 'just plain obligation'. Thus, I want to understand 'Why should I be
moral?' as equivalent to 'Why is it the case that I just plain ought to do
what I morally ought to do?' In order to make the meaning of the
question clear, we have to come to some understanding what's meant
by saying that someone 'just plain ought' to do something.

There are many concepts of obligation. I have discussed quite a few
of them in this book. I have attempted to show that, in many cases,
these concepts conflict. Moral obligation may conflict with legal obligation. Prudential obligation may conflict with etiquettical obligation. In a
given case, a person might know that he has a legal obligation to do one
thing, and a prudential obligation to do another, and an etiquettical
obligation to do yet a third. Knowing all this, he still might seek advice.
He might put his request in words such as these: 'I know that I legally
ought to do this, and that I prudentially ought to do that. But what I

want to know is what, all things considered, I ought to do.' When a person thus asks what, all things considered, he ought to do, he is asking about what I call his "just plain obligation". He wants to know what he just plain ought to do.

I propose to use JO*s, t, p* as a convenient abbreviation for the statement that *s* just plain ought, as of *t*, to see to *p*. I also propose to use JO as a name for the concept of just plain obligation.

JO is the most all-inclusive concept of obligation. It is not tied down to morality, or prudence, or law, or etiquette. It plays an important role in discussions of the relative stringency of these other, narrower, sorts of obligation. If we feel that moral obligation is more stringent than any other sort of obligation — that it "takes precedence over" them — then we may express our view by saying that we just plain ought to do what we morally ought to do. On the other hand, if we feel that morality must sometimes take a back seat to self-interest, we may say that there are some occasions on which we just plain ought to forget about morality, and do what's prudentially obligatory instead.

If we take the 'should' in 'Why should I be moral?' to express just plain obligation, and we take "being moral" to mean doing what we morally ought to do, then the question as a whole amounts to this: 'Why is it the case that I just plain ought to do what I morally ought to do?' If we understand the question in this way, we'll have to acknowledge that it presupposes a general principle on the order of (12), (13), and (14). However, it seems to me that this general principle is different from each of those in an important way. Whereas each of those principles is either trivial or false, the general principle here seems to me to be interesting and rather more plausible. The principle, of course, is that we just plain ought to do what we morally ought to do:

(15) $(s)(t)(p)(\text{MO}s, t, p \rightarrow \text{JO}s, t, p)$

Now the question may be understood as the question: why is (15) true?[12]

Some philosophers, apparently understanding the question in something like the way currently under consideration, have attempted to explain why we should be moral by appeal to some alleged social benefits of moral behavior.[13] They have proposed that each of us just plain ought to be moral because, if everyone were moral, then all of us, collectively, would be best off. This is a version of the principle of moral harmony. I have already explained (in Chapter 7) why I think it must be rejected. The problem is that there are many instances in which a very good world is accessible to a group, but, because others are not going to do their parts in the relevant group action, this good world is not accessible to a certain individual in the group. In this sort of case, the best worlds accessible to the individual may be ones in which he does things incompatible with what he does in the best world accessible to the group. So his moral obligations, based on what's possible for him, may fail to be components of the group action that would make the group best off.[14] In light of this, it is clear that we can't explain why each of us just plain ought to do what's morally obligatory by claiming that if each us were to do so, all of us would be best off. The problem with this explanation is that the general principle is simply false.

In order to come a little closer to a satisfactory answer to the question 'Why be moral?', let us draw out an implication of the view that we just plain ought to do what we morally ought to do. We have distinguished among a number of concepts of obligation. Each of these is tied down in a crucial way to some sort of value and to some sort of possibility. Moral obligation, if understood in the way I have proposed, is tied down to the intrinsic values of the accessible possible worlds. What counts here is not just how well you fare, or how well your friends fare, or even how well humanity fares in the various accessible worlds. Rather, what's of crucial concern here is the total intrinsic value of each of the possible worlds accessible to you. You morally ought to see to a certain state of affairs just in case it occurs in some world accessible to you, and its negation doesn't occur in any accessible world with as great an intrinsic value.

If we just plain ought to do what's morally obligatory, then our moral obligations override our prudential, social and civic obligations, as well as any obligations imposed upon us by the codes of law, etiquette, and "morality" of the various social groups to which we may belong. The idea that moral obligation overrides the others may be defended, I think, by appeal to certain features of the concepts of value and possibility to which these various normative concepts are tied. Let me attempt, briefly, to explain.

It is natural to assume that intrinsic value is more fundamental and important than any other sort of value. This intuition is based on the fact that intrinsic value is both necessary and unrelativized. In these respects, intrinsic value is unlike extrinsic value, value-for-the-agent, value-for-the group, and "lawfulness". It is an objective, necessary, and person-independent sort of value. Some of these other sorts of value may be explained by appeal to the concept of intrinsic value, but intrinsic value cannot be explained by appeal to them. It is easy to appreciate the notion that it is more important than any other sort of value.

Similarly, where the guidance of human action is concerned, regular accessibility naturally presents itself as being more important than any other sort of possibility. If the question is, 'what should I do?', it seems most fitting to focus first on what I *can* do. In my view, this is the same as focussing on the worlds accessible to me. Other sorts of possibility, such as metaphysical possibility, epistemic possibility, group accessibility, and world accessibility, seem much less relevant. For various reasons, things that are possible in these ways may be outside of my control. Although they are, in the specified ways, possible for someone or something, they may not be possible *for me*. I cannot assure their occurrence.

Since moral obligation, in my view, is tied crucially to intrinsic value and regular accessibility, while these other concepts of obligation are tied to other, less important concepts of possibility and value, we can readily appreciate the intuition that moral obligation overrides other sorts of obligation. Most simply put, the view is that we just plain ought to do what we morally ought to do because moral obligation is directly based on intrinsic value and regular accessibility, and these are the most important sorts of value and possibility for the appraisal of human action. Of all the available senses of 'best' and 'can', these give the most fundamental sense to the thesis that we ought to do the best we can.

Obviously, to give a full account of the sort of approach I am advocating, I would have to flesh out the notion of importance to which I have appealed. At present, unfortunately, I find that I cannot do so. Thus, what I have said about the question 'Why be moral?' is really just the outline of an answer. Nevertheless, it is the outline of an answer that seems to me to be on the right track.

CHAPTER 10

CONCLUSIONS

One of the main claims I want to make concerning the views I have presented in the preceding chapters of this book is a claim about their unity. I have been trying here to provide a unified set of accounts of the oughts and iffy oughts of ordinary English. When I say that this set of accounts is "unified", I mean to draw attention to the fact that, insofar as possible, I have analyzed these normative notions by appeal to closely related components of a single, relatively simple metaphysical and axiological system.

There are several reasons for proceeding in this way. For one, it makes for a simpler overall theory. The reader is asked to accept only a small number of basic assumptions, and it should be fairly easy to identify and keep track of these. (I acknowledge that some of the assumptions are somewhat controversial.) Another reason for proceeding in this way is that it enables us to see the connections among the various normative concepts more easily. Since they are all defined by appeal to the same basic vocabulary, their logical relations are relatively easy to discern. Finally, where two defined concepts differ in logical behavior, I can usually appeal to the conceptual basis of a straightforward (if somewhat questionbegging) explanation.

At any rate, I have made use of a relatively small collection of metaphysical and axiological concepts in this book. By appeal to these concepts, I have attempted to analyze or otherwise explain what I take to the most interesting concepts of obligation.

10.0.1. *Metaphysical Concepts*

Of the metaphysical concepts I have used, perhaps the most important is the concept of a possible world. I have not attempted to analyze this notion, but have assumed that it is familiar enough to stand on its own. As I see it, a possible world may be viewed as being nothing more than the conjunction of all the states of affairs that occur, or are true, there. I have also assumed throughout that even though many worlds are possible, only one possible world is actual.

Certain relations among worlds have played a prominent role in my discussion. One of these is "nearness". I appealed to it in my discussion of subjunctively conditioned absolute obligation. I have assumed, following David Lewis and others, that when a person seriously utters a subjunctive conditional of the form 'if p were true, then q would be true', he presupposes some way of arranging possible worlds in terms of similarity or nearness. The statement as a whole is meant to suggest (roughly) that in the nearest world in which p is true, q is true, too.

For my purposes, a more interesting sort of relation among worlds is "accessibility". I have made use of three main concepts of accessibility. The first of these, 'regular accessibility', relates a person, as of a time, to a world, from a world. The idea here, expressed by As, t, w', w, is that s still has it in his power as of t in w to see to it that w' occurs, or is actual. S can still behave in such a way that things will turn out as they do in w'. The second accessibility relation is group accessibility. This differs from regular accessibility only in that the first term of the relation must be a set of people, rather than a person. The final concept of accessibility is 'world accessibility'. Here the idea is that the history of a world, w, up to some time, t, does not physically rule out the possibility that from t onwards, things will go as they do in w'. Formally, these three concepts are much like. Each is transitive, reflexive, and symmetric — in special senses explained in the appropriate places.

The three accessibility relations are linked by some metaphysical principles. One of these says that regular accessibility entails world accessibility:

A/WA: $(s)(t)(w)(w')(\text{A}s, t, w', w \rightarrow \text{WA}t, w', w)$

Another says that group accessibility has the same feature:

GA/WA: $(k)(t)(w)(w')(\text{GA}s, t, w', w \rightarrow \text{WA}t, w', w)$

A final principle links regular accessibility to group accessibility:

A/GA: $(s)(t)(w)(w')(\text{A}s, t, w', w \leftrightarrow \text{GA}\{s\}, t, w', w)$

I have attempted to explain (mainly in Chapter 7, Section 4.1, and Chapter 8, Section 2) why various other attractive principles connecting these principles must be rejected.

10.0.2. *Axiological Concepts*

I have made use of three main value-theoretic notions. The most important of these, as I see it, is the notion of intrinsic value. The intrinsic value of a state of affairs is the value it has in its own right, independent of any value it has because of its consequences. This is a sort of value that a state of affairs has noncontingently. I have suggested a pluralistic axiology, according to which pleasure, justice, perhaps freedom, perhaps knowledge, and perhaps beauty are intrinsically good, while pain, injustice, perhaps bondage, perhaps ignorance, and perhaps ugliness are intrinsically bad. I have assumed that there are basic intrinsic value states, and that the intrinsic value of each basic intrinsic value state may be represented in numerical terms. If the assumptions are correct, it makes sense to say that the intrinsic value of a possible world is equal to the sum of the intrinsic values of the basic intrinsic value states that occur there.

My second value concept is the person-relativized notion I have dubbed "value-for-s". By this I mean something like individual welfare. The value of a world for a person is a measure of how well things go for that person in that world — how well he fares there. Given a sufficiently simple view about intrinsic value, we may be able to say that the value-for-s of a world, w, is determined by the extent to which s enjoys the intrinsic goods, and suffers the intrinsic evils, of w. On complex axiologies, this won't work, and the concept of welfare will become quite independent of the concept of intrinsic value.

The final value concept is just a group-relativized version of value-for-s. It is a measure of how well a group fares at a world. Given a subtle axiology, with goods such as justice, we may find that the welfare of a group may vary independently of the welfare of its members. Suppose, for example, that distributive justice is an intrinsic good. Next, assume that there is a group in which a fixed amount of goods is very poorly distributed. Without adding anything to the sum of the individual welfare measurements, we may add something to the group welfare measurement. All we have to do is redistribute the goods in a fairer way. Thus, we cannot safely assume that the welfare of a group is equal to the sum of the welfares of its members.

10.0.3. *Normative Concepts*

By appeal to these fundamental metaphysical and axiological concepts,

I have introduced six main concepts of absolute obligation. These may be catalogued as follows:

1. First, there is a defined neo-utilitarian concept of individual moral obligation. This is defined in MO (Chapter 2, Section 3) by appeal to regular accessibility and intrinsic value. Roughly, my idea that, as of a time, a person morally ought to do what he does in the intrinsically best worlds then accessible to him.

2. Individual prudential obligation was defined in PO (Chapter 5, Section 3.1) by appeal to regular accessibility and value-for-s. A person prudentially ought to do what he does in the best-for-him accessible worlds.

3. Group moral obligation was defined in GMO (Chapter 7, Section 4.2) by appeal to group accessibility and intrinsic value. A group morally ought to do what it does in the intrinsically best worlds accessible to it.

4. Group prudential obligation was defined in GPO (Chapter 7, Section 4.3) by appeal to group accessibility and value-for-k. The idea here is that a group prudentially ought to do what it does in the best-for-it worlds accessible to it.

5. Civic obligation was defined in CVO (Chapter 7, Section 4.4) by appeal to the concepts required for GPO as well as the notion of a "social group". An individual has a civic obligation, relative to some social group, to bring about p provided that he would have to bring about p if the group were to do its group prudential obligation. In this case, his doing p would be a part of the best-for-the-group group action.

6. The ought-to-be was defined in OB (Chapter 8, Section 2) by appeal to world accessibility and intrinsic value. What ought to be is what happens in the intrinsically best still possible worlds.

Two other important concepts of obligation were introduced, but neither was defined. These are the unanalyzed concept of individual moral obligation and "just plain" obligation. I maintain that the unanalyzed concept of moral obligation is necessarily equivalent to the concept defined in MO. An open question argument convinces me that these concepts are distinct. Just plain obligation, as I see it, is required in order to make sense of the concept of overriding, as well as to formulate properly the question 'Why should I be moral?'

Many of the most interesting problems concerning the logic of obligation essentially involve statements with both an 'if' and 'ought'. These so-called "iffy oughts" are particularly multifarious and tricky. In

Part Two, I attempted to distinguish among a startlingly large variety of
these. The most important of them may be organized as follows:

1. First there are the various forms of conditioned absolute obligation. Each of these is expressed by a syntactic structure in which there
is a factual statement as antecedent, a conditional connective, and an
absolute obligation statement as consequent. Materially-, subjunctively-,
and strictly conditioned absolute obligation are the paradigms of this
sort of iffy ought. They are explained in Chapter 4. By appeal to the
other sorts of absolute obligation, we may identify at least twenty one
other sorts of conditioned obligation.

2. Next we have the various forms of conditional obligation. These
include conditional individual moral obligation, conditional individual
prudential obligation, conditional group moral obligation, conditional
group prudential obligation, and the conditional ought-to-be. In Chapter 4, I attempted to explain the main formal differences between these
conditional structures and the various forms of conditioned absolute
obligation.

3. In Chapter 5, I discussed the hypothetical imperative. As I see it,
this is a close relative of individual conditional prudential obligtion. 'If
you want to get a reputation for honesty, then you ought to give correct
change' means, roughly, that in the best-for-you accessible worlds in
which you do gain a reputation for honesty, you give correct change.

4. Another sort of iffy ought is a special sort of conditional probability statement in which the "consequent" is a statement of absolute
obligation. Although I discussed only one main sort of probabilistic
obligation, it's pretty clear that we have the makings of at least eight
such things — one for each sort of absolute obligation (Chapter 6,
Section 4).

5. I noted (Chapter 6, section 3) the Chisholmian notion of requirement. So far as I can tell, it is not definable by appeal to the
metaphysical and axiological concepts to which I have appealed in this
book.

6. I also noted (Chapter 6) that there is a class of particularly
difficult statements, such as 'if you make a promise, you ought to keep
it' that seem to be immune to the sort of treatment I have proposed.
These statements of "defeasible commitment" are clearly distinct from
everything I have so far enumerated. They seem to be related to the
Chisholmian notion of requirement.

10.1. AN ATTEMPT AT JUSTIFICATION

Looking over this rather rich array of oughts and iffy oughts, the reader may be somewhat put off. 'Is there really any need for so many? Couldn't we make do with just two or three of these things?'

I too prefer to keep things simple. Thus, I would have been satisfied if things had not turned out quite so complicated. However, it seems to me that the oughts and iffy oughts of English in fact do take all of these forms. So my defense is that what I have said here seems to me to be true. I am reminded of the words of W. D. Ross: 'loyalty to the facts is worth more than symmetrical architectonic or a hastily reached simplicity'.[1]

Another sort of defense may also be appropriate. We may ask what benefits accrue to us if we adopt the proposed way of looking at things. I think there are many. I maintain that the approach I have adopted provides us with the materials for dealing with a large number of closely related problems in normative ethics. Most of these are problems concerning "the logic of obligation". That is, most are problems concerning the logical relations of some ought-statements either to some other ought-statements or to some factual statements. So, if we choose, we may say that these are problems in informal deontic logic.

Of these problems, the first was introduced by Castañeda in his 1968 paper, 'A Problem for Utilitarianism.'[2] This is the problem of formulating a normative theory that is both recognizably act utilitarian in spirit but which is also adequate to some strongly held deontic intuitions. I have attempted to show (in Chapter 2) that MO solves Castañeda's problem. MO incorporates the act utilitarian insight that we always ought to do the best we can. Furthermore, the formulation I have provided yields a fully satisfactory set of deontic principles. In the present context, one of the most important of these is a version of Castañeda's DC. If you ought to do a complex act, then you ought to do its components. My analysis explains why the individual utilities are irrelevant. What counts is that if the compound is performed in the best accessible worlds, then so are the components.

The concept introduced in MO in Chapter 2 also has some bearing on the Kantian doctrine that 'ought' implies 'can'. If we understand 'ought' as I have suggested, we can see why Kant was right. If you morally ought to do something, then you do it in the best accessible worlds. It follows, then, that worlds in which you do it are accessible.

To say this, however, is to say that you can do it. Variations on the Kantian theme turn out to be true in several other cases — individual prudential obligation, group moral obligation, group prudential obligation, and the ought-to-be. Each of these is a "doing-the-best-we-can" concept of obligation, directly definable by appeal to some concept of possibility and some concept of value. Civic obligation, as I indicated in Chapter 7, Section 4.4, fails to validate Kant's principle.

Although some will see it otherwise, I think these proposed concepts of absolute obligation shed light on the vexing question whether we can validly derive an 'ought' from an 'is'. As I pointed out (Chapter 2, Section 3.2; Chapter 5, Section 4.1) statements of absolute moral and prudential obligation may validly be derived from statements of unalterability. If you do a certain thing in every accessible world, then you do it in the best of the accessible worlds. Furthermore, if I'm right, we can derive statements of absolute moral obligation from statements about intrinsic value. Some may wish to count this as a case of deriving an 'ought' from an 'is'.

In Part Two of this book, I focussed on issues concerning the so-called "iffy oughts". In this category are various sorts of conditioned absolute obligation, as well as conditional obligation, hypothetical imperatives, statements of defeasible commitment and probablistic requirement.

Among the main claims I want to make in behalf of the proposed concept of conditional obligation is the claim that it provides the basis for a solution to the puzzle Chisholm set in his 1963 paper, 'Contrary to Duty Imperatives and Deontic Logic.'[3] Since factual detachment fails for conditional obligation, there is no conflict among the sentences Chisholm cited. (See Chapter 4, Section 6.)

Furthermore, I feel that the unified treatment of materially-, subjunctively-, and strictly conditioned absolute obligation, along with conditional obligation, clarifies a very confusing and ambiguous bunch of ordinary language sentences. The literature on the topic suggests that there is widespread disagreement about the formal structure of the iffy oughts. However, if I am right, there is much less disagreement than there appears to be. It is reasonable to suppose that philosophers have not really disagreed about one thing — rather, they have been talking about different things without realizing it. My treatment provides a clear and simple way to set these things apart, and it explains why each has the formal features it has.

The proposed treatment of hypothetical imperatives enables us to answer a variety of long-standing questions about these puzzling sentences. One of these was prompted by Prichard, who raised the question why factual detachment seems to fail for the hypothetical imperative.[4] My analysis (Chapter 5, Section 4) gives the answer. While unalterability detachment is valid, factual detachment fails for every sort of conditional obligation. The proposed treatment of hypothetical imperatives has another, perhaps even more important payoff. It helps us to understand the connection between these statements and statements of moral obligation. The difference, as I see it, is axiological. Hypothetical imperatives are based on the notion of value-for-s. Statements of moral obligation are based on the notion of intrinsic value. Since there is no interesting connection between the two systems of value, there is no interesting logical connection between the two sorts of statement. So even though a certain form of unalterability detachment is valid for the hypothetical imperative, the detachable ought-statement is only a statement of prudential obligation.

I also feel that my treatment of hypothetical imperatives goes a long way toward dispelling some of the confusion engendered by Kant's suggestion that the moral ought is the categorical ought, while the prudential ought is hypothetical. As I have attempted to show (Chapter 5, Section 4.2) Kant seems to have been wrong on this point. Moral oughts may be categorical or hypothetical. Equally, prudential oughts may be categorical or hypothetical. There is no syntactic mark of the moral. My own view is that Kant may have intended to make a claim about the overridingness of moral oughts. Perhaps, when he said that moral oughts are categorical, what he meant was this: if you have a non-moral obligation to do a certain thing, then it's possible that it's not the case that you just plain ought to do it. Maybe your non-moral obligation is overridden by some other obligation. However, if you have a moral obligation to do a certain thing, then you just plain ought to do it. Moral obligations cannot be overridden.

In Chapter 6, I attempted to show how hard it is to explain prima facie duty, defeasible commitment, and requirement by appeal to the notions of accessibility and intrinsic value. I wanted to drive home the fact that defeasible commitment is distinct from conditioned and conditional obligation. Though I have had relatively little to say about defeasible commitment and its allies, I think I've said enough to establish my main point: it's not analyzable as a form of conditioned or conditional moral obligation. It must be treated separately, perhaps along the lines Chisholm has suggested.

In Part Three, I developed a number of additional concepts of obligation, and attempted to extend my treatment into new areas. One of these concerns groups. If we suppose that groups have obligations, then we face the question concerning the relations between what groups ought to do and what their members ought to do. In this connection, some have assumed that our individual obligations must somehow be parts of the obligations of our social groups. Puzzles such as the prisoner's dilemma suggest otherwise. My treatment provides relatively straightforward answers. In virtue of the differences between group accessibility and individual accessibility, it turns out that group moral obligation and individual moral obligation do not necessarily harmon-ize. Perhaps we (collectively) ought to elect Smith in a landslide. It does not follow that I ought to vote for Smith, or that you ought to vote for Smith.

In order to make room for another way of viewing things, I have introduced the notion of civic obligation (Chapter 7, Section 4.4). As I have tried to show, this is a herring of a different color.

In a series of papers, Castañeda has drawn attention to the distinction between the ought-to-do and the ought-to-be.[5] I have attempted to develop an account of the ought-to-be (Chapter 8, Section 2) that shows just how it relates to my concept of moral obligation. As I see it, what ought to happen is what does happen in the intrinsically best worlds that are still world-accessible. By appeal to this analysis of the ought-to-be, I have provided answers to a collection of questions such as this one: ought it to be the case that we do the things that we ought to do? I have shown how the question is ambiguous, and how its answer is 'yes' on some readings, and 'no' on others (Chapter 8, Section 3).

My treatment generates an unequivocal answer to the question about conflicts of obligation. At any given time, an individual's absolute moral obligations cannot conflict. I have attempted to provide possible ex-planations for the attractiveness of the contrary view.

Finally, I have attempted to sketch the sort of answer I would give to the question 'Why be moral?' Once again, we must look to the meta-physical and axiological basis for the answer. We just plain ought to do what we morally ought to do because moral obligation is inextricably tied to the most important sort of value (intrinsic value) and the most important sort of possibility (regular accessibility).

Along the way, I have attempted to show how my approach suggests a unified set of answers to a variety of other questions in moral philosophy. If my treatment of most, or even some, of these problems has seemed plausible, then I think my overall approach is justified. Perhaps another moral philosopher, having made adjustments to the metaphysics or the axiology, or having developed variations on the normative concepts, will be able to make greater headway on the problems. My fundamental point — that there's still good reason to suppose that concepts of obligation may be analyzed by appeal to a small set of concepts of possibility and a small set of concepts of value — will have been vindicated.

NOTES

NOTES TO PREFACE

[1] 'A Problem for Utilitarianism,' *Analysis* **28** (1968), 141—142.

[2] Three especially impressive items are: Lennart Åqvist, 'Improved Formulations of Act Utilitarianism,' *Noûs* **3** (1969), 299—323; Lars Bergström, *The Alternatives and Consequences of Actions* (Stockholm: Almqvist & Wiksell, 1966); Howard Sobel, 'Values, Alternatives, and Utilitarianism,' *Noûs* **4** (1971), 373—384. Further relevant items are cited in Chapter I, note 3.

[3] 'Ought, Value, and Utilitarianism,' *The American Philosophical Quarterly* **VI** (1969), 257—275.

[4] *Analysis and Metaphysics*, ed. by Keith Lehrer (Dordrecht: Reidel, 1975), pp. 255—271.

[5] *Analysis* **24** (1963), 33—36.

[6] 'The Ethics of Requirement,' *The American Philosophical Quarterly* **1** (1964), 150.

NOTES TO CHAPTER 1

[1] The classic statements of utilitarinaism may be found in Bentham's *Introduction to the Principles of Morals and Legislation* (1789) and Mill's *Utilitarianism* (1865). Moore's utilitarianism is developed in *Principia Ethica* (Cambridge: Cambridge University Press, 1903) and *Ethics* (London: Oxford University Press, 1912). J. J. C. Smart's *An Outline of a System of Utilitarian Ethics* (Carlton: Melbourne University Press, 1961) contains a clear exposition and defense.

[2] I first encountered this puzzle in Harold Zellner's paper, 'The Inconsistency of Utilitarianism,' presented at the 69th Annual Meeting of the Eastern Division of the American Philosophical Association, Boston, December 27—29, 1972. An Abstract of the paper appears in *The Journal of Philosophy* **LXIX**, 19 (October 26, 1972), 676.

[3] Hector-Neri Castañeda, 'A Problem for Utilitarianism,' *Analysis* **28** (1968), 141—142. Castañeda's paper provoked several replies, including: Harold Zellner, 'Utilitarianism and Derived Obligation,' *Analysis* **32** (1972), 124—125; Fred Westphal, 'Utilitarianism and Conjunctive Acts: A Reply to Professor Castañeda,' *Analysis* **32** (1972), 82—85; R. E. Bales, 'Utilitarianism, Overall Obligatoriness and Deontic Logic,' *Analysis* **32** (1972), 203—205; Lars Bergström, 'Utilitarianism and Deontic Logic,' *Analysis* **29** (1968), 43—44. Castañeda responded to Westphal and Bergström in his 'On the Problem of Formulating a Coherent Act-Utilitarianism,' *Analysis* **32** (1972), 118—124.

[4] The concept of the "devilish machine" is derived from Lennart Åqvist, 'Improved Formulations of Act Utilitarianism,' *Noûs* **3** (1969), 299—323.

[5] For a detailed account of this approach, see Lars Bergström, *The Alternatives and Consequences of Action* (Stockholm: Almqvist & Wiksell, 1966). Bergström has discussed this approach in several papers, including: 'Alternatives and Utilitarianism,' *Theoria* **34** (1968), 163—170; 'Utilitarianism and Alternative Actions,' *Noûs* **5** (1971), 237—252; and 'On the Formulation and Application of Utilitarianism,' *Noûs* **10** (1976), 121—144. Bergström's approach is discussed at length in a critical review by R. E. Bales, in *Theoria* **40** (1974), 35—57.

[6] Mainly because it is so simple, I have used Robert Stalnaker's account of subjunctive conditionals. See his 'A Theory of Conditionals,' in *Studies in Logical Theory* ed. by Nicholas Rescher, American Philosophical Quarterly Monograph Series: Number 2 (Oxford: Basil Blackwell, 1968), pp. 98—112. Where it really matters, I guess I prefer David Lewis' view. See his *Counterfactuals*, (Cambridge: Harvard University Press, 1973).

[7] A case relevantly similar to this one, but more amusing than it, is discussed by Åqvist in 'Improved Formulations of Act Utilitarianism,' *Noûs* **3** (1969), 318—321.

[8] See, for example, G. E. Moore, *Principia Ethica* (Cambridge: Cambridge University Press, 1903), pp. 77—81. Several useful papers on this topic are mentioned by Dan Brock in 'Recent Work in Utilitarianism,' *American Philosophical Quarterly* **10** (1973), 242—243. Some attacks on qualitative hedonism are evaluated in Norman O. Dahl, 'Is Mill's Hedonism Inconsistent?,' in *Studies in Ethics*, ed. by Nicholas Rescher, American Philosophical Quarterly Monograph Series: Number 7 (Oxford: Basil Blackwell, 1973), pp. 37—54.

[9] G. E. Moore, *Principia Ethica* (Cambridge: Cambridge University Press, 1903), 117, 21ff. See also Moore's *Ethics* (London: Oxford University Press, 1912), pp. 24—25 and his *Philosphical Studies* (London: Routledge and Kegan Paul, 1922), pp. 253—275.

NOTES TO CHAPTER 2

[1] See my 'World Utilitarianism,' in *Analysis and Metaphysics*, ed. by Keith Lehrer (Dordrecht: Reidel, 1975), pp. 255—271. See especially the discussion of "life history worlds" on p. 265.

[2] This issue is discussed in David Lewis, 'Counterfactual Dependence and Time's Arrow,' *Noûs* **XIII** (1979), 455—476. Lewis there cites four philosophers who apparently have endorsed something like the "past-wise indiscernibility thesis". Lewis rejects it. See also Terence Horgan, '"Could", Possible Worlds, and Moral Responsibility,' *The Southern Journal of Philosophy* **XVII** (1979), 345—358; and 'Counterfactuals and Newcomb's Problem,' *The Journal of Philosophy* **LXXVIII** (1981), 331—356.

[3] Moore defends this view in *Principia Ethica* and in *Ethics*. See esp. *Ethics*, pp. 42—49. More recently, a version of it has been defended by Roderick Chisholm in 'Intrinsic Value,' in *Values and Morals*, ed. by A. Goldman and J. Kim (Dordrecht: Reidel, 1978), pp. 121—130. Chisholm's proposal is criticized in E. Bodanszky and E. Conee, 'Isolating Intrinsic Value,' *Analysis* **41** (1981), 51—53; and defended in Chisholm's 'Defining Intrinsic Value,' *Analysis* **41** (1981), 99—100.

[4] Roderick M. Chisholm, 'Objectives and Intrinsic Value,' in *Jenseits von Sein und*

Nichtsein, ed. by Rudolf Haller (Graz: Akademi: ches Druck; und Verlagsanstalt, 1972), p. 262.

5 *Proceedings and Addresses of the American Philosophical Association* **XLII** (1968—1969), p. 34. Moore seems to have held a similar view. See his 'The Conception of Intrinsic Value,' *Philosophical Studies* (London: Routledge and Kegan Paul, 1922), pp. 260—261.

6 For an interesting proposal concerning this further problem, see Warren Quinn, 'Theories of Intrinsic Value,' *American Philosophical Quarterly* **11** (1974), 123—132; and Edward Oldfield, 'An Approach to a Theory of Intrinsic Value,' *Philosophical Studies* **3** (1977), 233—249. Quinn's proposal is criticized in Peter Markie, 'Quinn, the Logic of Intrinsic Value, and Defeat,' *International Logic Review* 19—20 (1979).

7 This concept of obligation is a time- and agent-relativized version of concept developed by David Lewis. See his *Counterfactuals* (Cambridge: Harvard University Press, 1973). I am deeply indebted to Lewis here and elsewhere in this book. I am confident that he would not endorse the modifications I have made to his views.

8 Perhaps I should also mention that I reject the assumption that for each possible act, there always is exactly one possible world that would exist, if that act were performed.

9 See below, Chapter 9, Section 1.

10 "It is always in everyone's power to satisfy the commands of the categorical command of morality; . . ." Immanuel Kant, *Critique of Practical Reason*, transl. by Lewis White Beck (New York: The Liberal Arts Press, 1956), p. 38.

NOTES TO CHAPTER 3

1 This topic is discussed in Dan Brock's 'Recent Work in Utilitarianism,' *American Philosophical Quarterly* **10** (1973), 250—251. He there cites several relevant papers. In my view, one of the most interesting discussions can be found in R. E. Bales, 'Act Utilitarianism: Account of Right-Making Characteristics or Decision-Making Procedure?,' *American Philosophical Quarterly* **8** (1971), 257—265. See also J. J. C. Smart, *An Outline of a System of Utilitarian Ethics* (Melbourne: Melbourne University Press, 1961).

2 Kurt Baier, *The Moral Point of View*, abridged edition (New York: Random House, 1965), p. 109.

3 For an example of this sort of position, see Samuel Scheffler, *The Rejection of Consequentialism* (Oxford: The Clarendon Press, 1982).

4 An excellent, though somewhat dated, bibliography of this topic can be found in Nicholas Rescher, *Distributive Justice* (Indianapolis: The Bobbs-Merrill Company, Inc., 1966), pp. 137—139.

5 The article appeared in *The Philosophical Review* **85** (1976), 449—487.

6 In 'Utilitarianism and Past and Future Mistakes,' *Noûs* **10** (1976), 195—219.

7 The objection made by Goldman and Sobel provoked several comments, and eventually led to at least one reconsideration. Among these are: Lars Bergström, 'Utilitarianism and Future Mistakes,' *Theoria* **43** (1977), 84—102; Michael McKinsey, 'Levels of Obligation,' *Philosophical Studies* **35** (1979), 385—395; Holly Smith Goldman, 'Doing the Best One Can,' *Values and Morals*, ed. by A. I. Goldman and

J. Kim (Dordrecht: Reidel, 1978), pp. 185—214; P. S. Greenspan, 'Oughts and Determinism: A Response to Goldman,' *The Philosophical Review* **87** (1978), 77—83.

[8] The official account of conditional obligation is presented and explained in Chapter 4, Section 5.

[9] I am grateful to Ed Gettier for explaining the plausibility of this line of argument.

[10] Edited by Bernard Williams and J. J. C. Smart (Cambridge: Cambridge University Press, 1973), pp. 77—150. In subsequent notes, I refer to this work as 'Williams'.

[11] Useful discussion of Williams' essay can be found in: Nancy Davis, 'Utilitarianism and Responsibility,' *Ratio* **22** (1980), 15—35; John Harris, 'Williams on Negative Responsibility and Integrity,' *Philosophical Quarterly* **24** (1974), 265—273; Harry Silverstein, 'Utilitarianism and Group Coordination,' *Noûs* **XIII**, 3, (September, 1979), 335—360. Williams extended the discussion in 'Utilitarianism and Moral Self-Indulgence,' *Modern British Philosophy* 4th Series, ed. by H. D. Lewis (London: Allen and Unwin, 1976), pp. 306—321, as well as in other papers.

[12] Williams, p. 99.

[13] Williams, p. 116.

[14] Williams, p. 117.

[15] Williams, p. 99.

[16] Williams, p. 110.

[17] Williams, p. 116.

[18] Williams, pp. 115—116.

[19] Williams, p. 117.

[20] *Principa Ethica* (Cambridge: Cambridge University Press, 1903), p. 20.

[21] For an extended, insightful discussion of this point, see R. E. Bales, 'Act-Utilitarianism: Account of Right-Making Characteristics or Decision-making Procedure?', *American Philosophical Quarterly* **8** (1971), 257—265.

[22] Williams, p. 99.

NOTES TO CHAPTER 4

[1] Although a number of deontic logicians have used the term 'detachment' in the relevant sense, I first came across the current use of 'factual detachment', as well as the current use of 'deontic detachment' in P. S. Greenspan's 'Conditional Oughts and Hypothetical Imperatives,' *The Journal of Philosophy* **LXXII** (1975), 259—276.

[2] By Arthur Prior in 'The Paradoxes of Derived Obligation,' *Mind* **63** (1954), 64—65.

[3] My use of 'overrides' derives from Chisholm. See his 'The Ethics of Requirement,' *The American Philosophical Quarterly* **1** (1964), 148. Chisholm, in turn, cites W. D. Ross, *The Right and the Good* (New York: Oxford University Press, 1930), p. 18.

[4] Prior, op. cit.

[5] Once again, I am appealing to Stalnaker's account of the subjunctive conditional, even though I think that Lewis's account is in some ways preferable. My choice is based largely on considerations of simplicity. Most of the points I want to make could be made, albeit not so readily, on the more complicated account.

[6] Once again, I am indebted to David Lewis. My proposal is an agent- and time-relativized version of the concept of conditional obligation he presents in *Counterfactuals* (Cambridge: Harvard University Press, 1973), p. 100. See also his 'Semantic

Analyses for Dyadic Deontic Logic,' in *Logical Theory and Semantic Analysis*, ed. by Soren Stenlund (Dordrecht: Reidel, 1974), pp. 1—14.

[7] See, for example, John Robison, 'Who, What, Where and When: A Note on Deontic Logic,' *Philosophical Studies* **15** (1964), 89—92.

[8] A good discussion of this point may be found in Hans Lenk, 'Varieties of Commitment,' *Theory and Decision* **9** (1978), 17—37. See esp. pp. 22—25. See also Peter L. Mott, 'On Chisholm's Paradox,' *Journal of Philosophical Logic* **2** (1973), 197—211; and Judith W. DeCew, 'Conditional Obligation and Counterfactuals,' *Journal of Philosophical Logic* **10** (1981), 55—72.

[9] *Analysis* **24** (1963), 33—36.

[10] For an excellent review of some of the main treatments of Chisholm's puzzle, as well as a fine bibliography of recent work in deontic logic in general, see James E. Tomberlin, 'Contrary-to-Duty Imperatives and Conditional Obligation,' *Noûs* **XV** (1981), 357—375. Two other extremely useful works are: Azizah al-Hibri, *Deontic Logic: A Comprehensive Appraisal and a New Proposal* (Washington: University press of America, 1978) and Risto Hilpinen (ed.), *Deontic Logic: Introductory and Systematic Readings* (Dordrecht: Reidel, 1971). One of the most insightful discussions of Chisholm's problem may be found in Lennart Åqvist, 'Good Samaritans, Contrary to Duty Imperatives, and Epistemic Obligations,' *Noûs* **1** (1967), 361—379.

[11] For example, Peter Mott, in 'On Chisholm's Paradox,' op. cit.

[12] Criticism along these lines is also presented in DeCew's 'Conditional Obligation and Counterfactuals,' op. cit. For further criticism of Mott's approach, see Tomberlin's 'Contrary to Duty Imperatives and Conditional Obligation, op. cit.

[13] I don't claim to be the first to see things in this way. See, for example, Bas van Fraassen, 'The Logic of Conditional Obligation,' *Journal of Philosophical Logic* **1** (1972), 417—438, and David Lewis, 'Semantic Analyses for Dyadic Deontic Logic,' op. cit.

NOTES TO CHAPTER 5

[1] Von Wright is an example. See his 'A New System of Deontic Logic,' in *Deontic Logic: Introductory and Systematic Readings*, ed. by Risto Hilpinen (Dordrecht: Reidel, 1971), p. 109.

[2] Immanuel Kant, *Groundwork of the Metaphysic of Morals*, transl. by H. J. Paton (New York: Harper Torchbooks, 1964), p. 108.

[3] Ibid., p. 108.

[4] Ibid., pp. 82—83.

[5] Ibid., p. 85.

[6] Ibid., p. 86.

[7] Ibid., p. 87.

[8] Ibid., p. 109.

[9] Immanuel Kant, *Critique of Pure Practical Reason* in *The Philosophy of Kant*, ed. by Carl Friedrich (New York: The Modern Library, 1949), p. 213.

[10] H. A. Prichard, *Moral Obligation* (Oxford: The Clarendon Press, 1957), p. 91.

[11] R. M. Hare, *The Language of Morals* (New York: Oxford University Press, 1964), p. 91.

[12] Ibid., p. 34.

[13] Immanuel Kant, *Groundwork of the Metaphysic of Morals*, transl. by H. J. Paton (New York: Harper Torchbooks, 1964), pp. 82—84.

[14] Ibid., p. 108.

[15] Ibid., p. 85.

[16] Ibid., p. 85.

[17] Kant suggests this view in the *Groundwork*, pp. 84—86. It is also suggested by Thomas Hill in 'The Hypothetical Imperative,' *The Philosophical Review* **LXXXII** (1973), 425—450.

[18] This causal view also has its origins in Kant. See, for example, *Groundwork*, p. 65.

[19] The example is taken from Kant. See the *Groundwork*, p. 65.

[20] For an interesting discussion of this approach to the concept of prudence, see Phillip Bricker, 'Prudence,' *The Journal of Philosophy* **LXXVII** (1980), 381—401.

[21] *Critique of Pure Practical Reason* in *The Philosophy of Kant*, ed. by Carl Friedrich (New York: the Modern Library, 1949), p. 229.

[22] That is, it is like *FD4, discussed above in Chapter 4, Section 5.

[23] Strictly speaking, the antecedent of FDHI*2 tells us a bit more than this. It also tells us that there is an accessible $\sim q$ world. I beg the reader to forgive a certain looseness here. I am confident that it will not seriously affect the point at issue.

[24] See her 'Conditional Oughts and Hypothetical Imperatives,' *The Journal of Philosophy* **LXXII** (1975), 259—276. A similar view seems to be defended in Thomas Hill, 'The Hypothetical Imperative,' *The Philosophical Review* **LXXXII** (1973), 429—450. Valuable commentary on Hill's view may be found in John Marshall, 'Hypothetical Imperatives,' *The American Philosophical Quarterly* **19** (1982), 105—114. See especially pp. 109—110.

[25] Greenspan, op. cit., p. 273. See also the discussion of "the second assumption", p. 272.

[26] R. M. Hare, *The Language of Morals*, p. 34.

[27] It may be of interest to note that relevantly similar principles hold for MO as well. The most simple of these is: (Us, t, p & Ks, t, p) $\rightarrow$ MO$s, t, p$.

[28] Related points are discussed in Phillipa Foot, 'Morality as a System of Hypothetical Imperatives,' *The Philosophical Review* **LXXXI** (1972), 305—316; and in John Harsanyi, 'Ethics in Terms of Hypothetical Imperatives,' *Mind* N. S. **LXVII** (1958), 305—316.

[29] *Groundwork*, p. 85.

[30] Thomas Hill, 'The Hypothetical Imperative,' *The Philosophical Review* **LXXXII** (1973), 429—450.

[31] Hill, ibid., p. 434.

[32] Hill, ibid., p. 436.

[33] Hill, ibid., p. 436.

[34] Hill, ibid., p. 443.

NOTES TO CHAPTER 6

[1] W. D. Ross, *The Right and the Good* (Oxford: The Clarendon Press, 1930), p. 21.

[2] Ross, op. cit., pp. 41—42.

[3] See above, Chapter 4, Section 2.
[4] Chapter 4, Section 4.
[5] Chapter 4, Section 3.
[6] See above, Chapter 4, Section 5, for a discussion of unalterability detachment for CMO.
[7] An extremely insightful discussion of subjunctive conditionals and conditional obligation can be found in Judith W. DeCew, 'Conditional Obligation and Counterfactuals,' *The Journal of Philosophical Logic* **10** (1981), 55—72.
[8] R. M. Chisholm, 'The Ethics of Requirement,' *American Philosophical Quarterly* **I** (1964), 147—153.
[9] Op. cit., p. 147.
[10] Ibid.
[11] Ibid.
[12] Ibid.
[13] Op. cit., p. 149. I have taken the liberty of shifting the position of a quantifier.
[14] Op. cit., p. 150. I have taken the liberty of changing a 'q' to a 'p'.
[15] See below, Chapter 8, Section 3.
[16] Op. cit., p. 150.
[17] Op. cit., p. 148; pp. 150—151.
[18] This suggestion was presented to me by several people. I believe Eva Bodanszky was first.
[19] Chisholm, op. cit., p. 150.

NOTES TO CHAPTER 7

[1] Among the many advocates of this view are: George Berkeley, *Passive Obedience*, in Mary W. Calkins, ed., *Berkeley: Selections* (New York: Scribner's, 1929), pp. 427—469; Jeremy Bentham, *Introduction to the Principles of Morals and Legislation*, in E. A. Burtt, ed., *The English Philosophers from Bacon to Mill* (New York: Modern Library, 1949), p. 796; Stephen Toulmin, *The Place of Reason in Ethics* (New York: Cambridge University Press, 1950); Kurt Baier, *The Moral Point of View*, abridged edition (New York: Random House, 1965).
[2] The classic example here is Bentham. He maintained that '. . . it is but tautology to say that the more consistently [the principle of utility] is followed, the better it must ever be for humankind.' op. cit., p. 796.
[3] See, for example, Gerald Barnes, 'Utilitarianisms,' *Ethics* **LXXXII** (October, 1971), 56—64 and Donald Regan, *Utilitarianism and Co-operation* (Oxford: The Clarendon Press, 1980).
[4] Used by Gerald Barnes in 'Utilitarianisms,' *Ethics* **LXXXII**, 1 (October, 1971), 56—64.
[5] Used by me in 'The Principle of Moral Harmony,' *The Journal of Philosophy* **LXXVII**, 3 (March, 1980), 171—174.
[6] Used by Donald Regan in *Utilitarianism and Cooperation*, (Oxford: The Clarendon Press, 1980).
[7] See also Allan Gibbard, 'Rule Utilitarianism: Merely an Illusory Alternative?,' *Australasian Journal of Philosophy* **43** (1965), 211—220. Jordan Howard Sobel has written extensively on questions concerning individual obligations and group welfare.

See, for example: ' "Everyone", Consequences, and Generalization Arguments,' *Inquiry*
10 (1967), 373—404; 'Utilitarianism: Simple and General,' *Inquiry* **13** (1970), 394—
449; 'The Need for Coercion,' *Coercion: Nomos* **XIV**, edited by J. R. Pennock and John
W. Chapman, (Chicago/New York: Aldine-Atherton, Inc., 1972), 148—177; 'Interac-
tion Problems for Utility Maximizers,' *Canadian Journal of Philosophy* **IV**, 4 (June,
1975), 677—688; 'Utility Maximizers in Iterated Prisoner's Dilemmas,' *Dialogue*,
(1976); 'Everyone's Conforming to a Rule,' *Philosophical Studies* **48** (1985), 375—387.
[8] There is a large body of literature on group action. Bibliographies can be found in
David Copp, 'Collective Actions and Secondary Actions,' *American Philosophical
Quarterly* **16** (1979), 177—186; and Michael McKinsey, 'Obligations to the Starving,
Noûs **XV** (1981), 309—323.
[9] For an account of the concept of individual prudential obligation, see above, Chapter
5, Section 3.1.
[10] The objection is based on some suggestions presented to me in correspondence by
Howard Sobel.
[11] Donald Regan, *Utilitarianism and Co-operation* (Oxford: The Clarendon Press,
1980). In subsequent footnotes, I refer to this book as 'Regan'.
[12] Regan, p. 124
[13] Regan, pp. 135—136.
[14] Regan, pp. 109—123.
[15] Regan, pp. 177—178.
[16] It should be noted that this is a "total value" variant of PMH. Universal compliance
with CUO maximizes the total value of the outcome. It does not maximize the group's
share in the value of the outcome. It's pretty clear that modest tinkering with Regan's
theory would produce a relevantly similar theory that verifies a more straightforwardly
group-oriented version of PMH.
[17] *Noûs* **XVIII**, 1 (March, 1984), 152—159.
[18] For Regan's comment on this sort of objection, see Regan, pp. 172—174.
[19] Pointed out by Barley, op. cit., p. 157, as well as by Earl Conee in his review which
appeared in *The Journal of Philosophy* **LXXX**, 7 (July, 1983), 415—424.
[20] Regan, p. 177.
[21] Regan, pp. 177—185.
[22] This point is made by Conee, op. cit., p. 421.
[23] Regan discusses a case something like this one on pp. 174—176. He concludes by
saying that it 'deserves some further thought.'
[24] For Regan's definition, see Regan, p. 6.
[25] See Regan, pp. 18—19.
[26] The reader is invited to compare this argument with Regan's argument on pp.
18—19.
[27] A similar view is suggested by Conee, op. cit., p. 422.

NOTES TO CHAPTER 8

[1] For a discussion of group moral obligation, see Chapter 7, Section 4.2.
[2] This approach is based on things said by Jaakko Hintikka in 'Some Main Problems of

Deontic Logic,' in *Deontic Logic: Introductory and Systematic Readings* ed. by Risto Hilpinen (Dordrecht: Reidel, 1970), pp. 59—104. Hintikka's approach is criticized in R. L. Purtill, 'Deontically Perfect Worlds and Prima Facie Obligations,' *Philosophy* 3 (1973), 429—438.

3 See above, Chapter 1, Section 4, 'A Puzzle about Time'.

4 See above, Chapter 7, Section 4.1, 'Group Accessibility'. The main point is discussed in connection with *A5.

5 David Lewis, *Counterfactuals* (Cambridge: Harvard University Press, 1973), Chapter 5.

6 Alan McMichael, 'Too Much of a Good Thing: A Problem in Deontic Logic,' *Analysis* 38 (1978), 83—84.

7 Lewis replied to McMichael's criticism in 'Reply to McMichael,' *Analysis* 38 (1978), 85—86.

8 An extremely interesting discussion can be found in Terence Horgan's '"Could", Possible Worlds, and Moral Responsibility,' *The Southern Journal of Philosophy* XVII (1979), 345—358.

9 In *Counterfactuals*, David Lewis says, 'In the case of physical necessity, for instance, we have this restriction: the accessible worlds are those where the actual laws of nature hold true. Physical necessity is truth at all worlds where those laws hold true; physical possibility is truth at some worlds where those laws hold true.' (p. 5).

10 My approach is very similar to Horgan's. For comparison, see his article noted above in Note 8.

11 For a discussion of these notions, see above, Chapter 2, Section 1.2.

12 For a good discussion of this temptation, see Terence Horgan, 'Counterfactuals and Newcomb's Problem,' *The Journal of Philosophy* LXXVIII (1981), 331—356. See also David Lewis, 'Counterfactual Dependence and Time's Arrow,' *Noûs* XIII (1979), 455—476.

13 A relevantly similar point concerning regular acccessibility was discussed above in Chapter 2, Section 1.1, 'Indiscernibility with respect to the Past'.

14 Roderick M. Chisholm, 'The Ethics of Requirement,' *American Philosophical Quarterly* I (1964), 147—153.

15 Ibid., p. 150.

16 For further discussion of 'The Ethics of Requirement', see Chapter 6, Section 1.3, 'Defeasible Commitment and Chisholmian Requirement'.

NOTES TO CHAPTER 9

1 Ruth Barcan Marcus, 'Moral Dilemmas and Consistency,' *The Journal of Philosophy* LXXVII (1980), 121—136; Bas C. van Fraassen, 'Values and the Heart's Command,' *The Journal of Philosophy* LXX (1973), 5—19; Bernard Williams, 'Ethical Consistency,' in *Problems of the Self* (Cambridge: Cambridge University Press, 1973), pp. 173—176. Another defense of the view can be found in E. J. Lemmon, 'Moral Dilemmas,' *The Philosophical Review* LXXI (1962), 139—158.

2 J. P. Sartre, 'Existentialism is a Humanism,' in Walter Kaufman, ed., *Existentialism from Dostoevsky to Sartre* (New York: Meridian, 1956), pp. 295—298.

3 Op. cit., p. 125.

[4] Ibid.

[5] Marcus, op. cit., p. 131.

[6] Williams, op. cit., p. 175.

[7] Terrance C. McConnell, 'Moral Dilemmas and Consistency in Ethics,' *Canadian Journal of Philosophy* **VIII**, 2 (June, 1978), 276.

[8] Alan Donagan, 'Consistency in Rationalist Moral Systems,' *The Journal of Philosophy* **LXXXI**, 6 (June, 1984), 305.

[9] Remarks in his paper suggest that perhaps Donagan intends to avoid the inconsistency by retreating to a weakened version of the "ought implies can" principle. See pp. 300—302.

[10] See above, Chapter 5, Section 3.1.

[11] See above, Chapter 5, Section 3.1.

[12] The reader may wonder why I have formulated (15) as a mere conditional rather than as a biconditional. The answer has to do with Buridanical cases. Suppose twins are drowning, and I can save only one. Moral considerations are exactly balanced. Suppose I have flipped a coin, and have determined to save twin A. Then I just plain ought to save twin A, even though it is not the case that I morally ought to save twin A. Thus, in this sort of case I just plain ought to do something that is not morally obligatory. In non-Buridanical cases, moral obligation and just plain obligation coincide.

[13] For an example of this approach, see Kurt Baier, *The Moral Point of View*, abridged edition (New York: Random House, 1956), pp. 106—109.

[14] For a more detailed explanation of this point, see above, Chapter 7, Section 3.2.

NOTES TO CHAPTER 10

[1] W. D. Ross, *The Right and the Good* (New York: Oxford University Press, 1930).

[2] *Analysis* **28** (1968), 141—142.

[3] *Analysis* **24** (1963), 33—36.

[4] H. A. Prichard, *Moral Obligation* (Oxford: The Clarendon Press, 1957), p. 91.

[5] See, for example, 'Acts, the Logic of Obligation, and Deontic Calculi,' *Philosophical Studies* **XIX** (1968), 12—26.

INDEX OF NAMES

237

INDEX OF SUBJECTS

PHILOSOPHICAL STUDIES SERIES
IN PHILOSOPHY

Editors:

WILFRID SELLARS, Univ. of Pittsburgh and KEITH LEHRER, Univ. of Arizona

Board of Consulting Editors:

Jonathan Bennett, Allan Gibbard, Robert Stalnaker, and Robert G. Turnbull

1. JAY F. ROSENBERG, *Linguistic Representation*, 1974.
2. WILFRID SELLARS, *Essays in Philosophy and Its History*, 1974.
3. DICKINSON S. MILLER, *Philosophical Analysis and Human Welfare*. Selected Essays and Chapters from Six Decades. Edited with an Introduction by Lloyd D. Easton, 1975.
4. KEITH LEHRER (ed.), *Analysis and Metaphysics*. Essays in Honor of R. M. Chisholm. 1975.
5. CARL GINET, *Knowledge, Perception, and Memory*, 1975.
6. PETER H. HARE and EDWARD H. MADDEN, *Causing, Perceiving and Believing*. An Examination of the Philosophy of C. J. Ducasse, 1975.
7. HECTOR-NERI CASTAÑEDA, *Thinking and Doing*. The Philosophical Foundations of Institutions, 1975.
8. JOHN L. POLLOCK, *Subjunctive Reasoning*, 1976.
9. BRUCE AUNE, *Reason and Action*, 1977.
10. GEORGE SCHLESINGER, *Religion and Scientific Method*, 1977.
11. YIRMIAHU YOVEL (ed.), *Philosophy of History and Action*. Papers presented at the first Jerusalem Philosophical Encounter, December 1974, 1978.
12. JOSEPH C. PITT, *The Philosophy of Wilfrid Sellars: Queries and Extensions*, 1978.
13. ALVIN I. GOLDMAN and JAEGWON KIM, *Values and Morals*. Essays in Honor of William Frankena, Charles Stevenson, and Richard Brandt, 1978.
14. MICHAEL J. LOUX, *Substance and Attribute*. A Study in Ontology, 1978.
15. ERNEST SOSA (ed.), *The Philosophy of Nicholas Rescher: Discussion and Replies*, 1979.
16. JEFFRIE G. MURPHY, *Retribution, Justice, and Therapy*. Essays in the Philosophy of Law, 1979.
17. GEORGE S. PAPPAS, *Justification and Knowledge: New Studies in Epistemology*, 1979.
18. JAMES W. CORNMAN, *Skepticism, Justification, and Explanation*, 1980.
19. PETER VAN INWAGEN, *Time and Cause*. Essays presented to Richard Taylor, 1980.

20. DONALD NUTE, *Topics in Conditional Logic*, 1980.
21. RISTO HILPINEN (ed.), *Rationality in Science*, 1980.
22. GEORGES DICKER, *Perceptual Knowledge*, 1980.
23. JAY F. ROSENBERG, *One World and Our Knowledge of It*, 1980.
24. KEITH LEHRER and CARL WAGNER, *Rational Consensus in Science and Society*, 1981.
25. DAVID O'CONNOR, *The Metaphysics of G. E. Moore*, 1982.
26. JOHN D. HODSON, *The Ethics of Legal Coercion*, 1983.
27. ROBERT J. RICHMAN, *God, Free Will, and Morality*, 1983.
28. TERENCE PENELHUM, *God and Skepticism*, 1983.
29. JAMES BOGEN and JAMES E. McGUIRE (eds.), *How Things Are, Studies in Predication and the History of Philosophy and Science*, forthcoming.
30. CLEMENT DORE, *Theism*, forthcoming.
31. THOMAS L. CARSON, *The Status of Morality*, 1984.
32. MICHAEL J. WHITE, *Agency and Integrality*, 1985.
33. DONALD F. GUSTAFSON, *Intention and Agency*, 1986.
34. PAUL K. MOSER, *Empirical Justification*, 1985.